Scottish Cultural Review of Language and Literature

Volume 9

Series Editors
Rhona Brown
University of Glasgow

John Corbett
University of Glasgow

Sarah Dunnigan
University of Edinburgh

James McGonigal
University of Glasgow

Production Editor
Ronnie Young
University of Glasgow

SCROLL

The Scottish Cultural Review of Language and Literature publishes new
work in Scottish Studies, with a focus on analysis and reinterpretation of
the literature and languages of Scotland, and the cultural contexts that have
shaped them.

Further information on our editorial and production procedures can be
found at www.rodopi.nl

R.D.S. Jack

"Joyous Sweit Imaginatioun"

Essays on Scottish Literature in Honour of R.D.S. Jack

Edited by

Sarah Carpenter and Sarah M. Dunnigan

Rodopi

Amsterdam - New York, NY 2007

Cover image: The cover shows details from "The Ratification of the Marriage Contract of James IV and Margaret Tudor", written and decorated by Sir Thomas Galbraith (The National Archives UK, Document E39/81).

Cover design: Gavin Miller and Pier Post

The paper on which this book is printed meets the requirements of "ISO 9706: 1994, Information and documentation - Paper for documents - Requirements for permanence".

ISBN: 978-90-420-2313-0
©Editions Rodopi B.V., Amsterdam - New York, NY 2007
Printed in The Netherlands

Contents

Contributors

Sarah Carpenter is Senior Lecturer in English Literature at the University of Edinburgh. She has published chiefly on drama and performance of the medieval and Tudor periods, as in *Masks and Masking in Medieval and Early Tudor England* (2002) which she wrote with Meg Twycross. She is currently leading a project on performance at the Royal Courts of Scotland before 1650.

John Corbett is Professor of Applied Language Studies at Glasgow University. He is the author and editor of books and articles on diverse aspects of Scottish and English language and literature. He is principal investigator of two AHRC-funded projects, the Scottish Corpus of Texts and Speech, and the Corpus of Modern Scottish Writing (1700–1945): see www.scottishcorpus.ac.uk.

Sarah M. Dunnigan is Lecturer in English Literature at the University of Edinburgh. She has written on medieval and Renaissance Scottish literature, including *Eros and Poetry at the Courts of Mary Queen of Scots and James VI* (2002), twentieth-century Scottish literature, and Scottish ballads, and is presently writing a book on Scottish fairy tales.

Elizabeth Elliott completed a doctorate on the *Kingis Quair* and the medieval reception history of the *Consolation of Philosophy* at the University of Edinburgh, where she currently teaches.

Alastair Fowler is Regius Professor Emeritus of Rhetoric and English Literature of the University of Edinburgh. His influential publications on Renaissance literature include *Silent Poetry: Essays in Numerological Analysis* (1970), the edition of *Paradise Lost* (1971), *Conceitful Thought: the Interpretation of English Renaissance Poems* (1975) and *Renaissance Realism: Narrative Images in Literature and Art* (2003).

Jack MacQueen is Professor Emeritus of the University of Edinburgh and has written extensively on Scottish literature and on numerology. His publications include *Robert Henryson: a Study of the Major Narrative Poems* (1964), *Numerology: Theory and Outline History of a Literary Mode* (1985) and *Complete and Full with Numbers: the Narrative Poetry of Robert Henryson* (2006).

Sergi Mainer is a British Academy Postdoctoral Fellow at the Department of English Studies, University of Stirling. His main field of research is Older Scots literature with special interest in romance, literary translation, epic and comparative literature. His first book, *The Scottish Romance Tradition c.1375– c.1550: Nation, Chivalry and Literature* will be published by Rodopi. He is now working on a second monograph, *Literary Translation in the Reign of James VI of Scotland*.

David Moses obtained his first degree at Edinburgh University where he also gained a PhD in medieval English and Scottish Literature under the supervision of R. D. S. Jack. In 2005 he moved to Ampleforth College in Yorkshire, where he teaches English and is Head Tutor to Music Scholars. He continues to research and publish on areas as diverse as representations of Benedictines in Medieval Literature, and mysticism in the works of Neil M. Gunn.

John J. McGavin is a member of the Centre for Medieval and Renaissance Culture at the University of Southampton, where he is Professor of English. He has written on rhetoric, Chaucer, and on English and Scottish Drama, and is currently editing the provincial Records of Early Drama of Southeast Scotland with Dr Eila Williamson. His *Theatricality and Narrative in Medieval and Early-Modern Scotland* was published by Ashgate in 2007.

Kevin J. McGinley is assistant professor in English Language and Literature at Fatih University, Istanbul. He is editor (with R.D.S. Jack) of *Of Lion and of Unicorn: Essays on Anglo-Scottish Literary Relations in Honour of Professor John MacQueen* (Edinburgh, 1993) and of *New Bearings in Higher Education* (Istanbul, 2006). He has published articles on Robert Henryson, David Lyndsay, and John Home and is currently working on a study of John Home's drama on the international eighteenth-century stage.

Andrew Nash is Lecturer in English Literature at the University of Reading. In addition to many articles on J.M. Barrie and other aspects of Scottish Literature he is the author of *Kailyard and Scottish Literature* (2007), editor of *The Culture of Collected Editions* (2003), and co-editor of *Literary Cultures and the Material Book* (2007).

David J. Parkinson is Professor of English at the University of Saskatchewan where he teaches Scottish and medieval literature. His research concerns the circulation of late-medieval Scottish literature in the seventeenth century and after.

Murray Pittock is Bradley Professor of English Literature at the University of Glasgow and a Fellow of the Royal Society of Edinburgh and the English Association. His recent and forthcoming books include *The Reception of Sir Walter Scott in Europe* (2007), *James Boswell* (2007), *Scottish and Irish Romanticism* (2008) and *Scotland Since 1960* (2008).

Ken Simpson was Founding Director of the Centre for Scottish Cultural Studies at the University of Strathclyde and Reader in English Studies. He has twice been Neag Distinguished Visiting Professor in British Literature at the University of Connecticut and twice the W. Ormiston Roy Research Fellow in Scottish Literature at the University of South Carolina. He is also an Honorary Professorial Research Fellow in Scottish Literature at the University of Glasgow.

Acknowledgements

The editors would like to thank everyone who helped to bring this volume to publication. In particular, those who contributed to the conference in honour of Professor Ronnie Jack held in 2004 provided the warmth, initiative and impetus to create the collection: John Corbett, Elizabeth Elliott, Alastair Fowler, Jack MacQueen, Sergi Mainer, John McGavin, David Moses, Murray Pittock, Ken Simpson and Christopher Whyte. *Scroll*'s production editor, Ronnie Young, provided tireless and vital help in the final stages of bringing the volume to completion. We are extremely grateful to him, and also to Rodopi's editor, Marieke Schilling, for her advice and patience

Foreword

Jack MacQueen and Alastair Fowler

If my diaries are to be trusted, Ronnie Jack and I first met at 3 pm on Monday 13 April 1964 to discuss his admission as a PhD candidate to the department of English Literature in Edinburgh University. We met amid the splendours of the recently opened David Hume Tower. Mr Jack, as I addressed him in the formal language of the time, was a product of the ancient grammar school which later became Ayr Academy. From there he had gone to Glasgow University, where his first intention had been to study law. He soon realised the superior attractions of the humanities, and eventually gained a First in English Language and Literature.

His roots were in the West, and his initial attitude to an exotic Eastern institution like the University of Edinburgh was distrustful, even suspicious. To a degree this thawed when he heard that I too was a Glasgow graduate and that we both had sat under some of the same professors and lecturers. Even so, it took a little time for him to reconcile himself to Edinburgh, as eventually he so notably did.

On Tuesday 15 September we marked the beginning of his new existence by lunching together at the Chambers Street Staff Club of happy, but now (alas!) remote, memory. Thereafter Ronnie engaged himself furiously in research. The subject – on which I had expressed some initial doubt – was the Scottish Sonnet, and he soon showed how groundless my doubts had been. Supervisor was soon learning at least as much as supervisee. The quantity of good material Ronnie unearthed from what was then one of the obscurer corners of Scottish Literature was quite exceptional. In Glasgow he had, I think, taken "Italian for Honours English" as an optional course; his skill in that language combined with his research discoveries to produce an exceptional thesis. He and his fellow candidates – Tom Scott, Ian Jamieson, Judith Dale, Ian Campbell, to mention only a few – formed a stimulating group in a lively Department.

There were rumours that Ronnie was not only researching, but also writing a novel. To the best of my knowledge, no one, apart from himself, ever saw any chapter or episode of this great work. A pity, one must say.

At weekends Ronnie relaxed, if that is the word. He was a keen player of hockey and joined the Edinburgh Western club. He played, as he worked, with intensity. Every Monday morning he appeared, battered, bruised, but smiling, after the previous Saturday's encounter. He was, and probably still is, a golfer of accomplishment. Occasionally we played together. I have pleasant memories of being crushingly outplayed on the Pentlands and at Ayr Belleisle and Turnberry.

Ronnie left his heart in Ayr, but for only a relatively short time. My wife and I were invited to his wedding there – a joyous occasion – and soon afterwards we visited Kirsty and him in their new Penicuik establishment. By then, Ronnie had climbed the first rung of the academic ladder. He was an Assistant Lecturer, a probationary, often temporary, rank, fortunately no longer in existence. For Ronnie it posed no hazard, as the brilliant remainder of his University career bears witness.

Former supervisors of distinguished Professors do not often get the chance to contribute to the Festschrift which the Professor receives after his retirement. It is very much my pleasure to be able to do so, and to wish that Ronnie's retirement may be long, happy and productive.

Jack MacQueen

When I returned to Edinburgh University in 1972, many people helped me to get my bearings, but Ronnie Jack more than most. With his experience as Associate Dean he was a mine of information as to what could (and, more often, couldn't) be done administratively. No one had so many contacts and such various knowledge of the Department. This was particularly true where the role of Scottish literature was concerned; then a contentious matter, however hard that may be to credit now. To my relief, I found that Ronnie and I shared several convictions about Scottish literature. We agreed it was so good that it deserved to be in the mainstream of teaching rather than hived off on its own. We also shared the experience of teaching in the USA – at the University of Virginia – and knew the advantages of teaching in large classes. Again, there was never any need to convince Ronnie that literature is more than the literature of any one period or region: that it has to be taken holus-bolus (if I may resort to Medieval Latin).

Ronnie has so many strings to his bow that it is more of a lute than a violin. Facility with modern languages (French, Italian, German) has opened up comparative literature to him as a natural field of endeavour, and led to several books and articles on Scottish relations with European literatures. One such publication, *The Italian Influence on Scottish Literature* (1972), attracted so much attention that he was commissioned to write the Introduction on Scotland's literary debt to Italy for *Leopardi: A Scottis Quair* (1987), the volume he co-edited for presentation to the Italian President at the Edinburgh consulate. His medieval major (so to say), together with his love of theatre and an injection of Charlottesville theory, led to his *Patterns of Divine Comedy in Medieval Drama* (1989), a valuable study I read part of in manuscript and have since often returned to. Being as much at home in English as in Scottish literature, Ronnie is open to the flow of critical and theoretical ideas (while being far too good a linguist to feel any attraction to structuralism or deconstruction). Nor is he limited in historical period, as his books on James Barrie show. Perhaps for this reason he was early to grasp the experimental nature of Barrie's drama and his place in the context of European modernism. And this makes yet another string resound; for Ronnie's interest in drama is not only theoretical but practical, and has involved serving on the board of the Lyceum theatre.

All this makes him the ideal subject for a Festschrift in the traditional sense: a gathering of diverse essays by pupils, friends, and colleagues who have enjoyed very different friendly relations with him.

Alastair Fowler

Introduction

Sarah Carpenter and Sarah M. Dunnigan

Now is Perkin and these pilgrimes to the plow faren.
To erie this half-acre, holpen him manye.

[Now Perkin and these pilgrims set themselves to the plough. Many folk helped him
to turn over the soil in this half-acre of land.] (William Langland, *Piers Plowman*,
VI.105–6)

[…] I cannot think of a more exact analogy for the spirit in which I offer my own
attempt at guidance. I have had the privilege of labouring in the field of Scottish
Literature for over thirty years. Within that period, the subject has made rapid strides
forward. […] I have also published in all periods from medieval to modern. That
breadth of endeavour has given me a genuine regard for the skill with which different
kinds of ploughing are conducted within this small domain. So why should I – even in
Piers' humble spirit – claim the right to demand a pause on my terms? (Jack ed. 1997:
xxxiv–v)

This volume gathers together essays, diverse in the historical period,
mode, and form each explores, in honour of Professor R.D.S. Jack's
own particular scholarly "labour", to borrow his analogy of Langland's medieval ploughman. It represents just a selection of the
colleagues, students, and friends whose thinking on Scottish literature
has been touched by Ronnie's own. Many more have generously
contributed to various projects inspired by him and acknowledged his
intellectual and personal influence. The essays here reflect the diverse
interests and scholarship of their writers. Yet it is striking how they
complement and respond to the themes and preoccupations apparent
in Ronnie's own work. This is plainly a tribute to his personal influence both on individual scholars and on the subject as a whole; it is
also a demonstration of the Renaissance breadth of his interests and
engagement across the field of Scottish literature. Chronologically, the
collection sweeps from the early middle ages to the early twentieth
century, from Boethius to Barrie, conveying a sense of the identity
and continuity of the tradition of Scottish literature across the centuries. While engaging with many writers and topics that feature in

Ronnie's writing, it also responds to many of his own particular interests and qualities of scholarship. We hope that the volume not only attests the individuality of Ronnie's work but also reflects how it has anticipated, shaped, and inspired the broader field of Scottish literary studies. This brief introduction identifies what might be considered particularly salient features of Ronnie's work (whilst acknowledging how imperfect and limited such "summaries" must always be), suggesting the nature of their broader resonance and import and the ways in which they are mirrored in the individual essays collected here.

Until his recent retirement in 2004 Ronnie Jack held a Chair in Medieval and Scottish Literature at the University of Edinburgh, a position which reflected his "core" roots in the late medieval period but also, as he himself implies in the *Mercat* preface cited above, the way in which his interests have cut across and transcended demarcations of historical period, form, and genre. Whilst the litany of Scottish writers on which Ronnie has published is long and varied – Barbour, Dunbar, Montgomerie, Urquhart, Burns, Barrie, to name only some – what arguably unites them all is the different ways in which their work embodies the qualities of what Ronnie calls "mystery, allegory and the imagination" (Jack ed. 1997: xxxix). It is no surprise that Ronnie has devoted his attention to exemplars and practitioners of this type of art; not simply those of the medieval and Renaissance periods, where hermeneutical beauty and opacity is so obviously key, but beyond in writers such as J.M. Barrie and Burns. In the former's "magic" art, Jack discovers a labyrinthine quest "towards meaning, authorship, form, art and language" (Jack 1991: 252), and in the latter poet, for whom, he has argued, it is necessary to peel away layers of hagiography and inaccurate critical categorisation, he perceives the crafted, rhetorical voices which create an "anarchical cantata" (Jack ed. 1997: xxxi). Needless to say, it requires a particular kind of imaginative and critical acuity which can successfully elucidate such imaginatively high art.

One might argue, therefore, that Ronnie's criticism is underpinned by the intent to fashion a reader capable of this imaginative perception: one who is free, for example, of the narrow or limiting perspectives of an unthinkingly inward nationalist criticism. Ronnie's reader is resistant to the kind of critical vision which does not see the aesthetic, cultural, and linguistic landscapes opened up by far-reaching perspectives on the place of Scottish literature in a comparative framework. His own critical compass has pointed to the imaginative journeys undertaken by Scottish writers in European, and in particular Italian, literature. This impulse can first be charted in Ronnie's doctoral work on the Scottish sonnet which identified sources for the formal architectonics and thematic topoi of the Scottish Renaissance poets (Fowler, Montgomerie, James VI, Stewart, Alexander, Ayton, and Drummond) in the work of the French Grands Rhétoriqueurs and the Pléiade, and in Italian Renaissance poets such as Bembo, Guarini, and Marino. The original Renaissance period in Scotland has had a chequered critical history (itself an abiding interest of Ronnie's, as explained further below) but it is singularly his work in this period, from his first article in 1966 to one of the most recent in 2006, which has done most to shape our understanding of this complex period. In *The Italian Influence on Scottish Literature* (Jack 1972), Ronnie delineated the imaginative cross-currents between the two countries not just in the Renaissance but in the centuries preceding and subsequent to it (cf. also Jack 1986). In the current critical climate where national literary and cultural paradigms are more often questioned than asserted, such scholarship, lifting national and verbal borders to show what is elsewhere called the "linguistic internationalism" of Scottish writing (Jack ed. 1997: xv), can be seen as prescient. It is developed and sustained in his most recent work in a series of articles on early Scottish translation (Jack 1997; 2001; 2006; cf. also Jack and Hubbard eds 2006).

Ronnie's comparative interests necessitate an attentiveness to language which also manifests itself at all levels in his work, not just that directly concerned with issues of translation. Questions of rhetoric underpin Ronnie's critical inquiry at all times in his commitment to explore the infinitely diverse ways in which the artist "signs" meaning. His work on the medieval makars discloses the theoretical and poetic richness of their signs and symbols; in the Renaissance period, it has revealed the way in which William Alexander's neglected treatise, the *Anacrisis*, is a major contribution to traditions of Scottish rhetorical and humanist criticism (Jack ed. 1997: 474ff); and in relation to Burns it betrays his fascination for the poet's "verbal and narratorial ambiguity" (Jack and Noble eds 1982: 110).

If such a concern with the particularity, precision, and exactitude of literary form mirrors a contemporary renewal or "remembering" of the role of the aesthetic in criticism, then another of Ronnie's enduring concerns can also be seen as prescient: a questioning of "the canonical". Both by his focus on unfashionable and undervalued writers and works, and in his insistence on rethinking the parameters of literary judgement, he contributed to a movement which over his career has seen both an expansion and a refinement of the discipline of Scottish literature. Issues of literary judgement are frequently scrutinised in Ronnie's work, whether the short-sightedness of critics regarding the earlier period or the imperceptive and false mythologising of Barrie. His scholarly and editorial work in the Renaissance period in particular has meant a series of charged encounters with questions of literary value and "worth" not only because it has to contend with the great canonical weight of the English Elizabethan Renaissance but also with the prevailing biases of Scottish critical traditions. This has resulted in a long engagement with such issues, the most sustained of which is arguably the prefatory essay to the *Mercat Anthology*, edited with P.A.T. Rozendaal, which was importantly the first edition of pre-1700 Scottish material that could be used as a teaching text. Here, the case is trenchantly made against that type of Scottish critical discourse which arrays its own list of villains and heroes and, in so doing, becomes seriously prejudicial and seriously inaccurate. Further, Ronnie is unique in being a major voice which places the early period at the heart of any critical recalibration; aesthetically and intellectually, it is seen as vital for an understanding of Scottish literature which refuses conventional circumscriptions.

As has been suggested, from his earliest work, Ronnie was concerned to question, extend and revalue the accepted canon of Scottish literature. Many of the essays in this volume reinforce this movement by playing new light on Scottish writing which has been neglected or sidelined. Sarah M. Dunnigan's essay on William Drummond questions the common critical assessment of his work as a mere belated survival of sixteenth-century Petrarchanism, exploring the intellectual and philosophical sophistication and originality with which Drummond engaged with the concept of beauty. David Parkinson challenges the dominant critical acceptance of Gregory Smith's Caledonian antisyzygy to revalue Scottish seventeenth-century writing; the "Nonsensick Raptures" of Samuel Rutherford are shown in a new light, his reworking of late medieval dream vision and affective piety contributing to the beginnings of a new national literary canon. Murray Pittock reasserts the contribution of Scottish writing to the development of Romanticism, demonstrating the crucial place of Fergusson in the development of the Romantic aesthetic. Both Ken Simpson and Andrew Nash focus on James Barrie whose writing Ronnie has done much to reassess and re-establish. Each explores a relatively little recognised area of Barrie's work, the craftsmanship of the short fiction and the dynamic relationship of his journalism and drama. All these essays share Ronnie's commitment to re-calibrating the emphases of the Scottish literary canon.

Ronnie's desire to place Scottish literature in its wider context, uncovering the dynamic interaction between European and Scottish traditions, is also evident in a variety of the essays. Sergi Mainer helps to refine our perception of *Eger and Grime*'s ambivalent interrogation of the romance genre by setting it against earlier Occitan, Catalan and French models. Sarah Carpenter examines how Italianate performance of the court of Mary Queen of Scots was both intimately engaged with European practices and yet able to assert its own independent stance. John McGavin investigates the journey of an early seventeenth-century Scots gentleman, Thomas Ker, to Europe, showing how private writing of the time can testify not only to early modern Scottish aesthetic and cultural taste but to Scots involvement in high level governmental intelligence gathering.

As stated earlier, if his field is the wide map of Scottish literary geography, Ronnie's particular path through that field is laid down by his abiding interest in form, rhetoric and literary craftsmanship. Perhaps unsurprisingly, this is especially apparent in a number of the medieval essays. Elizabeth Elliott re-directs attention from the biographical contexts of the *Kingis Quair* to argue the poem's relationship to the medieval craft of memory, illuminating its appropriation and interpretation of its source in Boethius's *Consolation of Philosophy*. Kevin McGinley's delicate analysis of Henryson's puns in the

Testament of Cresseid reveals how competing spiritual and secular values are brought into play, enriching the polysemous complexity of the poem. David Moses examines the "nut and kernel" metaphor to show how Henryson draws on Augustinian sign theory to develop his own ideas of metaphoricity and interpretation. Such focus on rhetorical craft re-emerges through later stages of the collection. In his essay on Sir Thomas Urquhart, another of Ronnie's own subjects, John Corbett explores the extravagant imagination yet broad and learned scholarship with which Urquhart developed his proposals for a "universal language" which could transform both learning and literature. Ken Simpson's detailed analysis of the craftsmanship underlying the couthy manner of Barrie's *Farewell Miss Julie Logan* extends the analysis of form into the twentieth century.

The field of Scottish literary studies is different from what it was when Ronnie first began. Indeed, ten years on from when the *Mercat Anthology* was first published, arguably the ground beneath has shifted a little more, though "ploughing" of "the half acre called Scottish Literature" (Jack ed. 1997: xxxix) is still far from done. All the essays collected here pay tribute in one way or another to Ronnie's interests, scholarship and influence. Many, especially from former postgraduate students, bear more personal witness to his inspirational intellectual energy. He was able to kindle in generations of students his own responsiveness to the "Ioyous sweit Imaginatioun" which Gavin Douglas attributes to poetry in the *Palis of Honour* (Bawcutt ed. 2003: 69). Douglas's account of "the Court Rhetoricall" sums up many of Ronnie's lifelong concerns with the delight, the ornate craft and the persuasiveness of poetic rhetoric:

Yone is the court of joyus discipline
Quhilk causys folk thair purpos till expres
In ornat wyse provocand with gladnes,
All gentyll hartis to thare lare inclyne. (Bawcutt ed. 2003: 59)

This introduction has explored the distinctiveness and singularity of Ronnie's achievements as well as suggesting their most "anticipatory" and influential aspects – an imaginative and intellectual openness which is simultaneously focussed "inwardly" on form and method; an historical and generic breadth of vision which, to use

Ronnie's own words, is "equally intricate and equally interconnected" (Jack 1991: 252). In his writing, he often cites the famous analogy drawn by medieval writers between literal and metaphorical "building":

It is not without value to call to mind what we see happen in the construction of buildings, where first the foundation is laid, then the structure is raised upon it, and finally, when the work is all finished, the house is decorated by the laying on of colour. (Minnis ed. 1991: 74)

The *Palis of Honour* is arguably one of the most fantastical of allegorical edifices in which the poet-dreamer composes a "lay" celebrating the contemplation of "Ioyous sweit Imaginatioun" alluded to earlier. In that spirit, Ronnie's work has helped us comprehend the imaginative architecture of so many Scottish writers. This collection testifies both to the impact of his own work and to its continuing contribution to the development of the discipline of Scottish literary study.

Bibliography

Bawcutt, Priscilla (ed.) 2003. *The Shorter Poems of Gavin Douglas* [Scottish Text Society 5th Series no. 2.]. Edinburgh: Scottish Text Society.

Jack, R.D.S. 1972. *The Italian Influence on Scottish Literature*. Edinburgh: Edinburgh University Press.

—. and Andrew Noble (eds). 1982. *The Art of Robert Burns*. London: Vision Press.

—. 1986. *Scotland's Literary Debt to Italy*. Edinburgh: Edinburgh University Press.

—. 1991. *The Road to the Never Land: A Re-assessment of J.M. Barrie's Dramatic Art*. Aberdeen: Aberdeen University Press.

—. 1997. "Translating the Lost Scottish Renaissance" in *Translation and Literature* 6(1): 66–80.

—. 2001. "'Versi Strani': Early Scottish Translation" in Rose, Margaret and Emanuela Rossini (eds) *Italian Scottish Identities and Connections*. Edinburgh and Milan: Italian Cultural Institute. 111–20.

—. and P.A.T. Rozendaal (eds). [1997] 2003. *The Mercat Anthology of Early Scottish Literature: 1375–1707*. Edinburgh: Mercat Press.

—. and Tom Hubbard (eds). 2006. *Scotland in Europe*. Amsterdam and New York: Rodopi.

—. 2006. "Translation and Early Scottish Literature" in Jack, R.D.S. and Tom Hubbard (eds). *Scotland in Europe*. Amsterdam and New York: Rodopi. 39–54.

Minnis, Alastair and A.B. Scott (eds). 1991. *Medieval Literary Theory and Criticism c1100-c1375. The Commentary Tradition*. Oxford: Clarendon Press.

The Open Sentence: Memory, Identity and Translation in the *Kingis Quair*

Elizabeth Elliott

This paper associates the *Kingis Quair*'s treatment of the personal history of James I with the medieval craft of memory, as a tradition which suggests a precedent for the text's combination of allegory and autobiography, and illuminates its response to its source material, Boethius's *Consolation of Philosophy*.
Keywords: Allegory, Boethius, James I, *Kingis Quair*, Memory.

The fifteenth-century *Kingis Quair* is perhaps best known for its association with James I of Scotland, and for the first person narrative it presents as a record of the monarch's youthful experience. Although the king is never named within the poem, the narrator's account of his early life is telling, as he describes his capture at sea when "Noght ferr passit the state of innocence, / Bot nere about the nowmer of yeris thre" and his life as a prisoner in a foreign land thereafter, "Without confort [...] Nere by the space of yeris twise nyne" (Norton-Smith cd. 1971: ll.148–49, 171, 173; subsequent references are to this edition). This personal history has long been acknowledged to correspond to that of James Stewart, whose ship was taken by pirates as he sailed for France in 1406, and who remained a hostage in England until 1424, when he returned to Scotland as king (Brown 2000). The external evidence of the manuscript implies that, at the least, the poem's scribes and readers recognised this correspondence, as the identification is made explicit both in an original scribal colophon and in a later note, which describes the poem as "the Kingis Quair [...] Maid quhen his Maiestie wes in Ingland" (Norton-Smith ed. 1971: xix).

While the earliest modern editors and critics of the *Quair* readily accepted this identification as evidence of James's authorship, the attribution became the focus of a long-standing controversy with the publication of James Brown's *Authorship of The Kingis Quair* in 1896. The ensuing debate stimulated attempts to establish the context of the *Quair*'s production through analysis of the manuscript's provenance and language, and is usefully summarised by Petrina (1997: 53–59).

However, in recent years, few critics have done more than acknowledge those doubts which still remain as to the origin of this work or,
with a few notable exceptions such as Mapstone's article, have even
examined the significance of the poem's connection with James I
(Mapstone 1997). The debate has lapsed into silence, perhaps because
many critics have come to share Derek Pearsall's view that it had
already attracted too much attention, "the question of authorship
having diverted criticism from its main task of elucidation" (1966:
226–27). Yet this assessment serves to identify the limitations of past
attempts to address this subject, which have sought primarily to
confirm or deny James's role as originator of the text, treating the
work as the product of a unique consciousness whose identity can be
at least partially recovered through the project of criticism. Such an
individualist position is, to an extent, a prerequisite for attribution
studies, whose subject has been defined as "the uniqueness of each
human being and how this is enacted in writing" (Love 2002: 4).
However, it appears somewhat strange in view of more recent models
of authorship, which have denied the agency of the individual in recognising the determining influence of historical context, or the capacity of language to efface its own origins (Love 2002: 7). Moreover, the
aims of such criticism are at odds with medieval conceptions of
authorship, in which the unique qualities of the writer are typically of
less import than the role the text might play in the ethical development
of its readership, as writing takes on a communal purpose, reflected in
the cooperation of author, scribes, illuminators, and others involved in
the production of a manuscript (Minnis 1988).

The naive model of authorship which informs previous discussions of the *Quair*'s origins has tended to produce criticism that
disregards the poem as it draws attention to the author as historical
subject, rather than as a presence invoked and constructed within the
text itself. In this article, I seek to redress the balance in highlighting
some of the misreadings provoked by this model of authorship, and in
exploring the ways in which the *Quair* works to shape the personal
history of James I as a literary artefact.

It is significant that much past criticism of the *Quair* responds to
its treatment of James I's early life as chronicle history rather than

literature, a case in point being the poet's description of his capture, which alludes to his age at that time:

Noght ferr passit the state of innocence,
Bot nere about the nowmer of yeris thre –
Were it causit throu hevinly influence
Of goddis will, or othir casualtee
Can I noght say – bot out of my contree,
By thaire avise that had of me the cure,
Be see to pas tuke I myn auenture (ll.148–54)

In seeking to resolve the question of the *Quair*'s authorship, critics such as James Brown consider this as a bald statement of fact. Since the "state of innocence" is a conventional reference to the first seven years of life, the poem indicates that James was approximately ten years old at the time of his capture, and as James was probably born in late July of 1394, to interpret this in the strictest sense would suggest a date in 1405. For Brown this was proof positive that James could not have composed the *Quair*, since it was known that he had been taken hostage in 1406 (Brown 1896: 48–60). In seeking to challenge this argument, critics have proposed numerous practical solutions: the fallibility of human memory; the customs of a time less concerned with the measurement of age than our own; or the exigencies of the rhyme scheme within the verse (McDiarmid ed. 1973: 40–41). However, these counter claims largely admit the premise of Brown's argument, in treating the passage as a historical document rather than examining its poetic purpose and literary context.

As has often been observed, the opening of the *Quair*, "Heigh in the hevynnis figure circulere", invokes a circular form that was highly significant for a contemporary audience, since spheres and circles were thought to reflect the eternal being of God in their endlessness and their use often indicates a concern with divine matters (Jack 1989: 19–20; Jack and Rozendaal eds 1997: 56). Circles are invoked throughout the *Quair*, and especially at its beginning, where the orbits of the heavenly bodies are echoed in the "rolling" of the narrator's thoughts and the "tolter quhele" of Fortune (stanzas 8–10). As the opening line is repeated at the close of the poem, the circular structure of the work as a whole is revealed, in the poet's affirmation that the "f[a]tall influence" he has described was determined by God's providence, written "Hich in the hevynnis figure circulere" (1366, 1372). In this context, the poet's reference to "the nowmer of yeris thre", and his expression of doubt as to whether his capture was "causit throu hevinly influence / Of goddis will" are suggestive. For a contemporary audience, they might bring to mind the significance of fortunate numbers, which appear in popular works such as the Miracle Cycles as the sign of the perfection of the divine order, and such an impression would be reinforced by the poet's account of his imprisonment, "Nere by the space of yeris twise nyne" (Jack 1989: 18–19, 22–3). Three, as the first unified number, and nine, as its square, were commonly associated with the Trinity, so that the patterning of James's life in the poet's description prefigures the explicit statement that his fate was determined by providence at the close of the poem. Unlike the more complex numerological schemes discovered in the *Quair* by critics such as John MacQueen and Alice Miskimin, this interpretation would be available to a listening audience as well as to readers of the poem (MacQueen 1977: 187–92; Miskimin 1977). Moreover, for a medieval audience, such a reading would perhaps be more immediate and significant than the factual interpretation of modern critics, since the discipline of history was not so much conceived as an objective record of past events, but rather as a demonstration of God's personal care for man (Jack 1989: 33–34). The effective function of the numerological design of James's life in the *Quair* as an authorial sign recognising and emphasising such care would be of far greater importance than the historical fact of his age.

The effect of this tendency to read such allusions in the *Quair* in terms of the conventions of chronicle history and, correspondingly, to treat the analysis of James I's relationship to the poem as an activity that detracts from critical study of the work as literature can also be recognised in the perception of the autobiographical mode of the *Quair* as an anomaly. This is reflected in assessments of the work as an "uneasy cohabitation of dream and autobiography", where the "'modern' biographical mode" meets "medieval tradition" (Petrina 1997: 34, 38). Yet this apparent difficulty might be resolved if the *Quair* were considered in the light of a medieval tradition which treats personal experience as a textual entity in itself: the diverse body of practices that modern scholarship calls the craft of memory, and which has been most fully analysed by Mary Carruthers (1990).

The primary importance of memory in the preservation and transmission of both individual experience and the documents of past events and knowledge, at a time when few of the learned could depend on regular access to libraries, in itself provides a link between contemporary perceptions of the literary and the personal. Such a link is reinforced by the Aristotelian conception of character as the effect of habit that informed the craft of memory. In experiencing the same sensations and repeating the same actions, the individual's character is formed over a period of time, so that the memory of this experience becomes a definitive influence on personality and future behaviour (Aristotle 1984: 2: 1742). This personal experience derives its ethical meaning from contact with the memory of a community, through education, and the literary text plays an important part in this interaction (Carruthers 1990: 68–69, 24–25). Rather than adopting the "objective" stance which continues to underwrite much modern scholarship, the medieval scholar makes his reading a part of himself, adding it to the memory that mediates his experience of the present time. In this context, the primary object of literary study was not the text as an entity with its own intrinsic meaning, but the ways in which the text might contribute to a subject's ethical behaviour on a specific present occasion. As Carruthers argues, the tenor of this approach may be traced in the custom of *sortes*, in which the opening of a book at random, and the treatment of the words found there as a source of personal guidance, reflect a conception of ethics as coincident with rhetoric, as a practice which entails the adaptation of a generalised content to a specific set of circumstances (1990: 163). Since the aim of this practice is ethical development, the relationship between reader and text is conceived as one of mutual alteration, an idea reflected in the use of rumination as a metaphor for memory work, with its associations with the transformative process of digestion (Carruthers 1990: 164–65).

If the craft of memory offers a parallel for the *Quair*'s treatment of personal experience and identity as textual elements, however, it also presents a model for the poem's approach to those texts which it evokes, either explicitly or implicitly. Indeed, to a medieval audience, the opening lines of the *Quair* in themselves might suggest a work that would deal with memorial themes. Practitioners of the art of memory sought to organise their mental materials according to schemata which enabled them to locate and manipulate information at will, and one source of such schemata was astronomy. Not only were celestial maps useful as mnemotechnical devices, but cosmology was also associated with inventive meditation, in schemes such as the Six Days of Creation in Genesis, or the angelic circles which appear in the commentary tradition (Carruthers and Ziolkowski 2002: 15–16). In this context, the opening of the *Quair*, "in the hevynis figure circulere", appears particularly suggestive as the first stanza of a work which deals so prominently with the recollection of past events and the difficulties of poetic composition. Moreover, the prologue goes on to focus on an act of reading performed by the narrator, who chooses the *Consolation of Philosophy* to while away a disturbed night, and is afterwards moved to write about his own experience. A contemporary reader who was familiar with the techniques of mnemonic work might be struck by the juxtaposition of the *Quair*'s celestial opening with the situation of a solitary reader working at night, as seclusion and the silence of the nocturnal hours were often recommended as being the most favourable conditions for the exercise of memory (Carruthers 1990: 86, 173). The requirements of medieval mnemotechnique remain prominent as the poet describes the book which will inspire his own composition:

Of quhich the name is clepit properly
Boece (efter him that was the compiloure),
Schewing [the] counsele of Philosophye,
Compilit by that noble senatoure
Of Rome, quhilom that was the warldis floure,
And from estate, by Fortune for a quhile
Foriugit was to pouert in exile (ll.15–21).

Mnemotechnique is dependent on the establishment of systematic associations, and requires a firm starting-point to act as the key to that order. For the medieval practitioners of the art of memory, the starting-point of a text was its title (Carruthers 1990: 86). In this respect, the poet of the *Quair*'s concern with the proper name of the work suggests that his description is intended to serve the requirements of memorisation Further statements on the subject and order of the *Consolation*, both here and in the following stanza, bear a strong resemblance to those found under the headings which make up academic prologues, which were themselves designed as external supports for the memory (Minnis 1988: 4–30; Carruthers 1990: 194).

From its inception, then, the *Quair* may be said to invoke the techniques of a memorial practice which treats the authoritative text as a means to ethical behaviour, so that the reader might anticipate that the poet's treatment of Boethian philosophy will follow a similar pattern. However, modern criticism of the *Quair* has tended to read the poet's engagement with the *Consolation* in terms of the validity of his interpretation of the Boethian text (Petrina 1997: 44–48, 92–93). More controversially, critics such as Vincent Carretta and Clair F. James interpret the poem as a sceptical meditation on courtly love, depicting the narrator's loss of reason and fall into sin, in readings which complement Katherine Heinrichs' argument that the use of Boethian material in an amatory context typically parodies the *Consolation,* substituting the philosopher's deliverance from Fortune's bondage for the misguided lover's submission to love *par amours* (Carretta 1981; James 1993; Heinrichs 1990: 184, 217–18). Such arguments attribute a fixed meaning to the Boethian text, a position that not only ignores the role of the reader in an interpretive practice whose focus is ethical development, but also fails to acknowledge the rhetorical context in which the poem situates itself.

To offer an analogy with medieval academic practice, the opening of the *Quair* corresponds to the circumstantial topic *cur* or *causa*, also known as *intentio auctoris*, the prologue heading in which the scholar identifies the aims and circumstances that moved the author to write (Copeland 1991: 76–82). Although other dream poems, including Guillaume de Deguileville's *Pèlerinage de la vie humaine* and Chaucer's *Book of the Duchess* and *Parliament of Fowls*, also depict a text as their point of origin, the *Quair* is distinctive because the act of reading it describes does not provoke the dream it relates. Instead, the narrator's contact with Boethius' *Consolation* offers "mater new[e]" for a literary composition that is apparently more concerned with the poet's own past than with the work he has just encountered (1.54). The process described suggests a notion of rhetorical invention that identifies composition with the creative adaptation of traditional literary subjects rather than the treatment of unfamiliar matters, and this notion reflects a tendency in later medieval poetics which has been examined by Rita Copeland. In particular, Copeland highlights the development of conceptions of the roles of poet and translator as sharing common ground in their handling of received material, but diverging in the degree of innovation in their treatment of such sources. While the translator responds explicitly to a source, assuming a subservient position, the poet seeks to gain possession of such material (1991: 171–79).

The role of the source text in this model of literary invention reflects the contemporary understanding of rhetoric as a means of carrying out the transfer of learning and empire between cultures, the notion of *translatio studii et imperii* which interpreted Charlemagne's Empire as a renewal of the power of imperial Rome, and saw translation as a way of transferring the authority of the classical authors to other languages through translation, commentary and the invention of new literary forms (Evans et al. 1999: 318–19). As Copeland argues, the classical idea of translation, expressed in the desire of Romans such as Cicero to bring the eloquence of conquered Greece to the Latin tongue, is "founded on a historical agenda of conquest and supremacy through submission" (Copeland 1989: 17). In treating the source text like a poet, with innovation, the classical author sought not only to assimilate but also to surpass his material. While medieval writers did not tend to adopt this stance overtly, since poet, like *auctor*, was a term that implied authority and was most often applied to the authors of respected works in the classical languages, the project of translation might still act as a means of appropriation (Brownlee 1984: 7–23). The fidelity of the translator lies in making the meaning of the source text readily accessible, as a prologue to the later edition of the Wycliffite Bible expresses it, to "let the sentence euere be hool and open" (Burnley 1989: 50–51). As David Burnley argues, this is not a reference to the sentence as a syntactical unit, but to the meaning of the text, which the translator must seek to clarify even at the expense of the order or literal meaning of the words of the source (1989: 50–51). In a culture which approached literary texts as a source of knowledge to be added to the memorial store in order to improve the ethical character of the scholar, this meaning is not the particular message the author intended to convey, but rather what the text has to teach the reader about living a moral life. It is a method epitomised by the interpretation and allegorisation of pagan *auctores* such as Ovid so that their works may be understood in a way which conforms to Christian teaching: the intention of the interpreter thereby displaces that of the original producer (Minnis 1988: 20–21). Handled in this way, the source text could undergo significant changes, since the translator or commentator is effectively rewriting its substance in order to reveal the significance he has himself determined.

In this sense, the vernacular translation displaces the original as the object of interest, an effect which increased as text, critical apparatus and commentary came to be rendered into the vernacular. In the later Middle Ages, the practice of translation was understood to include approaches ranging from explicit subservience to the source text to approaches which seek to displace the source text, presenting the resulting vernacular composition as an independent work (Copeland 1991). Gradually, this posture of translation enabled vernacular writers to locate responsibility for the work in themselves rather than their sources, to take on the authorising function. This shift in the conception of the vernacular writer and the relationship he bears to his work is reflected in the practice of Chaucer, who reserves the term "poet" for the authors of works in the classical languages and Italian, and adopts the posture of translator even in his most imaginative works like the *Prologue* to the *Legend of Good Women*. However, his appropriation of the discourse of academic theory causes the reader to perceive the translator as *auctor*, identifying the writer's nature and personal experience as the direct cause of the text rather than emphasising the classical matter his work incorporates (Copeland 1991: 193–94). A similar shift is reflected in the extension of the word "poet" in the French language to include the producers of vernacular, contemporary works, being first applied to Guillaume de Machaut (Brownlee 1984: 7–23).

The *Kingis Quair* both articulates and responds to this redefinition of the role of the vernacular writer, producing a work which acknowledges its origins in an act of reading, yet at the same time strictly delimits its reliance on any traditional source. The opening of the poem sets up a contrast between the narrator's experience of misfortune and that of Boethius, whose *Consolation* describes his own imprisonment, brought about by his attempts to preserve the Roman government, and his consolation by Lady Philosophy, who teaches him about the nature of fortune and free will. The *Consolation* is precisely the kind of work a vernacular author might introduce to valorise his own text, yet in the *Quair*, Boethius is not described as an author, but as "the compiloure" of "counsele of philosophye". This use of a term derived from academic theory is significant, since it denotes a practitioner who orders materials written by others, a role distinct from that of *auctor* as it underlines the absence of creative input (Minnis 1988: 94, 100–2). In contrast with the later description of Boethius as "enditing" (composing) his work, this perhaps implies an awareness of the synthetic nature of Boethius' composition, while it also emphasises the relationship between the writer and his text as it is portrayed within the *Consolation*, in which Boethius presents himself as the recipient of Philosophy's counsel rather than its author. Although Boethius' ability to benefit from the personal experience of "infortune, pouert and distresse" in making them the foundation of "his verray sekernesse" is highlighted, the value of his work is asserted only to be immediately undermined:

With mony a noble resoun (as him likit)
Enditing in his fair[e] Latyne tong,
So full of fruyte and rethorikly pykit,
Quhich to declare my scole is ouer yong;
Therefore I lat him pas, and in my tong
Procede I will agayn to my sentence
Of my mater, and leve all incidence (ll.43–49)

The rhetorical figures and fruitful meaning of the Latin text are acknowledged to be beyond the poet's academic skill to "declare" (interpret), or perhaps even beyond the scope of the vocabulary offered by the vernacular, if "scole" is understood as a reference to his language, as a recent edition has argued (James I 1999). If the poet of the *Quair* were seeking to valorise his work as a subservient exposition of an authoritative text, this would present a serious problem. However, rather than preventing the fulfilment of the writer's literary project, this deficit is dismissed as relating to "incidence", incidental matter which is irrelevant to the "sentence" or meaning of his material. The poet's "mater new[e]", revealed to him through the reading of Boethius, is rather "how that eche estate, / As Fortune lykith, thame will [ay] translate", a subject further refined and personalised in the injunction he attributes to the matins bell: "tell on, man, quhat thee befell" (ll.54–56, 77).

Far from adopting the posture of a translator, the writer is composing within a context in which near contemporaries and notable producers of vernacular works, Gower and Chaucer, may be acknowledged as "poetis laureate" (l.1376). Not only does the writer's adoption of the modesty topos emphasise his own rhetorical training but, in an opening which identifies the aims and circumstances which moved the author to write, as the conventions of the academic prologue required, he describes the causes of his own work and asserts its status as an innovation: "I tuke conclusione / Sum new thing to write" (ll.88–89). This "buke" is to be set against his past use of "ink and paper spent / To lyte effect", presumably unsuccessful works which had been completed, rather than failed attempts to write, since memory and wax tablets, not expensive paper, remained the usual media of composition (87–88). The vernacular writer, and not Boethius, is to bear responsibility for the matter of the text, adopting the position of *auctoritas*.

The first person perspective of the narrative, whose opening juxtaposes the personal history of Boethius with that of the narrator, reinforces this emphasis on subjective experience. Moreover, the temporal arrangement of the narrative significantly positions the reading of Boethius, not as the catalyst for the allegorical vision that the poet will describe, but as an event which provokes the writer to reassess his past experience. In this way, the knowledge of Fortune and the workings of necessity the protagonist obtains through his vision are framed as revealed knowledge rather than adaptations of Boethian textual matter. While the unanticipated effects of the narrator's reading of the *Consolation* appear to suggest an initial contact with the work, however, this is not stated directly, and caution is necessary since allusions to books as physical objects can serve as figurative references to the memorial store, the bookcases that furnish the private room of the memorial cell (Carruthers 1998: 108). Yet, if the opening of the work is not an unambiguous denial of prior knowledge of the *Consolation*, it shifts the focus from the authoritative text as the source of transcendent and ethically beneficial meaning to an essential significance transmitted to both Boethius and the protagonist through visionary experience and, in so doing, it valorises a focus on personal experience over the mediation of textual authority.

The idea that the experiences of both Boethius and the James I persona of the *Quair* are invested with similar meaning can once again be attributed to the work's affinity with memorial craft. As Carruthers argues, the characteristic approach of the craft of memory, which seeks a transcendent meaning in its source and applies this generalised content to the specific context of an individual's character, is embodied in the collections known as *florilegia*. In these works, the formal arrangement of illustrations under topical headings reproduces the ordering principle of mnemotechnique, in a practice that reflects a conception of knowledge as a series of universal truths which only find expression in contingent forms. Each articulation of a concept such as justice thereby contributes to human understanding of this truth, in adding to the copiousness of its definition. Within a community which shares this epistemology and training, this activity can also be performed before a present audience, and Carruthers cites the example of Heloise, who quotes the lament of Cornelia from Lucan's *Pharsalia* on taking holy orders. In doing so, she is not acting the part of Cornelia, but articulating the sense that her own experience repeats that of Cornelia by associating the "public memory" derived from Lucan's text with her own action. Her speech creates a commonplace to be held together within a common memory locus, provided by her present audience, which contributes to the definitional copiousness of both the text and her own experience (Carruthers 1990: 26, 174–85). By linking his own narrative to that of Boethius, the protagonist of the *Quair* might be said to create a similar commonplace, in which the shared elements of their experience take on new meaning.

In using the title "Boece", the poet of the *Quair* immediately identifies the text with its producer, a relationship which is reinforced as Boethius' status and the circumstances that inspired him to write are alluded to: his fall from grace into "pouert in exile" (4). This emphasis reflects the interest in Boethius' life displayed in the translations and commentaries on the *Consolation*, and the *vitae* that were often included in Boethian manuscripts (Patch 1935: 9–20; McCosker 1993: 108–10). Such an interest might be read as an acknowledgement of the vital contribution which Boethius' identity and circumstances make to the meaning of the *Consolation*, and of the particular influence of the first book, which discusses his involvement in politics at some length as the immediate cause of his imprisonment and misfortune. His status as a nobleman becomes particularly significant since, in his role as interlocutor, Boethius exemplifies the work's target audience, who are described as a body of wise and virtuous men identified with the Senate (Boethius 1999: I pr. 4). Moreover, his suffering is depicted as the effect of his desire to work for the common good, in accordance with Philosophy's charge that her students must concern themselves with government to prevent the wicked from holding sway (I pr. 4). The notion of such an obligation reflects Platonic teaching, and is also manifested in the prevalence of the belief in the Middle Ages that a good ruler should also be a philosopher (Courcelle 1984: 60–66).

In the context of a reading practice conceived as the foundation of moral character, these features of the *Consolation* are inscribed within an interpretation of the text as a work which reflects the teachings of the mirror of princes tradition (Minnis and Machan 1993: 167–68). Significantly, the *Consolation's* form, a model which demonstrates the progress of its subject from a state of sorrow to one of effective consolation through the healing influence of music and argument, is echoed in the *remède* and *confort* modes adopted by French love poets in order to address the political misfortunes of the nobility during the Hundred Year's War (Poiron 1980: 149–50). Moreover, the text's philosophical education is apparently perceived as a means of overcoming the fear of personal loss which engagement in political life might entail, a reading implicit in the use of its form in a didactic text such as Guillaume de Machaut's *Confort d'ami*, a work which draws directly on the materials of the *de regimine principium* tradition as it offers advice to Machaut's imprisoned patron, Charles II of Navarre (de Machaut 1921: 3). Indeed, the *Confort* makes such a reading explicit in the narrator's plea to the reader:

Je te pri que tu te conseilles
A bonnes gens et que tu veilles
A faire le commun pourfit,
Einsi com Boësses le fit
Et com maint philosophe firent
Qui mainte doleur en souffrirent
Et furent chacié en essil.
L'escripture le dit, mais cil
Qui en ce faisoient, verité
Destruisoit leur iniquité (133, ll.3749–58)

[I implore you to be advised by good people and aspire to work for common profit as Boethius and many other philosophers did, suffering great pain in doing so, and being hunted into exile. Scripture says that, for those who do so, truth will destroy their iniquity]

Here both scripture and Boethius are cited as authorities that bear complementary readings, whose value arguably lies in their ability to inspire people to work for common profit despite the risk of pain and suffering incurred in so doing.

Against this background, the emphasis placed on the shared elements of Boethius' and James's experience in the *Quair* serves to highlight their status as political prisoners. In particular, the narrator's identification of Boethius' fate as that of "exile" manipulates the metaphor which Philosophy employs to describe the estrangement of the human soul from the knowledge of its true object to present a more compelling parallel between his circumstances and those of the Scottish exile (Boethius 1999 I: pr. 5). Moreover if, as Philosophy argues, adversity should be understood as a revelation of Fortune's disposition, the experience of political misfortune in particular becomes significant as a means to enable the subject to grasp the nature of the human condition, since it offers an immediate knowledge of the terms used to represent that metaphysical state (II pr. 1). Therefore, Boethius' imprisonment is not simply a menace to the stability of his worldview, but might even be seen as a necessary circumstance for the completion of his philosophical education, and the same might be said for that of James. More work is necessary to demonstrate the extent of the *Quair*'s debt to the medieval reception history of Boethius, but such a context holds out the promise of a reading of the poem which does not dismiss its engagement with the *Consolation* as a substitution of earthly love for the rejection of the material world as the means of attaining the supreme good (Fuog 2001: 43). Instead, the depiction of James as the recipient of a vision which brings him a knowledge of fortune and assuages the pain of his imprisonment may be read as an indication that he, like Boethius, has achieved the wisdom that a good ruler must possess. Here, his final action in the vision, in climbing on Fortune's wheel despite his knowledge of its unstable nature, does not represent a proof of his moral decay or interest in worldly things, but rather a willingness to pursue his worldly duties as a potentate despite the threat of personal loss (171–72).

Bibliography

Aristotle. 1984. *The Complete Works of Aristotle* (ed. Jonathan Barnes) 2 vols. Princeton: Princeton University Press.

Boethius. 1999. *The Consolation of Philosophy* (trans. Victor Watts). Harmondsworth: Penguin.

Brown, J.T.T. 1896. *The Authorship of* The Kingis Quair: *A New Criticism*. Glasgow: MacLehose.

Brown, Michael. 2000. *James I*. Rev. ed. East Linton: Tuckwell.

Brownlee, Kevin. 1984. *Poetic Identity in Guillaume de Machaut*. Wisconsin: University of Wisconsin Press.

Burnley, J.D. 1989. "Late Medieval English Translation: Types and Reflections" in Ellis, Roger, (ed.) *The Medieval Translator: The Theory and Practice of Translation in the Middle Ages*. Cambridge: Brewer. 37–53.

Carretta, Vincent. 1981. "The *Kingis Quair* and the *Consolation of Philosophy*" in *Studies in Scottish Literature* 16: 14–28.

Carruthers, Mary J. 1990. *The Book of Memory: A Study of Memory in Medieval Culture*. Cambridge: Cambridge University Press.

—. 1998. *The Craft of Thought: Meditation, Rhetoric, and the Making of Images, 400–1200*. Cambridge: Cambridge University Press.

—. and Jan M. Ziolkowski (eds). 2002. *The Medieval Craft of Memory: An Anthology of Texts and Pictures*. Philadelphia: University of Pennsylvania Press.

Copeland, Rita. 1989. "The Fortunes of 'Non Verbum Pro Verbo': Or, Why Jerome is not a Ciceronian" in Ellis, Roger (ed.) *The Medieval Translator: The Theory and Practice of Translation in the Middle Ages*. Cambridge: Brewer. 15–35.

—. 1991. *Rhetoric, Hermeneutics, and Translation in the Middle Ages: Academic Traditions and Vernacular Texts*. Cambridge: Cambridge University Press.

Courcelle, Pierre. 1984. *La Consolation de Philosophie dans la tradition littéraire*. Paris: Etudes augustiniennes.

de Machaut, Guillaume. 1921. *Œuvres de Guillaume de Machaut* (ed. Ernest Hœpffner). 3 vols. Paris: Firmin Didot.

Evans, Ruth, et al. 1999. "The Notion of Vernacular Literary Theory" in Wogan-Browne, Jocelyn et al. (eds) *The Idea of the Vernacular: An Anthology of Middle English Literary Theory, 1280–1520*. Exeter: University of Exeter Press. 314–30.

Fuog, Karin Edie Capri. 2001. "Placing Earth at the Center of the Cosmos: *The Kingis Quair* as Boethian Revision" in *Studies in Scottish Literature* 32: 140–49.

Heinrichs, Katherine. 1990. *The Myths of Love: Classical Lovers in Medieval Literature*. Pennsylvania: Pennsylvania University Press.

Jack, R.D.S. 1989. *Patterns of Divine Comedy: A Study of Medieval English Drama*. Edinburgh: Brewer.

—. and P. A. T. Rozendaal (eds). 1997. *The Mercat Anthology of Early Scottish Literature 1375–1707*. Edinburgh: Mercat.

James I of Scotland. 1999. *"The Kingis Quair:* Opening" in Wogan-Browne, Jocelyn et al. (eds) *The Idea of the Vernacular: An Anthology of Middle English Literary Theory, 1280–1520.* Exeter: University of Exeter Press. 300–4.

James, Clair F. 1993. *"The Kingis Quair*: The Plight of the Courtly Lover" in Chamberlain, David (ed.) *New Readings of Late Medieval Love Poems.* Lanham, Maryland: UP of America. 95–118.

Love, Harold. 2002. *Attributing Authorship: An Introduction.* Cambridge: Cambridge University Press.

MacQueen, John. 1977. "The Literature of Fifteenth-Century Scotland" in Brown, Jennifer M. (ed.) *Scottish Society in the Fifteenth Century.* London: Arnold. 184–208.

Mapstone, Sally. 1997. "Kingship and the *Kingis Quair*" in Cooper, Helen, and Sally Mapstone (eds.) *The Long Fifteenth Century: Essays for Douglas Gray.* Oxford: Clarendon Press. 51–69.

McCosker, S. 1993. *The Politics of Philosophy: Latin and English Interpretations of Boethius'* Consolatio *up to 1066.* DPhil thesis. University of Sydney.

McDiarmid, Matthew P. (ed.) 1973. *The Kingis Quair of James Stewart.* London: Heinemann.

Minnis, A.J. 1988. *Medieval Theory of Authorship: Scholastic Literary Attitudes in the Later Middle Ages.* 2nd edn. Aldershot: Wildwood.

—. and Tim William Machan. 1993. "The *Boece* as Late-Medieval Translation" in Minnis, A. J. (ed.) *Chaucer's* Boece *and the Medieval Tradition of Boethius.* Cambridge: Brewer. 167–88.

Miskimin, Alice. 1977. "Patterns in the *Kingis Quair* and the *Temple of Glass*" in *Papers on Language and Literature* 13: 339–61.

Nims, Margaret F. (tr.) 1967. *Poetria Nova of Geoffrey of Vinsauf.* Toronto: Pontifical Institute of Medieval Studies.

Norton-Smith, John (ed.) 1971. *James I of Scotland: The Kingis Quair.* Oxford: Clarendon.

Patch, Howard Rollin. 1935. *The Tradition of Boethius: A Study of His Importance in Medieval Culture.* New York: Oxford University Press.

Pearsall, Derek. 1966. "The English Chaucerians" in Brewer, D.S. (ed.) *Chaucer and Chaucerians: Critical Studies in Middle English Literature.* London: Nelson. 201–39.

Petrina, Alessandra. 1997. *The* Kingis Quair *of James I of Scotland.* Padova: Unipress.

Poiron, Daniel. 1980. "Traditions et fonctions du *dit poétique* au XIVe et au XVe siècle" in Gumbrecht, Hans Ulrich (ed.) *Literatur in der Gesellschaft des Spätmittelalters.* Volume 1. Heidelberg: Winter. 147–50.

"In brief sermone ane pregnant sentence": Perspectivism in Robert Henryson's *The Te___ Cresseid*

Kevin J. McGinley

Henryson's *Testament of Cresseid* uses puns to juxtapose competing secular and spiritual understandings of the narrative, alternative levels of meaning which highlight each others' limitations. The puns help create a polysemous text with a model of representation where, for fallen humanity, comprehensive truth is diffracted into imperfect counterposed perspectives.
Keywords: Christian; Henryson; *Testament of Cresseid*; language; medieval; perspectivism; polysemy; puns; secular; wordplay.

Robert Henryson frequently uses wordplay to produce thematic complexity in *The Testament of Cresseid*. William Stephenson has shown how the poem employs the acrostic "fictio" in lines 57–63 to raise issues about authorship and sources (Stephenson 1994) while R.J. Lyall has drawn attention to how the poem's final stanza enriches the significance of the word "cheritie" l.612) through syntactic ambiguity (Lyall 1982: 184–85). The most commonly occurring form of wordplay in *The Testament*, however, is the pun. A pun, of course, occurs when one word simultaneously suggests two distinct meanings. Henryson uses two key types of pun: those based on homonymy, where different words have the same graphic and phonetic form, and those based on polysemy, where "one word has different but related senses" (Delabastita 1997: 5).[1] But it is the pun's capacity to yoke together and juxtapose different and even heterogeneous meanings that is crucial to its function in *The Testament*. Henryson's puns evoke contrasting spiritual and secular perspectives on the poem's action to produce a polysemous text which registers different perspectives that reflect critically on each other by exposing each other's relative limitations.

---

[1] The definitions and forms of pun focused on here should be taken as heuristic rather than definitive. For more extensive discussion, see Debastita 1997: 1–9; Heller 1974; Freidhof 1984.

The question of whether *The Testament of Cresseid* is a worldly or a spiritual tale has been a central point of critical debate (see Patterson 1973). Starkly summarised, the narrative seems bleakly tragic. It tells of Cresseid's infidelity and concupiscence and her subsequent blasphemy against Venus and Cupid for failing to ensure that she remained "the flour of luif" (l.128). These lead to the gods inflicting her with leprosy, her exile to the leper colony and finally her death. But many critics have considered that the poem depicts Cresseid's suffering not in terms of tragic loss but of moral gain. Her experience is seen to have led her away from a state of sin to experience spiritual regeneration:

> The consequences [of Cresseid's actions] are not the mere facts that Cresseid was punished and died a leper, but that through the working of God's will she was punished, brought to penitence, and ended by taking the blame on herself: in fact the story of her salvation according to the Christian scheme. (Tillyard 1948: 17; see also MacQueen 1967: 45–93; Fox 1968: 34–58.

The planetary gods who inflict leprosy on Cresseid are thus considered to represent natural and astrological forces operating on human life to enact the benign will of God (Fox 1968: 34–35; MacQueen 1967: 69–70; Tillyard 1948: 19–22). Critics who have taken this view have often dismissed any focus on Cresseid's material pain as a superficial perspective that fails to see the underlying positive spiritual dimension of her experience. Hence the narrator's sympathy for Cresseid's suffering leads Denton Fox to dismiss him as "morally imbecilic", and "stupidly and passionately involved" (Fox 1968: 57n; see also Lyall 1982: 188–89). From this perspective, to focus on the tragic worldly dimensions of the poem's action is to remain blind to the fact that Cresseid's fate has a purifying and redemptive function within a benevolent providential order. Viewed in terms of Cresseid's spiritual progress, the poem depicts not loss but gain, and the narrated events have been all for the good, making sorrow over them unnecessary and foolish.

Other critics, however, have stressed the material significance of Cresseid's suffering. As Douglas Duncan has pointed out, the *Testament* depicts Cresseid's leprosy in a graphic manner, powerfully evoking horror and sympathy for her suffering. This aspect of the poem demands that Cresseid's fate be understood with reference to the human misery to which she finds herself exposed, and invites an appreciation of the positive value of the secular happiness which she has lost (Duncan 1961: 129). The narrator's sympathy for Cresseid is also important from this perspective as a humane response to the pathos of her circumstances. Thus H.E. Tolliver notes that "only by seeing Cresseid through his [the narrator's] eyes can we judge her properly" (Tolliver 1965: 306). But those who take account of Cresseid's material suffering have often been dismissive of claims that the poem has a spiritual dimension. C.W. Jentoft and Dolores Noll view the poem as promoting a secular morality located in the values of courtly love so that the faithful love of Troilus which Cresseid loses takes on a positive value independent of any religious concerns. Jentoft argues that "Cresseid's sin is courtly, not Christian" (Jentoft 1974: 100), while Noll states that "Henryson has created, for the purposes of this poem, a love universe which is both self-contained and eclectic. Its self-containment precludes a relationship to a larger, Christian world" (Noll 1979: 18). For A.C. Spearing, the poem recommends no positive system of values whatsoever: there is, he affirms, "no suggestion of healing" (Spearing 1964: 144) and the poem simply displays "the inescapable factuality of physical and mental anguish" (139). He remarks that

At the end of *Troilus and Criseyde*, Chaucer is able to make the transition from earthly to heavenly love acceptable on at least an emotional level, because the love of Troilus and Criseyde has been presented as sharing the universal qualities of the love of God. But in Henryson's poem, by the very nature of his story, earthly love has no such qualities, and no positive alternative can be proposed. (141)

If the metaphysically-inclined critics tend to dismiss the pathos of Cresseid's material suffering and the value of earthly happiness, then the secular-minded are equally disposed to ignore any possible spiritual dimensions of the poem's actions.

Both sides of this critical debate, however, may have a point. A number of critics have suggested that *The Testament* is in fact a multi-layered text which includes distinct levels of concrete and metaphysical significance, encompassing sympathy and moral denunciation (Kindrick 1993: 204–7; Tolliver 1965: 305–6). This idea fits neatly with R.D.S. Jack's stress on the comprehensive character of medieval thought, which focuses on the ways in which writers aimed to encompass diverse and seemingly conflicting perspectives within a harmonising framework. In a fallen world the Word of God must be communicated using diverse and incomplete arguments which necessarily fragment the unity of divine truth, but which do so in order to present that truth in a manner adapted to the specific moral, spiritual or educational needs of different audiences. This enables medieval writers to embrace seemingly conflicting viewpoints, often within the same text. Such conflict is itself a sign of the imperfection of human knowledge and reminds the audience that the significances they derive from a text are not the ultimate truth, but a version of that truth adapted to their own flawed vision. (Jack 2001: 4–5; Jack 1989: 96–103)

In *The Testament*, the pun is an important device for signalling the text's plural levels of significance and for resisting attempts to close the poem's meaning on a single interpretation. This appears clearly in a homonymic pun early on in the poem: "Thocht lufe be hait" (l.29). The primary sense here is clearly that "hait" is an adjective meaning "hot", as is indicated by the following references to love as something which is kindled like fire (l.30). But the word "hait", especially when paired so closely with "lufe", also evokes the noun "hate". Although this meaning is not developed in the stanza, the idea that love and hate might be in some ways equivalent is thematically resonant in a poem in which, as some critics have it, romantic passion leads the protagonist into sin and moral degeneracy while merciful providence intervenes on her behalf by inflicting leprosy on her. This pun also introduces the idea that an action's value can vary radically according to the perspective from which it is viewed. Occurring so near the beginning of the poem it signals the need to mindful of this when evaluating the positive or negative significances of the subsequent actions.

A later example further illustrates how Henryson uses puns to indicate the importance of shifts in perspective in the poem. Cresseid's "Complaint" features a warning about the fragility of worldly pleasure: "Be war in tyme, approchis neir the end" (l.455), followed by a statement that failure to heed this warning might lead one to suffer a fate like hers or even worse: "As I am now, peraduenture that ye / For all your micht may cum to that same end, / Or ellis war, gif ony war may be" (ll.456–58). Here, there is a homonymic pun on "war". Its two meanings – "wary" and "worse" – seem to be opposed in that caution is being recommended in positive terms as a defence against the negative degenerative influence of fortune. But the echo produced by their occurring so closely together suggests a deeper complicity between these two senses of "war", perhaps implying that the deterioration of one's fortunes might itself be a cautionary indication of fortune's true nature, allowing one to see that "Fortoun is fikkil" (l.567). The point is Boethian, and leads to the paradoxical conclusion that the best fortune is bad fortune, as Boethius has Dame Philosophy remark:

> What I want to say is a paradox, and so I am hardly able to put it into words. [...] Good fortune always seems to bring happiness, but deceives you with her smiles, whereas bad fortune is always truthful because by changing she shows her true fickleness. Good fortune deceives, but bad fortune enlightens. (Boethius 1969: 76, Bk. II, Prose VIII)

The doubleness of "war" thus signals that a Boethian philosophy underlies *The Testament* and, in reminding us of the possibility that things which are bad in material terms may be good in spiritual terms, draws attention to the ways our understanding of an event's significance can change according to whether it is viewed from a worldly or an otherworldly outlook.

At least one other pun in the poem similarly signals that we should look beyond the factual circumstances of Cresseid's fate to find deeper layers of significance. The judgement which Saturn and Cynthia bring to bear on Cresseid is referred to as a "sentence", in the sense of a punishment determined by a court (ll.309, 327, 333). But "sentence" can also refer to the inner meaning of a text and is used thus frequently in Henryson's *Moral Fables* (ll.12, 117, 588, 1100, 1894, 2590) as well as earlier in *The Testament*: "In brief sermone ane pregnant sentence wryte" (l.270). This extra layer of significance suggests that the judicial punishment can also be read as revealing the inner truth of Cresseid's actions. In this it works together with the symbolic implications of how the physical symptoms of Cresseid's leprosy reflect the descriptions of Saturn and Cynthia. Both deities are described as of leaden complexion (ll.155, 257) while Saturn is associated with cold and "ouirfret with froistis hoir" (l.163) and Cynthia described as wearing a grey cloak "full of spottis blak" (l.260). Cresseid's leprosy brings these same qualities to her: Saturn changes her bodily humours from moist and hot to cold and dry (l.318). Cynthia makes Cresseid's voice "hoir" (l.338), presumably meaning "hoarse" but punningly echoing Saturn's "froistis hoir" (l.163), and also covers her face "with spottis blak" and "lumpis haw" (ll.339–40). As Saturn and Cynthia are conventional symbols of time and vicissitude, this imposition of their attributes on Cresseid turns her into a living emblem of mutability. In this, Cresseid's leprosy drastically reveals the transitory nature of the sensual pleasures to which she has been dedicated at the beginning of the story. The gods' "sentence" on Cresseid can thus be seen as an act of interpretation which makes apparent the deeper significance of her actions. The pun thus points to the idea that the punishment of leprosy might have an educative function in revealing otherwise hidden truths.

But if these puns suggest that Cresseid's leprosy and subsequent suffering might constitute a progress towards moral and spiritual enlightenment, others suggest that this is an unbalanced outlook which needs to be countered by sensitivity to the material suffering which the poem so vividly depicts. When the parliament of the pagan gods discusses how Cresseid should be dealt with, Cupid urges that she should receive "bitter panis" (l.277) and that "with pane we suld mak recompence" (l.291), while Mercury appoints Saturn and Cynthia to make a judgement on "the pane of Cresseid". (l.299) "Pane" is an example of a polysemous pun, in which the same word has different connotations (Preminger 1986: 224; Fuog 2001: 20), as it can mean either "punishment" or simply "pain". The legal setting of the parliament and the use of terms, such as "meid", "recompence", and "modifie", associated with matters of compensation and legal judgements suggest that "pane" should be understood in terms of justly deserved punishment and possibly even atonement. Thus Fox, for instance, argues that Cresseid's leprosy is "a punishment sent by God" (Fox 1968: 38) but that it has a spiritually purifying and expiatory function which ties in with the view that lepers underwent purgatory on earth (Fox 1981: lxxxviii–ix).

Matthew P. McDiarmid, however, questions this positive view of Cresseid's punishment. Noting the evident malice and hostility of the gods evident in Cupid's appeal "ga help to reuenge, I yow pray" (1.294), he comments trenchantly that "No sensible man would suppose, yet it has been usually supposed, that in their collective 'wisdom' they could set up as spokesmen for God" (McDiarmid 1981: 102). The pun on "pane", by allowing the sense of "punishment" to be shadowed by the starker meaning "pain", incorporates a similar questioning of the concept of divine punishment even as it also registers this providential vision. By reminding us of the harsh factuality of Cresseid's material trauma, the pun highlights the limitations of the optimistic providential interpretation of the poem, always recalling that this eternal justice proceeds by a ruthless denudation of all joy from earthly life.

The narrator's sympathy for Cresseid is another feature of the poem around which debate over the poem's spiritual or secular emphasis has revolved. This issue too is problematised in a pun. In the narrator's opening comments on Cresseid's story, after recounting her fall into licentiousness he responds to her situation with pity: "I haue pietie thow suld fall sic mischance!" (1.84). There is much in the poem to support the views of Fox and Lyall that this pity results from a carnal perspective in which worldly happiness is positively valued. For instance, the narrator shares Cresseid's dedication to Venus and fleshly pleasure, as indicated by his prayer to Venus to restore his youthful virility (ll.22–35). Moreover, there are parallels in the imagery which Cresseid and the narrator use to describe their predicaments. Cresseid complains to Venus that

3e causit me alwayis vnderstand and trow
The seid of lufe was sawin in my face,
And ay grew grene throw 3our supplie and grace.
Bot now, allace, that seid with froist is slane (ll.136–39)

The imagery of verdure being slain by frost in this passage echoes the narrator's desire that "my faidit hart of lufe scho [Venus] wald mak grene" (1.24), and the thwarting of this wish as he is driven from his oratory by the cold. The frost and cold symbolise the natural processes of decay to which all sensual pleasure is prone, as is indicated by the wintry imagery employed in the poem's depiction of Saturn, who is a conventional figure of time (ll.155–68). The permanence which both the narrator and Cresseid expect from temporal pleasures is based on a failure to understand the Boethian point that such pleasures are by their very nature ephemeral. Craig McDonald's comment on Cresseid can thus be extended to include the narrator:

> Cresseid, like Boethius (II, Prose 1), is being punished for committing a fatal error of judgement, the failure to recognise her own mortality. She has placed herself in the hands of a variable goddess and has expected her fortune to remain stable. (McDonald 1977: 16)

These parallels and the Boethian terms in which they are couched seem to confirm the view that the narrator is disposed to be lenient towards Cresseid because he shares her materialistic outlook and foolish expectation of stability from the impermanent pleasures of the world. This in turn suggests that sympathy for Cresseid's loss of status as "the flour and A per se / Of Troy and Grece" and her subsequent decline into leprosy is based on a worldly mode of judgement which the poem criticises (Fox 1968: 56–57; Lyall 1982: 188–89). The narrator's pity is thus framed in a context which ascribes it morally negative implications.

But the word "pietie" is a homonymic pun which can also mean "piety" and this overtone sits very uncomfortably with the suggestion that sympathy for Cresseid is a product of a merely carnal viewpoint. Moreover, the word "pietie" appears elsewhere in the poem in a positive light. When Troilus encounters but fails to recognise Cresseid, the experience combines with his "knichtlie pietie" (1.519) to move him to an act of charity in giving a purse of gold to the lepers which in turn moves Cresseid to a final recognition of her own moral culpability: "Nane but my self as now I will accuse" (1.574). "Pietie" is thus associated with a movement away from concupiscence towards virtue. The pity/piety pun reinforces this aspect of the term's meaning and suggests that, even though focused on the pathos of worldly loss, the narrator's pity should be seen as a positive moral force. Again, Henryson uses the pun to problematise interpretation by countering a negative appraisal of the narrator's pity with a more affirmative interpretation while providing no clear means to choose between them.

Another possible pun near the poem's close continues this juxtaposition of opposing perspectives: Cresseid, on the point of dying, leaves her spirit to the goddess Diana: "'My spreit I leif to Diane, quhair scho dwellis, / To walk with hir in waist woddis and wellis'" (l.587–88). The word "waist", here, can be understood as equivalent to the modern English word "waste", meaning "desolate". The word also occurs with this sense and in the same collocation in the *Moral Fables*: "woddis waist" (l.2376); "wodds waist" (l.2441). This meaning of the word "waist" highlights the negative direction of the poem's action, focusing on Cresseid's progressive dislocation from the world of human comforts and implying a grief over this alienation which is far from any simple *contemptus mundi* attitude. This reading is sensitive to the sympathy with which Cresseid's plight is depicted and to the graphic emphasis on her physical decay, both of which invite one to consider the narrative as a portrayal of material degradation and human loss (McDiarmid 1981: 113).

But another possible meaning of "waist" is "familiar" (as past participle of the verb with the present tense "wait" (l.572), meaning "know").This past participle form is not listed in the *Dictionary of the Older Scots Tongue* and in fact the *DOST* list of past participles of "wit" and its cognate forms are almost exclusively formed with <-in> and <-en> suffixes, such as "wittin" and "witten". Nonetheless, "wist" was a common past participle form of "wit" in Middle English: the *Oxford English Dictionary* lists occurrences of this form in a range of well-known texts from 1300 to Henryson's time and beyond, including Gower's *Confessio Amantis*, *Cursor Mundi* and Malory's *Morte d'Arthur* (*OED*, wit, v1, A. 7β; B. 2; had-I-wist, hadiwist, www.oed.com). By analogy with this structure of present tense "wit" with past participle "wist", Henryson's "waist" might reasonably be taken as the past participle of his preferred present tense form "wait", especially as the last occurrence of present tense "wait" in *The Testament* – "I wait richt few ar thai" (l.572) – occurs only sixteen lines before "waist woddis and wellis" (l.588).

To read "waist" in this way as meaning "familiar" authorises the Christianising interpretation of the poem whereby the narrative delineates the process of Cresseid's moral and spiritual regeneration. From her earlier expectation of stable happiness from worldly things (ll.136–39), Cresseid progresses through a recognition in her "Complaint" of the necessarily ephemeral nature of sensual pleasures (ll.461–69), to a final grasp of her own moral culpability and spiritual deficiency in having actively embraced carnality (ll.554–59). This realisation is immediately followed by her departure from earthly life. To construe "waist" as "familiar", then, is to view the narrative as depicting an optimistic movement towards a spiritual homecoming which ends the spiritual exile in which Cresseid's initial moral disposition had placed her.

Thus, if one accepts "waist" as a homonymic pun, the word structures the poem's narrative as entailing two distinct movements contrapuntally arranged. In presenting Cresseid's ultimate spiritual destination as a wasteland, it indicates that the poem can be seen in terms of a "worldliness of moral judgement" (MacQueen 1967: 86) which views it as an account of tragic loss. At the same time, by raising the possibility that Diana's woods and springs will feel familiar, "waist" signals that the poem can be read in terms of an "otherworldly morality" (Tillyard 1948: 24–25) which views it optimistically as a spiritual regeneration.

Henryson's use of puns to juxtapose competing perspectives on the narrative which call each other into question may owe something to his main source for the poem, Chaucer's *Troilus and Criseyde*. Rosemary P. McGerr has analysed *Troilus and Criseyde* as an "open text" which juxtaposes different possible meanings while resisting attempts to close its significance on any one (McGerr 1988: 96–118), and has observed that a key device that Chaucer employs to this end is wordplay (1988: 98). Moreover, Robert Shoaf has argued that elsewhere in his works Chaucer similarly uses puns to prevent his texts from closing on one single meaning:

The pun is a device for delaying, interrupting, or otherwise frustrating closure. Often when a character insists on closure and its unisemy [...], a pun emerges to suggest polysemy and a ludic re-opening of the text. (Shoaf 1988: 45)

Henryson's puns achieve a similar effect, signalling that the poem has multiple possible significations and refusing to allow either the secular or spiritual perspective to predominate.

Furthermore, the different meanings which Henryson's puns raise often exist in a relation of mutual critique, each exposing the other as providing only a limited, partial image of Cresseid's tragedy. Puns themselves were widely viewed in the Middle Ages, along with other forms of wordplay and multiple significations, as instances of the inadequacy of human representation. They were frequently analysed in terms of the Biblical account of the tower of Babel (Genesis 11: 1–9) and seen as being a consequence of human language's fall away from the perfect Adamic tongue into a condition of linguistic confusion (Gellrich: 1985: 98–101; Steiner 1992: 60–62). Henryson's use of double meaning thus both exposes the deficiencies of human representation and exemplifies those same deficiencies.

This aspect of Henryson's use of puns is consonant with other aspects of the poem which foreground the problems and possible deceptiveness of linguistic representation. The god Mercury, for instance, is described as a rhetor and a poet and thus strongly associated with language: "Richt eloquent and full of rhetorie, / With polite termis and delicious, / With pen and ink to report all reddie, / [...] Lyke to ane poeit of the ald fassoun" (ll.240–45). But he is also described as a "Doctour in phisick" (l.250), bearing "fine electuairis" and "sugerit syropis" (ll.246–47). This might be considered a dubious image given the earlier reference to the narrator's morally questionable use of "phisike" (l.34) as a supplement for his fading virility. This impression is strengthened when one considers the portrayal of medicine in Henryson's burlesque poem "Sum Practysis of Medecyne" (Henryson 1981) where medical ingredients include curd from the speaker's buttocks (l.30), hedgehog bristles (l.32) a piece of a drake's penis (l.42) and the leg of a louse (l.43). Mercury's medical credentials might, then, associate him with quackery as much as with wisdom. This untrustworthiness is also indicated when Mercury is described as "Honest and gude, and not ane word culd lie" (l.252), a point which brings up the suggestion of lying even as it claims it dismiss it. The description of Mercury thus raises the possibility that rhetoric and linguistic representation are associated with deception and fakery, and

suggests that the powers of eloquence might be as much poison as cure.

These suggestions about the deficiencies of language are further evident in the narrator's lament about how Cresseid has been vilified by posterity (See Mieszkowski 1971). His desire to excuse her "as far furth as I may" (1.87) indicates that he is aware that some blame may be appropriate as is also indicated by his use of the terms "filth", "maculait", "gigotlike" and "foull pleasance" (ll.80–83) to describe her licentious behaviour. But he also reminds us of positive characteristics, "womanheid [...] wisdome and fairnes" (1.88), which this blackening of Cresseid's name excludes from its picture of her. In this the narrator foregrounds the gap between sign and referent, indicating that Cresseid's detractors have provide only a distorted and limited picture of her, a textual construct constituted by those exclusions which the narrator seeks to counter.

These aspects of the poem work together with its use of puns to highlight the inadequacies and omissions of the different proposed levels of interpretations. In this *The Testament* squares with what Derek Attridge observes of puns more generally – that by highlighting the exclusions on which any one representation depends, the pun enables "a glimpse of the infinite possibility of meaning kept at bay" and "a sense that the boundaries upon which our use of language depends are set up under specific historical conditions" (Attridge 1988: 208). Henryson's wordplay similarly displays an acute awareness of the biases and limitations of perspective upon which human constructions of meaning are contingent.

Attridge, however, goes on to propose that puns do not merely invite a negative perception of the deficiencies of any given representation: they can also open up positive vistas of meaning, since to be conscious of the failings of any one perspective "is to be made aware of a universe more open to reinterpretation and change than the one we are usually conscious of inhabiting" (Attridge 1988: 208). Ultimately, *The Testament* appears to make a similarly positive point, foregrounding the limitations of spiritual and secular perspectives in order to urge the importance of each and show the dangers of focusing on either one exclusively as being the sole truth.

Thus there are elements of the poem's treatment of love which suggest that earthly love and divine love can in fact coexist harmoniously. When Cresseid at the end of the poem perceives the ephemeral character of the pleasures she sought, this does not lead to a rejection of earthly love as a thing of no value. Rather, it leads her to a deeper appreciation of Troilus' faithful love which she had rejected:

Thy lufe, thy lawtie, and thy gentilnes
I countit small in my prosperitie,
Sa efflated I was in wantones,
And clam vpun the fickill quehill sa hie. (ll.547–50)

That Cresseid should thus value Troilus' sublunary love for her at the very point where she recognises the transience of sensual pleasures clearly suggests that Troilus's love is considered to be of a more permanent and enduring nature, less prone to the vicissitudes of Fortune, than the lust to which she gave herself over.

Moreover, there is a parallel between Cresseid's moral progress and a change in the narrator's perspective (Lyall 1982: 188–89) and this introduces a third term for understanding the nature of love in the poem in addition to Troilus' fidelity and Cresseid's licentiousness. The opening depiction of the narrator as a devotee of Venus (ll.22–35) indicates that his concerns in his own life have been dominated by sensuality. At the close of the poem, however, his position has changed significantly:

Now, worthie wemen, in this ballet schort,
Maid for ȝour worschip and instructioun,
Of cheritie, I monische and exhort,
Ming not your lufe with fals deceptioun [...]. (ll.610–13)

The key word here is "cheritie", which establishes a contrast between the narrator's initial devotion to Venus and his final disposition. The narrator's perspective has shifted from his original concern with *voluptas* towards a mode of understanding founded in *caritas* – love orientated towards the divine. Rather than presenting a stark opposition between earthly love and divine love, then, the *Testament* seems to present a trinal hierarchy (cf. Jack 1989: 22–23). Cresseid's merely sensual lust entails a dedication to transient pleasures which is dangerously unstable. It is contrasted with Troilus' faithful human love which, while still worldly and therefore transient, can enjoy a greater degree of stability. In this, Troilus' fidelity shadows the certitude of *caritas* which, being directed towards eternal spiritual things, is wholly unaffected by change. *The Testament* thus gives a comprehensive depiction of love, providing a metaphysically-grounded framework of understanding which ascribes the divine love of *caritas* and faithful earthly love their own relative validity.

   The Testament thus proposes a mode of moral judgement which enables consideration of both mundane and otherworldly concerns, suggesting that, despite any interference that occurs between these perspectives as a result of their different emphases, they ultimately represent different paths to the same truth. This point is reinforced in the final stanza where the narrator's closing remarks, while signalling the spiritual value which fidelity derives from its participation in *caritas*, also invite the female audience to view the value of fidelity in worldly terms. Hence he urges them to "Beir in ʒour mynd this sore conclusion / Of fair Cresseid" (ll.614–15). While the bookish narrator concludes with a reference to the divine love of "cheritie" which suggests that he is attuned to the metaphysical ramifications of Cresseid's actions, his injunction to his female readers directs them to consider the graphically depicted material consequences of her licentiousness. This makes the desire to avoid temporal misery such as Cresseid's a major motivation for embracing fidelity. The poem thus endorses Troilus' faithful love and discommends Cresseid's licentiousness in a manner which permits their conduct to be understood equally in terms of its metaphysical relation to divine love and of its pragmatic value in promoting temporal happiness. Each of these different focuses is shown to be incomplete but nonetheless useful and appropriate for directing different readerships towards moral virtue.

   The double meanings which Henryson uses to so unsettlingly juxtapose seemingly contrary ways of reading of *The Testament* are thus aimed at affirming that moral judgement should not view spiritual and worldly concerns as mutually exclusive. By emphasising the partiality of the poem's mundane and otherworldly levels of significance, the puns warn of the dangers of privileging one at the expense of the other and point towards a unitary vision which comprehends both. At the same time, the ambiguities and interpretative tensions generated by Henryson's wordplay remain a reminder that fallen humanity perceives such unified truth obliquely in variegated forms that give rise to manifold and often divergent truths adapted to differing circumstances. What R.D.S. Jack observes of J.M. Barrie's work is thus equally apt as a description of *The Testament of Cresseid*: the poem provides not a set of "consistently reinforcing truths", but rather "a series of counterpointed (sometimes even mutually contradictory) visions and a truth of many believed 'truths'" (Jack 1991: 93).

Bibliography

Aswell, E. Duncan. 1967. "The Role of Fortune in *The Testament of Cresseid*" in *Philological Quarterly* 46: 471–87.
Attridge, Derek. 1988. *Peculiar Language: Literature as Difference from the Renaissance to James Joyce*. London: Routledge.
Boethius. 1969. *The Consolation of Philosophy* (ed. and tr. V.E. Watts). Harmondsworth: Penguin.
Culler, Jonathan. 1988. "The Call of the Phoneme: Introduction" in Culler, Jonathan. (ed.) *On Puns: The Foundation of Letters*. New York: Blackwell. 1–16.
Delabastita, Dirk. 1997. "Introduction" in Delabastita, Dirk (ed.) *Traductio: Essays on Punning and Translation*. Manchester: St Jerome; Namur: Presses Universitaires de Namur. 1–22.
Douglas Duncan. 1961. "Henryson's *Testament of Cresseid*" in *Essays in Criticism*, 11: 128–35.
Fox, Denton. 1968. "Introduction" in Henryson, Robert. *The Testament of Cresseid* (ed. Denton Fox). London: Nelson. 1–58.
—. 1981. "Introduction" in Henryson, Robert. *The Poems of Robert Henryson* (ed. Denton Fox). Oxford: Clarendon. xiii–cxxiii.
Freidhof, Gerd. 1984. "Zur Typologisierung von Wortspielen mit Hilfe von oppositiven Merkmalen" in Rehder, Peter (ed.) *Slavistische Linguistik 1983*. Munich: Otto Sagner. 9–37.
Fuog, Karin. 2001. "Weaving Words: Puns in *The Kingis Quair*" in *English Language Notes* 38(13): 20–34.
Gellrich, Jesse M. 1985. *The Idea of the Book in the Middle Ages: Language Theory Mythology and Fiction*. Ithaca and London: Cornell University Press.
Heller, L.G. 1974. "Toward a General Typology of the Pun" in *Language and Style* 7: 271–82.
Henryson, Robert. 1981. *The Poems of Robert Henryson* (ed. Denton Fox). Oxford: Clarendon.
Jack, R.D.S. 1989. *Patterns of Divine Comedy: A Study of Mediaeval English Drama*. Cambridge: Brewer.
—. 1991. *The Road to the Never Land: A Reassessment of J.M. Barrie's Dramatic Art*. Aberdeen: Aberdeen University Press.
—. 2001. "Henryson and the Art of Precise Allegorical Argument" in Caie, Graham et al. (eds) *The European Sun: Proceedings of the Seventh International Conference on Medieval and Renaissance Language and Literature*. Tuckwell: East Linton. 1–11.
Jentoft, C.W. 1974. "Henryson as Authentic 'Chaucerian': Narrator, Character and Courtly Love in *The Testament of Cresseid*" in *Studies in Scottish Literature* 10(2): 94–102.
Kindrick Robert L. 1993. *Henryson and the Medieval Arts of Rhetoric*. New York and London: Garland.
Lyall, Roderick J. 1982. *Narrative and Morality in Middle Scots Poetry*. PhD thesis. University of Glasgow.

MacQueen, John. 1967. *Robert Henryson: A Study of the Major Narrative Poems.* Oxford: Clarendon.

McDiarmid, Matthew P. 1981. *Robert Henryson.* Edinburgh: Scottish Academic Press.

McDonald, Craig. 1977. "Venus and the Goddess Fortune in *The Testament of Cresseid*" in *Scottish Literary Journal* 4(2): 14–24.

McGerr, Rosemarie P. 1998. *Chaucer's Open Books: Resistance to Closure in Medieval Discourse.* Gainesville, Fl: University Press of Florida.

Mieszkowski, Gretchen. 1971. "The Reputation of Criseyde 1155–1500" in *Transactions of the Connecticut Academy of Arts and Sciences* 43: 71–153.

Noll, Dolores L. 1979. "*The Testament of Cresseid*: Are Christian Interpretations Valid?" in *Studies in Scottish Literature* 9(1): 16–25.

Patterson, Lee W. 1973. "Christian and Pagan in *The Testament of Cresseid*" in *Studies in Philology* 52: 696–714.

Preminger, Alex. 1986. *The Princeton Handbook of Poetic Terms.* Princeton NJ: Princeton University Press.

Shoaf, Robert A. 1988. "The Play of Puns in Late Middle English Poetry: Concerning Juxtology" in Culler, Jonathan (ed.) *On Puns: The Foundation of Letters.* New York: Blackwell. 44–61.

Spearing, A.C. 1964. *Criticism and Medieval Poetry.* London: Edward Arnold.

Steiner, George. 1992. *After Babel: Aspects of Language and Translation.* Second edition. Oxford: Oxford University Press.

Stephenson, William. 1994. "The Acrostic 'Fictio' in Robert Henryson's *The Testament of Cresseid* (lines 58–63)" in *Chaucer Review* 29(2): 163–65.

Tillyard, E.M.W. 1948. "Henryson: *The Testament of Cresseid*, c.1470" in *Five Poems: 1470–1870.* London: Chatto and Windus. 5–29.

Tolliver, H.E. (1965). "Robert Henryson: From *Moralitas* to Irony" in *English Studies* 46: 300–9.

A Tough Nut to Crack: Robert Henryson's Nut and Kernel Metaphor

David Moses

St Augustine of Hippo asserts that contingent, worldly symbols are only significant when internalised and approached with faith. Henryson can be seen to draw on the idea of Augustine's illustrative nut and kernel as a metaphor about metaphoricity and its interpretation, and to explain doctrinal understandings about the contingent nature of the written word.
Keywords: St Augustine; Robert Henryson; sign-theory; interiority; logocentrism, metaphor; symbolism; allegory.

Robert Henryson famously describes, in the prologue to *The Morall Fabillis of Esope the Phrygian*, how the moral kernel contained within each of his animal fables may only be revealed if its audience work hard to crack the literary nut in which it is contained: in a stanza which promotes the moral benefits of studying the tales, we are told

The nuttis schell, thocht it be hard and teuch,
Haldis the kirnell, sueit and delectabill;
Sa lyis thair ane doctrine wyse aneuch
And full of frute, under ane fenyeit fabill. (Henryson 1987: Prologue 15)

Few commentators have taken issue with Henryson's reference to doctrine or its connection with the image of the nut and kernel. This may be because it is seen as self evident in its broadest sense of being a wise and fruitful teaching, or perhaps on the contrary because there are so many interpretative possibilities. Most obviously, the "doctrine" referred to might be identified with the fable's *moralitas*. Yet might it also be that type of scholarly labour which will bring spiritual reward, something like the *curriculum vitae* or race through life having kept the faith (2 *Timothy*: 4: 7)? This would give the sense that the wise doctrine is itself the devotional act of reading and "cracking" the fable, the moral of which will become available to whoever approaches it from the correct perspective of devout faith.

Does it again mean that this poetic writing must necessarily be included along with mainstream Christian doctrine? However apparently trivial the text or tale, says Chaucer in his "Retraction", there is probably a message of some importance. He defers to the authority of scripture, saying that "Al that is writen is writen for oure doctrine" (citing 2 *Timothy*, 3: 16). In the *Nun's Priest's Tale* "For Seint Paul seith that al that writen is, / To oure doctrine it is ywrite, ywis" (Chaucer 1988: 4631) appears as part of the modesty topos or *excusatio* for the instructive beast fable. Helen Cooper observes that though St Paul meant it to apply to scripture, by the later Middle Ages it was "applied as the justification for the study of pagan authors in order to extract the moral kernel – by allegorisation if necessary" (Cooper 1983: 240). Henryson's prologue is dominated by the modesty topos, and he is indeed claiming to reproduce the writing of a "pagan" author. Moreover, in denying responsibility for the text's authorship, the writer might merely be indicating that God is the primary author of the text. R.D.S. Jack makes the all-important point that:

Medieval authors, seeing themselves as "efficient" (that is, "caused") causes of their own work, readily accepted authorities greater than their own *because* they saw themselves humbly. Their aesthetics made them word artisans. Their metaphysics placed them as shadow-signs of the first cause using an inadequate signing system (words) within a referential mystery. Seen from this perspective, the phrase, "Of quhome the name it neidis not record" [Fox 1987: Prologue 34] becomes a series of particularly ambiguous strokes of the pen or sounds in the air. They suggest at once, that the exact identity of the "first cause" of Henryson's tales is "unimportant" (human; rhetorical) and that its identity is "so obvious that I need not name it" (God; metaphysical). (Jack 1993: 7)

If the writer is the worldly medium of God the author, poetic fiction may be claimed to be of equal doctrinal importance to the "official" discourses of theology and philosophy, because the ultimate author and ontological origin are the same.

The above distinction between the rhetorical and metaphysical content of the *Fabillis* enables the consideration of another understanding of the reference to doctrine. It is the sense in these lines that what the nut and kernel metaphor signifies is a pre-existing doctrinal discourse which is to be elucidated through this poetic fiction. This would not merely mean that we should include the *Fabillis* as part of the broad canon of Christian teachings, but that a specific teaching is being amplified by the "animal" mode of the fable, which employs non-human animals to emphasise the paradoxical position of the human animal in the worldly context. That doctrinal position and its relation to the nut and kernel metaphor is the point of focus in this study.

St Augustine of Hippo (354–430) uses an analogous image with regard to the false representations of the pagan gods. Explaining that pagan signs are worthless because they refer not to spiritual truths, as true signs should, but to literal ones, he states: "inside its attractive shell this husk is a jangle of fine sounding stones: but it is the food of pigs, not men" [*Haec siliqua intra dulce tectorium sonantes lapillos quatit; non est autem hominum sed porcorum cibus*] (St Augustine 1995: 3. 27 [VII; 11]). He thus devalues any sign or interpretation which involves literal senses alone. Indeed, Augustine earlier explains in that work that meanings that are difficult to ascertain can be more pleasurably found in other ways: "no-one disputes that it is much more pleasant to learn lessons presented through imagery, and much more rewarding to discover meanings that are won only with difficulty" [*Nunc tamen nemo ambigit et per similitudines libentius quaeque cognosci et cum aliqua difficultate quaesita multo gratius inveniri*] (St Augustine 1995: 2. 13 [VI; 8]). He develops the fallen flesh / fallen language analogy when he states that "For when something meant figuratively is interpreted as if it were meant literally, it is understood in a carnal way" [*Cum enim figurate dictum sic accipitur tamquam proprie dictum sit, carnaliter sapitur*] (St Augustine 1995: 3. 20 [V; 9]). He is referring to mankind's inability to understand the spiritual significance of corporeal things now that they are fallen.

Augustine's use of the nut and kernel metaphor illustrates how the fallen things of the world are not trustworthy signs, but merely contingent signs which humans must see beyond. While it might seem a big leap to move from such a metaphor to human / animal relations, it is clear that Augustine's discourse is one that highlights mankind's obligation to transcend his physical state and to see beyond his corrupted corporeal context to the transcendent. Similarly in the *Fabillis* Henryson bestows his animals with a fabled though often flawed subjectivity in order both to highlight the human state itself as a problematically animal one, as well as to establish the need for individual interpretation of their "human" nature. "Cracking the nut" takes the audience through the processes of understanding metaphors about the difficulty of interpreting earthly things, to *the* ontological concern of the fiction: the state of the human soul in relation to earthly conduct.[1] Indeed, the complex artistic structures of the *Fabillis* are posited on a simple theologically commonplace premise which has biblical author-ity:

> [...] those who walk according to the flesh in the lust of uncleanness and despise authority. They are presumptuous, self-willed; they are not afraid to speak evil of dignitaries. [...] these, like natural brute beasts made to be caught and destroyed, speak evil of the things they do not understand and will utterly perish in their own corruption. (2 *Peter* 2. 10–12)

That mankind has habitual and bestial tendencies after the fall, and that he should be mindful to aspire to a higher purpose indicates a basic tenet of Christian thought, and is especially evident in those instances where Henryson draws attention to the dual characteristics of mankind's nature. He takes doctrinal correlations between human and beast, and presents them in such a way as to complicate each fable by suggesting that the audience must make moral distinctions and evaluations for themselves. In other words, the audience should be using its reason to see the spiritual truth of each fable, rather than re-maining content with seeing themselves reflected in the animals of the literal sense of the narrative.

Consequently, the correlation between man and animal, used in conjunction with the nut and kernel metaphor, provides Henryson with an established doctrinal basis for his teaching and discussion and, as R.D.S. Jack has emphasised, a critical model for his audience and an illustration of the dialectic need of figurative and metaphorical lan-guage. The balance of this discussion will attend to the way that Augustine employs the nut and kernel metaphor to illustrate both the duality of man as carnal and spiritual, and the duality of written lan-guage [*littera*] as fallen yet expressing truth. It will then focus on

---

[1] For a discussion of the theological context and contemporary literary attitudes to it see Moses 2006: 213–212.

Henryson as *makar* constructing a similar metaphor which evokes the notion that the doctrine on which his *Fabillis* are built requires the audience to see above a corrupted language. As with Chaucer's use of the word doctrine, which is commonly glossed as "instruction", Henryson highlights firstly his intention to present fictions for the delight of the audience, but secondly, and encapsulated at a figurative level, a didactic and moralistic Christian teaching as the authoritative basis and foundation of the fiction. This metaphor illustrates not just the problems of corrupted signs, but also the theological doctrine of mankind's corruption and fallenness.

Augustinian literary theory and the notion of interiority

Augustine posits a crucial relationship between the nut and kernel metaphor and the concept of inwardness. As explained below, this can be seen to inform Henryson's description of the particular kind of labour required to grasp the moral meaning of the *Fabillis*. In both writers the metaphor highlights the crucial role of individual agency, vital in interpreting the *Fabillis*. As literal tales alone they would be, in Augustine's words, a meaningless "jangle" of sounds appealing merely to mankind's animalistic desire for titillation, rather than serious spiritual instruction or, as Augustine puts it, the "food of pigs". Rather, if the things of the world are to be understood at all they must be viewed from the perspective of devout faith, which may then allow individuals to look into themselves, where by grace, illumination will be granted.

In the Prologue of his *Fabillis*, Henryson highlights the mode of his moral message by collocating the carnal with the spiritual. He explains that animals will be used to highlight human spiritual predicaments (Fox 1987: Prologue 43-56). He also chooses to illustrate how we must toil to gain the essential spiritual sustenance contained in the text, by providing the agricultural and victual metaphors of tilling the soil and cracking the nut. In doing so he subtly reminds his reader that they inhabit a corrupted fallen world of hardship and labour, and that mankind's chief goal must be to aspire to the heavenly paradise, now that the earthly one is forever beyond reach. Comparing man with animal highlights the negative aspects of mankind's post-lapsarian behaviour. Indeed, there is nothing new about the mode, for St Augustine frequently makes such comparisons, equating the things of the fallen world and a literal understand of them, with a negative view of the animal attributes of a beast.

Augustinian thought on fallenness and on the corrupted nature of signs became omnipresent in later medieval thought. His remarks on signs are not developed in a single unified discussion, but over several of his writings. Neither do they offer a completely uniform concept of sign theory, though they were fundamental to the development of medieval semiotics. The sign theory defined by Augustine embodies influential notions and is important not only in a medieval context, but can be seen to prefigure a fundamental premise of post-structuralist attitudes to language. He deals expressly with the contingency and corrupted nature of all signs, finding that the truth of their meaning may only be retrieved with the aid of divine illumination. Although Augustine regards words as a fundamental expression of reality, and of God's intention, this is conditional upon those signs being mediated by God in the *internal* world of the perceiver. This *interiority* is surprisingly akin to what we now broadly term post-structuralist theory and criticism. For Augustine, as for post-structuralism, meaning is not inherent in words, things – or animals. Rather, the plurality of all signs leaves them potentially open to multiple interpretations.

Where the similarity would seem to end is that for Augustine, this contingency may be overcome by faith, fixity of meaning attained, and the "transcendental signified" found. In his understanding, while the play of meaning is endlessly fallen and contingent, individuals who have faith may turn inward to find illumination. This particular notion of inwardness is what we mean when we refer to his *logocentrism*. While Post Structuralism is caught in an eternal present outside of which there seems to be no meaning and from which God is absent, Augustine's thought positively encourages faith, as that alone may result in Grace being granted, and things understood. At the centre of the Christian self, Derridean *différance* is delimited, the *Logos* found, and God's meaning revealed. Thus, the process of reading for Augustine requires and assumes a meaning system which is fideistically enclosed: have faith in God and by his grace understanding will follow. Correspondingly, reading things and words in the medieval world requires its subjects to utilise what may be termed the free-ranging hermeneutic of a comprehensive system of interrelated meanings; but this is perceivable only to one with faith. Is Augustine's sign theory so little referred to by modern literary theorists because such *logocentrism* is perceived as naïve and unquestioning? Logically, a world which can only be read fideistically would indeed seem to presuppose the established, approved and often comfortable interpretations of an existing belief system.

While Augustine's semiotics do rely upon the *logos* as both source of and solution to indexical signs, that understanding is far less naïve and far more helpful to modern as well as medieval study than is generally credited. Augustine's sign theory may be summed up by the word *interiority* or inwardness. Interiority for Augustine encompasses three interrelated concepts: the inner self, inward turns or revolution, and outward signs as expressions of inner things. Correspondingly, Augustine's thought establishes first the concept of the self as a private, though densely populated, inner space:

Behold, in those innumerable fields, and dens, and caves of my memory, innumerably full of innumerable kinds of things, brought in, first, either by the images, as all bodies are: secondly, or by the presence of things themselves, as the arts are: thirdly, or by certain notions and impressions, as the affections of the mind are. (St Augustine 1912: 10. 17)

[ecce in memoriae meae campis et antris et cavernis innumerabilibus atque innumerabiliter plenis innumerabilium rerum generibus, sive per imagines, sicut omnium corporum, sive per praesentiam, sicut artium, sive per nescio quas notiones vel notationes, sicut affectionum animi.]

Secondly, he develops the notion of personal revolution and illumination by which we turn into this inner space to look for God – the theological project of *Confessions*: "I entered even into mine own inwards [...] and saw [...] the unchangeable light of the Lord" [*intravi in intima mea* [...] *et vidi* [...]. *lucem incommutabilem*] (St Augustine 1912: 7. 10). Thirdly, he develops the conception of words as outward signs expressing inner realities when he says that a sign is something which, offering itself to the senses, conveys something other to the intellect: "For a sign is a thing which of itself makes some other thing come to mind, besides the impression that it presents to the senses" [*Signum est enim res praeter speciem quam ingerit sensibus aliud aliquid ex se faciens in cogitationem venire*] (St Augustine 1995: 2. 1 [I; 1]). In addition, metaphor in *De Doctrina Christiana* is itself defined as a kind of sign where things signified by appropriate terms are usurped by others signifying something else:

[Signs] are metaphorical when the actual things which we signify by the particular words are used to signify something else: when, for example, we say *bovem* and not only interpret these two syllables to mean the animal normally referred to by that name but also understand, by that animal, "worker in the gospel". (St Augustine 1995: 2. 33 [X; 15])

[Translata sunt, cum et ipsae res quas propriis verbis significamus, ad aliquid aliud significandum usurpantur, sicut dicimus bovem et per has duas syllabas intellegimus pecus quod isto nomine appellari solet, sed rursus per illud pecus intellegimus evangelistam]

For Augustine the assistance of a spiritual metaphor allows the usurpation and transformation of the things of the world – which are carnal or literal – once we reflect on and understand their meaning through the grid of anagogic reflexivity.

Augustine's interior world not only contains images of the exterior world, but also contains the very reality [*res ipsa*] of intelligible things:

Yet is not this [i.e. sensory images] all, that this unmeasurable capacity of my memory bears in mind. Here also be all these precepts of those liberal sciences as yet unforgotten; couched as it were further off in a more inward place, though properly no place: nor is it the images of the precepts which I bear, but the sciences themselves. [...] I have perceived with all the senses of my body those numbers which we name in counting; but those numbers by which we count, are far different; nor are they the images of these, and therefore they have a real existence. (St Augustine 1912: 10. 9; 10. 12).

[Sed non ea sola gestat immensa ista capacitas memoriae meae. hic sunt et illa omnia quae de doctrinis liberalibus percepta nondum exciderunt, quasi remota interiore loco, non loco; nec eorum imagines, sed res ipsas gero. [...] sensi etiam numeros omnibus corporis sensibus quos numeramus, sed illi alii sunt quibus numeramus, nec imagines istorum sunt et ideo valde sunt.]

It is not just a private world, therefore, but the world of eternal truth –
in literary terms the realm of the potential – where the soul finds
intelligible truth and ultimately the one eternal Truth which is God, by
turning to the Divine Mind. This is articulated first in *De libero
arbitrio*, where Augustine agrees "that by reason we comprehend that
there is a certain interior sense to which all things are referred by these
five well known senses" [*nos ratione comprehendere esse interiorem
quendam sensum ad quem ab istis quinque notissimis cuncta
referantur*]. He goes on to say that "he would not be sure that he
wants to be wise, and that he ought to be, unless that notion of wisdom
were inherent in his mind" [*Non enim* [...] *certus esset uelle se esse
sapientem idque oportere, nisi notio sapientiae menti eius inhaereret*].
(St Augustine 1937: 2. 3; 2. 15). In *Confessions* the notion of *logo-
centric* illumination is clearer still:

I entered even into mine own inwards [...] and with the eyes of my soul (such as it
was) I discovered over the same eye of my soul, over my mind, the unchangeable
light of the Lord. [...] I had by this time found the unchangeable and true eternity of
truth, residing above this changeable mind of mine [...] But another faculty there is
[...] which the Lord hath framed for me: commanding the eye not to hear, and the ear
not to see, but the eye for me to see by, and this for me to hear withal; assigning what
is proper to the other senses severally, in their own seats and offices; which being
divers through every sense, yet I the soul being but one, do actuate and govern. I will,
I say, mount beyond this faculty of mine. (St Augustine 1912: 7. 10; 7. 17; 10. 7).

[intravi in intima mea ... et vidi qualicumque oculo animae meae supra eundem
oculum animae meae, supra mentem meam, lucem incommutabilem ... inveneram
incommutabilem et veram veritatis aeternitatem supra mentem meam commutabilem.
... est alia vis, ... quam mihi fabricavit dominus, iubens oculo ut non audiat, et auri ut
non videat, sed illi per quem videam, huic per quam audiam, et propria singillatim
ceteris sensibus sedibus suis et officiis suis: quae diversa per eos ago unus ego
animus. transibo et istam vim meam.]

In *Confessions* this is not a continuous argument, though the
recurrence of the discussion in that work emphasises the importance
of the topic. However, it is in *De Doctrina Christiana* that Augustine
turns to the rather more concrete modes of signification of written
words [*littera*] or conventional linguistic signs, and in doing so uses
the "nut and kernel" metaphor to question the difference between literal and figurative levels of representation. We have seen that he

claims of pagan signs, in which corporal things represent further corporal things: "inside its attractive shell this husk is a jangle of fine
sounding stones: but it is the food of pigs, not men" (St Augustine
1995: 3: 27 [VII; 11]). In his use of this particular metaphor it can be
seen that Augustine is devaluing interpretation which involves literal
senses alone and where the sign is seen ambiguously as thing [*signa
pro rebus*]. Against this, he values the interpretation of the more significant figural signs and meanings, citing Paul as his authority: "the
letter kills but the spirit gives life" (2 Corinthians: 3: 6):

> To begin with, one must take care not to interpret a figurative expression literally.
> What the apostle says is relevant here: "the letter kills but the spirit gives life." For
> when something said figuratively is interpreted as if it were meant literally, it is un-
> derstood in a carnal way. No "death of the soul" is more aptly given that name than
> the situation in which the intelligence, which is what raises the soul above the level of
> animals, is subjected to the flesh by following the letter. (St Augustine 1995: 3. 20 [V;
> 9]).

> [Nam in principio cavendum est ne figuratam locutionem ad litteram accipias. Et ad
> hoc enim pertinet quod ait apostolus, littera occidit, spiritus autem vivificat. Cum
> enim figurate dictum sic accipitur tamquam proprie dictum sit, carnaliter sapitur.
> Neque ulla mors animae congruentius appellatur quam cum id etiam quod in ea bestiis
> antecellit, hoc est intellegentia, carni subicitur sequendo litteram.]

Augustine refers to the delusory nature of corporeal things in a
fallen world, and in the context that he has constructed he poses the
question of how we may understand anything from an irretrievably
fallen creation? His answer is that those with faith become the subjects of divine illumination. We understand by figurative reading
combined with *intelligentia*. The discussion is not exclusive to *De
Doctrina Christiana*. In *De Magistro* Augustine states that while
earthly teachers can never actually teach anything absolute, they may
assist the pupil to see truth not by didactic narratives but by dialectic
dialogue involving choices facilitated by a fortunate fall. The only true
teacher, Augustine points out, is the *logos* or "inner word" that sets
standards and mediates human choices of ascent and dissent. The
logical conclusion for Augustine is that Christ alone is our true
teacher:

If the one who hears me [a teacher] likewise sees those things with an inner and undivided eye, he knows the matter of which I speak by his own contemplation, not by means of my words. Hence, I do not teach even such a one, although I speak what is true and he sees what is true. For he is taught not by my words, but by the realities themselves made manifest to him by God revealing them to his inner self (St Augustine 1950: 12: 40).

The soul is the recipient of divine truth whether this is by experience of the "real" by *scientia* – knowledge through the senses – or in abstraction to the words which would enable *sapientia* or wisdom from the contemplation of God. The student must employ reasonable discrimination to perceive arbitrary and attenuant signs while inwardly he comes to understand by the grace of God. A reader of signs should have faith, and understanding will follow. In this respect Augustine's nut and kernel metaphor prescribes *how* we should read, while implying that religious allegory and doctrine is itself the literary representation of the contemplative practice which occupies the mental space.

Thus can it be seen that for Augustine, "Truth" is superior to the human intellect, and is not constructible by the human mind from worldly signs alone. From this position animals as signs have only limited meaning. Indeed, a text such as Henryson's, which uses animals to indicate some fundamental truth or moral reading would merely provide material for reflection: "for medieval thinkers reading was rarely an end in itself, most often it was conceived as a means to an end, which is the creation of a contemplative state of mind" (Stock 2001: 17). Truth cannot be exterior but interior, coming from the light of the inner man, who is intrinsically empowered to know the truth because he is created in the image of God.

"Al that is writen is writen for oure doctrine"

In the *Didascalicon* (*c.*1120) of the Augustinian Hugh of Saint-Victor (*c.*1096–1141) Augustine's thought on the nature of the sign is understood in essentially the same way, with Hugh privileging worldly signs over grammatical ones (Minnis and Scott 1998: 66). Such discussion of sign theory is often illustrated by reference to animals, which are perceived to be ideal explanatory signs. An apparent vestige of Augustine's words suggests that Hugh has Augustine in mind when he explains the process of illumination: "the idea in the mind is the internal word [...] And the divine wisdom, which the father has uttered out of his heart, invisible in itself, is recognised through creatures and in them" (Hugh of Saint-Victor 1961: 122). Similarly, the "Scottish" Augustinian Richard of Saint-Victor states: "all bodies have a likeness to good things which are invisible" [*Habent tamen corporea omnia ad invisibilia bona similitudinem aliquam*] (Migne 1844–64: 196: col. 90). In the visible world animals are evidence of things unseen; in the poetic mode where animals are distinctly human, their meaning in relation to man may be *made* to be apparent, in Cooper's words, "by allegorisation if necessary". Broadly speaking, though characteristically so, the medieval mind privileges the unseen over the seen, and displays an absolute passion for the truth, while its idea of evidence remains ineluctably different to ours.

Such exposition of the doctrinal comparison between carnal and spiritual, literal and metaphorical, comes into its own when placed next to a text which refers directly to it. It is particularly evident in the "nut and kernel" metaphor which Henryson employs in his *Fabillis*, and which can be seen as the citation of a multiplicitous metaphor concerning reason and *logos*:

> The nuttis schell, thocht it be hard and teuch,
> Haldis the kirnell, sweit and delectabill;
> Sa lyis thair ane doctrine wyse aneuch
> And full of frute, under ane fenyeit fabill. (Henryson 1987: Prologue 15–18).

Ian Jamieson demonstrates how Henryson takes the image of the nut's shell and kernel directly from the Aesopic source by Gualterus Anglicus, and understands the doctrine as the kernel contained *within* the shell itself, noting too that Henryson's words here would "seem to condemn those who refuse to take his ethical and religious preoccupations seriously" (Jamieson 1964: 30). In penetrating the meaning of each fable, Henryson explains, the doctrine will be revealed. This effectively indicates that his discourse has the authority of a range of exegetical writers and that as such, accepted authorities are present within his poetry and provide it with the "doctrine wyse aneuch" which he develops. If Henryson's nut and kernel metaphor is also a direct reference to Augustine, he would be citing the ideal theological authority to support the poetic focus on man's fallenness. Simultaneously, the reference ensures the accretive significance of the husk of the human body and the meaning or *logos* contained within it. At the literal level, this "signs" the metaphysical nature of the argument to be employed in the *Fabillis*; the "nuttis schell, thocht it be hard and teuch" contains a "delectabill" kernel, indicating that an understanding of each fable and of the doctrine which it elucidates will only come with some considerable effort.

At this level of analysis it is hard to see Henryson's image as referring directly to Augustine, since Henryson is discussing a different kind of figurative sign which leads to an apparent reversal of the meaning. For Augustine the beautiful husk of the falsely literal sign is full of rattling stones; for Henryson the tough shell of the truly figurative sign holds fair fruit. But what is made clearer by other exegetes who treat the metaphor as an important one, is that in the literary context such an image should be treated as a *verbum sapienti*, as though by its nature the metaphor implies the need for the further, more explicit statement or qualification. This qualification would be that for the "rattling stones" to have any meaning at all they would need to be approached with faith – fideistically enclosed – or indeed in the literary context understood as a type of allegory. In terms of literary convention, the metaphor is aptly explained by reference to a twelfth century commentary on the *Thebaid* of Statius, which observes that:

the compositions of poets seem not uncommonly to invite comparisons with a nut. Just as there are two parts to a nut, the shell and the kernel, so there are two parts to poetic compositions, the literal and the allegorical meaning. As the kernel is hidden under the shell so the allegorical interpretation is hidden under the literal meaning; as the shell must be cracked to get the kernel so the literal must be broken for the allegories to be discovered. (Whitbread 1971: 239).

Augustine's "spiritual" sense becomes metaphorised, and the term allegory in this passage refers to the meanings which are concealed beneath the primary, literal sense of poetry. While the literal sense provides access to meaning, it is necessary to break the surface tension of the literal sense, or in metaphorical terms, the husk. At the literal sense a cock is a cock and a nut just a nut; but within the accretive scheme of the poem the meaning of the metaphor extends from literary self-exposition to moral signifier. For the commentator even to refer to the nut and kernel suggests a *topos* signalling a discourse on the metaphoricity of metaphors. Indeed, what the above commentary makes clear is that fictions such as fables only really have metaphorical truth, being "not al grundid vpon truth" in the literal sense (Henryson 1987: Prologue 2).

Figuratively, the metaphor evokes theological issues concerning both the nature of corrupted signs, and mankind's corruption. When Henryson states that "Sa lyis thair ane doctrine wyse aneuch" under a feigned fable, the word that stands out is, of course, *doctrine*, implying as it does that both the nut and kernel metaphor, and the doctrine which it contains, is taken from a significant authority who brings theological validity to the poetic text. Jamieson suggests that a useful theological context for the *Fabillis* is *The Cloud of Unknowing*, especially chapter 35 (Jamieson 1964: 37). The text is useful in providing a *paratext* on theological attitudes to man's fallenness and his ability to control his animal instincts:

Before man sinned was the sensuality so obedient unto the will [...] But now it is not so: for unless it be ruled by grace in the will [...] all our living shall be more beastly and fleshly, than either manly or ghostly. (McCann 1952: ch. 66)

There is no evidence that Henryson was aware of or had access to a copy of *The Cloud of Unknowing*, and the use of the word doctrine would seem to suggest a much broader relevance to the metaphor employed than a single textual analogue. Nonetheless, what setting the two texts together reveals is the shared theme of mankind's choices. Man is at once a perfect soul abiding in a beastly, deadly body. Reason, as part of his nature, might have been all that man needed before the fall, but now it is so blinded with the original sin that it cannot work this work unless it is illumined by Grace (McCann 1952: ch. 64). Significantly the *Cloud*-poet explains elsewhere that "by a man's brain is ghostly understood imagination; for by nature it dwelleth and worketh in the head" using the illustration of a nut and kernel metaphor: "therefore let us pick off the rough bark and feed us with the sweet kernel" (McCann 1952: ch. 55). This particular use of the metaphor is significant because it draws primarily on Augustine, citing him as the authority on fallenness and illumination (Clark 1980: 83–110).

Henryson's evocation of the nut and kernel metaphor not merely assists the critical criterion that he has laid down with an authorised, imagistic metaphor, but indicates that signs in the fallen and temporally contingent world cannot signify anything precisely, though they *may* indicate spiritual or absolute truth. Once again the "real" or the "truthful" exists in the realm of the potential rather than the actual: metaphorical truth may signify and assist access to the spiritual truth, which a fallen creation can never contain or signify absolutely. Indeed the metaphor that Henryson uses to illustrate his suggested interpretative strategy in the *Fabillis* is also, as in *The Cloud of Unknowing*, the human skull, the kernel or lesson already contained within the mind or *logos*.

Henryson's, like Augustine's use of this metaphor, most readily highlights the dynamic instability of the human-animal dichotomy by observing that meaning is present in the human animal *and* in the significance of the beast, but that such meaning will always be contingent to the perceiver, who must look to himself and to God for the truth of the sign.[2] On the one hand Augustine's doctrine of illumination is paradoxical in suggesting that doctrine itself is a bad reflection of ontological reality, requiring a creative exegesis by individuals in order better to understand God's intention. But by his choice of the metaphor Henryson also answers the charge that fables are a lie with the response that all discourses, be they "official" or "poetic" are distorted truth, unless fideistically enclosed by the pre-existent faith which will guide the reader to a "correct" understanding of the moral content of the text, and the Truth which it signifies.

---

[2] Julian of Norwich has a similar understanding of the significance of her vision of a hazelnut, which for her represents creation in microcosm, and at the same time provides her with an understanding that it contains its creator: "And in this he [God] shewed a little thing, the quantitie of an haselnott, lying in þe palme of my hand, as me semide, and it was as rounde as a balle. I looked theran with the eye of my vnderstanding, and thought: What may this be? And it was answered generally thus: / It is all that is made" (Julian of Norwich 1978: 299).

While Henryson's poetic treatment of theological problems concerning mankind's similarity to the animal leaves him open to the
charge that his fables are a lie, which intentionally disrupt or distort an
understanding of "truth", it is also the case that where doctrine is not
examined in detail by "official" discourses, it is explored more fully in
a poetic mode. By observing at the outset that "Brutal beistis spak and
vnderstude" (Henryson 1987: Prologue 44) in the *Fabillis*, Henryson
emphasises the ironic disturbance between a person or thing and their
sign, which is always inclined to generate ambiguity, play and paradox. This is clearly a deliberate aspect of the discourse at hand. The
daring use of fiction for which Henryson has to apologise with a conventional *topos*, facilitates illustration and exploration of the existing
discourse on a fallen perspective. This needs little prefacing once the
striking nut and kernel metaphor has been used to indicate that
doctrine as the subject matter of the *Fabillis*. In the process, the
problems of linguistic interpretation are made obvious in the same
way, and so narrowly aligned with the usage of other writers that the
metaphor itself would seem to justify the august tag of *topos*. There
are, however, inevitable and inherent inconsistencies revealed by such
an analysis. Augustine's *logocentrism* is based upon a closed matrix
of interpretation where understanding requires the seeker to have
Christian faith before approaching knowledge. In the same way,
Henryson's suggestion that there is a moral to be found for the diligent
and faithful scholar implies that the kernel gained will be those
Christian morals sought. Indeed, from this perspective meaning is not
necessarily inherent in the *Fabillis* at all. As Fables they are full of
possibilities indicating a single if illusory Truth. Approach with faith,
or what you read may just be a story: have Christian faith and the
signs will reveal their Christian meaning. The hermeneutic is
enclosed, and Henryson goes as far as to cap-off (or perhaps disrupt)
meaning further, by giving his audience morals to the fables in the
form of an additional *moralitas*. But that, as Augustine would have
pointed out, is just another story.

Bibliography

St Augustine. 1912. *Confessions* (tr. W. Watts). 2 vols. London: W. Heinmann.

—. 1937. *De libero arbitrio* (ed. and tr. F.E. Touscher). Philadelphia: Peter Reilly Co.

—. 1950. *The Greatness of the Soul & The Teacher* (ed. J. Quasen and J.C. Plumpe; tr. J.M. Culleran). London: Longman, Green and Co.

—. 1995. *De Doctrina Christiana* (ed. and tr. R.P.H. Green). Oxford: Clarendon Press.

Chaucer, Geoffrey. 1988. *The Riverside Chaucer*. (ed. Larry D. Benson). Oxford: Oxford University Press.

Clark, J.P.H. 1980. "Sources and Theology in 'The Cloud of Unknowing'" in *The Downside Review* 98: 83–109.

Cooper, Helen. 1983. *The Structure of the Canterbury Tales*. London: Gerald Duckworth & Co. Ltd.

Fowler, Alistair. 1987. *A History of English Literature: Forms and Kinds from the Middle Ages to the Present*. Oxford: Blackwell.

Henryson, Robert. 1987. *The Poems of Robert Henryson* (ed. Denton Fox). Oxford: Clarendon.

Hugh of St Victor. 1961. *The Didascalicon of Hugh of St. Victor: A Medieval Guide to the Arts* (tr. Jerome Taylor). London: Columbia University Press.

Jack, R.D.S. 1993. "Henryson and the Art of Precise Allegorical Argument" in Caie, Graham et al. (eds) *The European Sun: Proceedings of the Seventh International Conference on Medieval and Renaissance Language and Literature*. Tuckwell: East Linton. 1–11.

Jamieson, I.W.A. 1964. *The Poetry of Robert Henryson: A Study of the use of Source Material*. PhD thesis. University of Edinburgh.

Julian of Norwich. 1978. *A Book Of Showings to the Anchoress Julian of Norwich* (ed. Colledge E. and J. Walsh). 2 vols. Toronto: Pontifical Institute of Mediæval Studies.

Kirwan, Christopher. 1989. *Augustine*. London: Routledge.

McCann, Justin (ed.) 1952. *The Cloud of Unknowing and Other Treatises*. London: Burns Oates.

Migne, J. P. (ed.) 1844–1864. *Patrologia Latina Cursus Completus*. 221 Vols. Paris. Citations reproduced from the *Patrologia Latina* database version. 1993. Copyright © Chadwyck-Healey Inc.

Minnis, A.J., and A.B. Scott (eds). 1998. *Medieval Literary Theory and Criticism c.1100–c.1375: The Commentary Tradition*. Oxford: Oxford Clarendon Press.

Moses, D. 2006. "Sole Food and Eating Habits: What's at Steak in the Diet of a Medieval Monk?" in *Downside Review* 436: 213–222.

Plotinus. 1991. *The Enneads*. (tr. S. Mackenna). Harmondsworth: Penguin.

Stock, Brian. 2001. *After Augustine: The Meditative Reader and the Text*. Philadelphia: University of Pennsylvania Press.

Whitbread, L (tr.) 1971. *Fulgentius the Mythographer*. Ohio: Ohio State University Press.

Eger and Grime and the Boundaries of Courtly Romance[1]

Sergi Mainer

As a late version of middle-Scots romance, *Eger and Grime* raises questions about the values and direction of the whole medieval romance tradition. Comparison with earlier European models suggests how by challenging the relation between romance and realism and between the courtly and bourgeois, and by destabilising the primacy of *fin'amors*, the tale becomes an ironic and self-parodic meta-romance.
Keywords: *Eger and Grime*; Romance; Scottish; Realism; *fin'amors*.

In fifteenth-century Scotland, there was an oscillation in the patronage of literature and the arts. Whereas during the reigns of James II (1437–60) and James III (1460–88), the nobility rather than the monarchy subsidised the vast majority of the literary production, in the times of James I (1406–37) and James IV (1488–1513), the royal houses eagerly supported and promoted cultural activity (Mapstone 1991: 416–19). By the end of the century, in the second of these periods of royal patronage, we find the first reference to *Eger and Grime*, when James IV listened to it at his royal residence in Stirling in 1497 (Dixon and Balfour eds 1877: 1: 330). It is not surprising that James enjoyed the recitation of a romance which, as we shall see, undermined the *topoi* of the genre/mode. Some of the most famous compositions by his poet laureate, William Dunbar, challenge the audience by playing with literary conventions. Poems such as the *Goldyn Targe*, *The Thrissill and the Rois* or *Tretis of the Twa Mariit Wemen and the Wedo* are good examples of this: the dreamer of *Goldyn Targe* hardly progresses spiritually by the end of the vision; in *The Thrissill and the Rois*, the narrator's detachment operates as an ironic comment on an otherwise celebratory poem; and, in the *Tretis*

[1] I would like to acknowledge the support of the British Academy, whose Postdoctoral Fellowship has allowed to pursue my research on medieval and early modern Scottish literature. I would also like to thank Sarah Carpenter and Sarah Dunnigan for their invaluable editorial suggestions. I would finally like to express my ever-lasting gratitude to R.D.S Jack, who infected me with his passion for Scottish literature as an undergraduate and postgraduate student, and more importantly, as a friend.

of the Twa Mariit Wemen and the Wedo, the high style in which the
locus amoenus is depicted contrasts with the satirical nature of the rest
of the *Tretis*. Furthermore, Dunbar's only surviving romance, *Schir
Thomas Norny*, is nothing but a parodic view of a romance hero.

The exact date of composition of *Eger and Grime* is nevertheless
uncertain as is its origin. Despite its popularity in late medieval and
early Renaissance Scotland, the two surviving editions are rather late
ones: from 1687 (known as the Percy version and containing 1474
lines) and 1711 (known as the Huntington-Laing version and consist-
ing of 2860 lines). Unfortunately, both texts are profoundly altered
and modernised, making it almost impossible to determine the actual
origin or date of composition. Deanna Delmar Evans suggests that the
safest thing to say is that it was written in the Borders, either in the
south of Scotland or in Cumberland (Evans 2001: 283). Some of the
facts surrounding the romance, however, may suggest a Scottish origin. Not only is *Eger and Grime* first alluded to in the court of James
IV, but the many references to the poem during the late fifteenth and
sixteenth centuries are exclusively found in Scottish documents
(Hasler 2000: 200). Out of the two existing versions, the Huntington-
Laing – the Caldwell edition of which I shall be using in this essay –
is more attentive to detail and its spelling practice is closer to Middle
Scots. However, the major divergence between the two is in their
endings. The longer version's unexpected conclusion posits questions
about the exhaustion of medieval romance on the verge of the sixteenth century: how much further could it go after more than 300
years? In what ways should it be transformed?

Romance, the courtly and the real

The *roman courtois* had travelled a long way from its origins in the
mid and late twelfth century. Even the early texts such as those of
Chrétien de Troyes or the Old Occitan *Jaufre* (c. 1170–c.1225)
humorously explored the incongruities between realism and the idealised courtly world they were creating. In the latter, for instance,
Jaufre, the main character, is found at the verge of starvation owing to
his courtly oath not to eat again until he encounters some adventure,

revealing the ludicrousness of such an unrealistic way of action. At the same time, however, those early romances also disseminate a chivalric discourse in which idealised behavioural parameters were put forward as examples of conduct for the growing courtly audience during and after the twelfth-century Renaissance, a time when the establishment of royal and aristocratic courts in Europe contributed to an interest in courtliness. Feudal concepts such as loyalty or honour were at scrutiny within a knight's personal progression to find a place for himself in society. Love, as adapted from its different constructions in troubadour poetry, tended to play a central role and helped in the examination of feudal ideas. Since their early conception and all through the Middle Ages, romances, as narratives of heroic feats and courtly ideals, necessarily underwent transformations in constant dialogue with the time and society in which they were written. By the time Scottish works such as *Eger and Grime* or Sir David Lyndsay's *Squyer Meldrum* (c.1550) were composed, verse romances were old-fashioned in continental Europe, which was moving towards prose. On the other hand, the makars, in all literary genres, still favoured verse as a more demanding and rhetorically sophisticated means of expression (Jack and Rozendaal eds 1997: xvii). Albeit written in verse, then, these late Scottish romances did not aim to revert to older romance paradigms; instead they scrutinised the narratorial and thematic limits of romance through the convergence of the autochthonous Scottish tradition and the subversion of *topoi*.

The beginning of *Eger and Grime* detaches the romance from the reality of late medieval marriage amongst the upper classes. The only heiress to the kingdom of Bealm is a single lady, Winliane. However, to marry her and, consequently, take possession of the realm is not going to be an easy task since:

Husband would she never have nane,
Neither for gold, nor yet for good,
Nor yet for highness of his blood,
But only he, that through swords dint
Ever wan, and never tint. (ll.8-12)

Strikingly, Winliane shows stalwart determination and independence from her parents, whose opinion regarding Winliane's preferences on whom to marry is never mentioned. By omitting her progenitors' position, the narrator detaches the plot from the real world, in which a single heiress to a realm would have but little choice about her future. Winliane articulates the dialectics of romance idealisation, introducing the *amor et militia topos*, in which love, and more often than not a suitable wedding securing a high place in society, are attained through military prestige. Courtly ideals and feudal aspirations are thus reconciled. Winliane is not looking for a *human* husband, but for an indestructible romance hero.

The apparently logical progression of *Eger and Grime* leads to the introduction of Eger, who seems to be the perfect incarnation of Winliane's dreams. He is valiant and has gained honour on the battlefield (ll.26–29). Conveniently, Eger's older brother has inherited their father's lands (ll.23–24), leaving the former as a *chevalier errant*, who has to progress in society through his knightly prowess. Everything works perfectly well, apart from the fact that the romance is coming to an end after less than thirty lines. Romances in which non-adulterous love is at the core of the narrative traditionally finished with marriage after the knight had proved his martial worth and accomplished his *aventure*. Good illustrations of this are the abovementioned *Jaufre*, the Old Catalan *Blandín de Cornualla* (late thirteenth or early fourteenth century), in which the two heroes Blandín and Guillot are wed to Brianda and Yrlanda respectively; or the Medieval French *Cleriadus et Meliadice* (c.1450–70), which was later translated into Middle Scots as *Clariodus* in the first half of the sixteenth century. The narrator of *Eger and Grime* implies that those narratives are exhausted and cannot go further than thirty lines.

The conflict between the idealistic world of Winliane and Eger and the realism of a knight's career in the late Middle Ages is problematised through the confrontation with the supernatural. The defiance of the ghostly and magical appears in many romances either to posit questions about the real world or, as part of the hero's initiation as a civilising knight, replacing the magic and the supernatural with the feudal and Christian. In the late fourteenth-century Middle English *Sir Gawain and the Green Knight*, Gawain's first encounters with uncanny and wild animals in the forest operate on this interpretative level. In *Eger and Grime*, the demonic figure of

Sir Gray-Steel, who guards the forbidden land, serves more central and disturbing purposes: he bridges the large gap existing between the courtly and knightly perfection as represented by Winliane's and Eger's pledge of betrothal and real warfare, where victory over the enemy is not always possible. The supernatural generates a tension which will remain focal for the rest of the narrative: the frictions, anxieties and difficult correspondences between the real and the ideal.

Interestingly, even the uncanny is filled by a flavour of realism. This rationalisation of supernatural elements is very typical of the Scottish romance tradition. Both in John Barbour's *Bruce* and in Blind Hary's *Wallace*, the presence of the supernatural is either dismissed or given a specifically spiritualised significance. In Book IV of *The Bruce*, a woman who is giving shelter to the King of Scots relates a prophecy, which foresees the ultimate success of Robert Bruce (ll.638–61). Yet, the hostess's words are said simply to "confort him [Bruce] sumdeill" (l.670) as the Scottish sovereign doubts the truthfulness of her speech. In *The Wallace*, Book VII, Wallace dreams of Saint Andrew and the Virgin Mary, who both re-affirm the rightfulness of his fight and elevate his enterprise to the realm of the sacred. In *Eger and Grime*, according to David E. Faris, all the potentially supernatural elements in the poem are treated in a rational manner (Faris 1981: 97–98). On his way to meet Gray-Steel, Eger has one last chance to stay within the confines of romance. A mysterious and solitary man, who could be a rationalised version of an emissary from the Other World, suddenly appears in the middle of nowhere. He begs Eger not to confront Gray-Steel (ll.101–2). Again the text sets up a situation in which Eger will become a victim of his own knightly demeanour and ambitions. The one possibility to be safe from his own downfall and the clash with reality would be to follow that man's advice; yet it is precisely because he sticks to the knightly code that he cannot turn down the challenge. Irony is strong: Eger's way of thinking and way of action are dictated by romance conventions, leaving him no choice.

His entering into the Other World follows the tenets of the genre, with a forest, a deep river, and the self-evident "land that was forbidden" (ll.122–28). Among the many examples of this motif in romances, the best-known is probably Lancelot's crossing of the

Sword Bridge in Chrétien's *Chevalier de la Charrette*. But for Lancelot, the Other World signifies a necessary step to achieve his double *aventure* to attain Guenevere's heart (and body) and to liberate the people from Logres. *Eger and Grime* displaces the traditional meaning and significance of the forest. If the other of the supernatural, magical Other World is the courtly, civilised idealisation of romance, the other of this courtly, civilised idealisation of romance is *also* the harsh reality of knighthood and warfare. Both the Other World of the forest and reality operate as the alterity of romance. Within this reasoning, it is logical that Gray-Steel's Other World reveals the paradoxes of knightly behaviour in a potentially realistic world.

Unlike most romances in which the hero is bound to overpower the supernatural, here it is Gray-Steel who vanquishes Eger. But instead of killing him, Gray-Steel just cuts off the knight's little finger. By remaining alive, Eger is exiled from his own romance paradigms into the world of reality, with which now he will be forced to come to terms. Physically, his missing finger is a constant reminder of his defeat, both to himself and to those around him. It is a sign he cannot hide from others: he will have to accept his new position as a peripheral figure in his own romance world; he will have to learn how to accept reality and shame. At the same time, beside the physical injury, there stands the figurative loss. Lee C. Ramsey suggests that the loss of his little finger may be interpreted as phallic imagery (Ramsey 1983: 138–39). Indeed, when Eger relates his eventful adventure to Grime, his first words are:

I am wounded and hurt full sore,
And tint my man-hood for evermore:
Lost the lady, for she is gone! (75–77)

The double reference to his pain (wounded and hurt) seems to allude to both his physical and figurative dolour. Even if "man-hood" can simply refer to "knighthood" in general, it nevertheless suggests emasculation and exposes Eger's most profound worries as both a knight and a lover. As a knight, his identity is intrinsically connected to his performance on the battlefield. If he can no longer win battles, his identity as a knight, man or lover is not only threatened but rather non-existent. The active and complete Aristotelian man is feminised:

for the best part of the narrative, Eger will become a convalescent knight, who is symbolically stripped of the masculine attributes of knighthood. *Eger and Grime*, then, goes beyond the hero's inner progression from knightly anonymity to fame, better understanding of the self and final marriage. At the beginning of the story Eger enjoys a central and hegemonic position, which should facilitate his marriage to Winliane. Yet, as soon as he is faced with the real world, in which defeat is possible, he is transformed into a marginal individual, who can no longer fight for himself.

At this point in the narrative, Lillias, in her double role as a lady helper and some sort of white sorceress, appears to aid Eger. She is constructed as yet another rationalisation of the supernatural, in this case, as Ramsey proposes, the fairy lady who assists the hero (Ramsey 1983: 148). In Chrétien's *Chevalier de la Charrette*, Lancelot is assisted at different stages by lady helpers; however, their role is less devious or problematic than that of Lillias. She gives Eger a magic potion which makes him heal quickly. But the curative effect of the drink will only work under certain circumstances:

As soon as love makes you agast,
Your ointments will you nothing last;
Your wounds they will both glow and gell,
Sow full sore, and be full ill;
But ye have mends, that ye may mean,
Unto your love where ye have been;
And bid her do as I have done,
And they will soft and sober soon. (ll.405–12)

Lillias's help is thus ambiguous. Instead of detaching the hero from the real world and restoring him to the kingdom of Bealm's courtly security, the magic transports Eger to a painfully realistic setting where his weaknesses will always be apparent. Ironically, the more he experiences the vicissitudes of supernatural encounters (first with Gray-Steel, then with Lillias), the more he becomes immersed in a realistic world. He will no longer be the perfect embodiment of the invincible knight, whose courage would be rewarded with his damsel's love. On the contrary, the subversion of one of the most recurrent *topoi* of chivalric romances, that of *amor et militia*, will open Eger's eyes to the harshness of real warfare. If the only way to keep his wounds closed is by asking his beloved Winliane to apply ointment to them periodically, he will have to tell her the truth about the outcome of his contest with Gray-Steel. But if he confesses this to her, she will not marry him as she will only accept someone who has never been defeated on the battlefield. Reconciliation with the romance hero he used to be proves unattainable. The now incomplete knight will have to choose between the two main features of a *roman courtois* hero, either *amor* (Winliane's affection) or *militia* (successful knighthood).

Doubles

To recover the idealised balance in the romance, which the interference of reality has destabilised, Eger needs a more pragmatic mediator than himself; someone who can negotiate between the intricacies of the real world and the idealism of romance. This is where Eger's best friend and brother in arms, Grime, comes into play. The friends could be considered doubles, representing two facets of the same character. Doubleness also applies to the two main female characters, Winliane and Lillias. Late medieval romances experiment assiduously with the possibilities of doubling. In Chrétien de Troyes' *Chevalier de la Charrette*, for example, the characters of the Arthurian court seem to be doubled, or at least shadowed, by their counterparts in the otherworldly kingdom of Logres: Lancelot and Maleagant (hero and villain, desiring Guenevere from a courtly and a menacingly aggressive perspective respectively), Guenevere and Maleagant's sister (both desiring Lancelot), or Arthur and Baudemagus (the two monarchs, Arthur losing Guenevere first when she is abducted and then to the hands of Lancelot; Baudemagus protecting Guenevere and offering an alternative model of kingship to that of Arthur). In the Tristan corpus this duality is even more evident with Blancheflor, Isolde, and Isolde of the White Hands with Rivalin, Tristan and the Dwarf Tristan – the six of them offering different visions of love, suffering and loss. But probably the best example to compare to *Eger and Grime* is *Amis and Amiloun*, in which the two main characters are overtly constructed as doubles. The two are said to be born the same day and, although they are not brothers, they look like twins so the only way to differentiate them is by their attire.

Whereas in *Amis and Amiloun* doubleness problematises moral and religious aspects of chivalric norms and practices, in *Eger and Grime* it is used to scrutinise the strain between excessively knightly attitudes and vows and soldierly reality. Eger and Grime formulate alternative ideological propositions, investigating the limits of romance in the close of the fifteenth century: Grime's behaviour and matter-of-factness are diametrically opposed to Eger's knightly and courtly ethos, which proves to be unsuitable to deal with realistic situations of warfare. The two main female characters' duality is not symmetrical to that of Eger and Grime. Winliane and Lillias are developed as the two major yet opposite woman stereotypes in chivalric literature: the lover or bride-to-be who is the hero's inspiration for knightly feats; and the lady helper (and in *Eger and Grime* also sorceress) who assists but, at the same time, challenges Eger and his courtly world. Through them, the author explores how different female stereotypes negotiate the new circumstances arising from *Eger and Grime's* fusion of romance motifs and realism.

Grime's ambivalent *modus operandi* is beyond the boundaries of romance conventions; he is the only one with sufficient non-chivalric resources to resolve Eger's quandary. Eger and Winlaine's Manichean conception of the world does not apply to Grime. While *Trouthe* is a vital feature in the construction of the identity of romance heroes such as Chaucer's Troilus, Grime feels entitled to twist it for the greater good. He has no qualms about suggesting that Eger lie to Winliane at first until they sort out what happened in the Other World.

When Winliane uncovers their deception and rejects Eger, Grime puts forward an apparently shocking proposal to her: "You love not him, will you love me?" (l.680). Such an unexpected question in the light of the two knights' intimate friendship and commitment can only be understood along the lines of their duality. In the aforementioned *Amis and Amiloun*, a similar exchange of partners is taken much further: Amis lies beside Amiloun's wife in bed when Amiloun has disguised himself as Amis to save the latter's honour. Antony J. Hasler argues this is one of the factors which reinforces the bond between the heroes (Hasler 2000: 213). Indeed, the two instances exemplify the interchangeability between both Eger and Grime and Amis and Amiloun. They project an extreme image of knightly *amicitia*: If they can share not only a spouse/fiancée, but by courtly implication also their *amor*, their selves dilute into just one, emphasising their doubleness.

When Winliane ignores his offer, the ever ingenious Grime proposes yet another plan to deceive both Winliane and everyone else in the kingdom of Bealm: he will take advantage of his interchange-ability with Eger. Grime will go to fight Gray-Steel and the super-natural, disguised as Eger his comrade-at-arms, to save both the latter's honour and love, which should rebalance the *amor et militia topos*. This ability and resourcefulness beyond knightly convention, in which cunning and pretence are at the service of an ostensibly good chivalric cause, re-codify Grime's construction along the lines of a proto-renaissance hero rather than of one of Chrétien's main charac-ters or Chaucer's Troilus. Despite their obvious differences, to some extent Grime could be regarded as an anticipation of characters such as Shakespeare's Prince Hal in *Henry IV part I*, whose Machiavellian inventiveness and way of action is contrasted with the Eger-like Hotspur's single-minded and unthinking obsession for heroic action.

The Three Estates

In fourteenth-century Europe, factors such as the constant growth of towns, the lack of labourers as a consequence of the Black Death, and the development of new professions shook the basis of European feudal societies. In this context, there was a rise of literature dealing with the position of the Three Estates in a fast changing world (Mohl 1933: 97–98). Scotland was not an exception: there are several instances of the increasing power of the bourgeoisie during the late Middle Ages. Ronald Tanner explains how, in fifteenth-century Scotland, the burgesses attending parliament dealt with non-political legislation relating to the burghs' administration and trade. Their chief influence was probably during the reign of James I, when their financial support for the monarch seems to have been rewarded by a negotiation *quid pro quo* with James (Tanner 2001: 268).

Traditionally, burgesses played a marginal role – or no role at all
– in romances. Even when they are alluded to, it is usually *en passant*,
as figures alien to the main action. For instance, in the Older Scots
Rauf Coilyear, when Charlemagne invites Rauf to visit him in Paris,
Rauf's ignorance of the city's location expresses not only geographical unawareness but also figuratively his alienation from the courtly
and knightly norms the French court represents. However, *Eger and
Grime* enacts the contemporary, contextual emergence of the
bourgeoisie. The first time a burgess is mentioned is simply to give
directions to Grime as to where Lillias's castle is (ll.1713–36), just as
a yeoman has previously informed Grime about the lord of the land,
the misfortunes of his family and Gray-Steel (ll.1142–60). At this
juncture, the bourgeoisie and the peasantry are undifferentiated
representatives of the Third Estate both in a similar literary periphery
to romance. Yet an uncharacteristic displacement occurs when the
burgess joins Grime as if he were a comrade-at-arms or his squire, that
is a member of the nobility, after his combat against Gray-Steel. Such
a transgression of a well-established convention contributes to the
overall attempt in *Eger and Grime* to re-write and re-codify romance,
trying to imagine new ways of accommodating the genre to the late
fifteenth century.

Some lines further on, when Grime, as a *chevalier errant*, needs
to rest, it is again the burgess who offers him shelter in a burgh.
Challenging as ever, the text destabilises romance norms once again.
In romance, giving shelter was largely confined to noble lords, in
whose castle the knight would recover from long travelling and
exhaustion. For instance, in *Sir Gawain and the Green Knight* Gawain
has a rest at Bertilak's dwelling, despite its supernatural connotations,.
In *Eger and Grime*, however, the aristocratic magnate's role is played
by the burgess, and the castle, the emblem of noble birth and medieval
rule, is replaced by a city, the new emergent centre of economic
power. In this way, the narrative disseminates the social changes of
the time.

Nevertheless, it would be a mistake to claim that the author had a
hidden agenda to promote the rights of the bourgeoisie in late
medieval Scotland. A close reading of the burgess's attitude indicates
otherwise. On talking to his servant, he commands:

Go! hy thee home with all thy mood,
And see that there be ready dight
A royal supper for the knight:
This is a knight of aventour,
To me it were a great honour,
In company sen we are met,
That I had him in my reset;
For we must now wit, ere he pass,
Into what countrey that he was;
Where he was born, and what degree,
Or in what land that he would be. (ll.2198–208)

The burgess's fascination for knightly life reveals a longing for the honours he will never have. Although the author relates that "The burges is a man of might" (l.2191), financial prosperity will never equal high birth even if the nobleman is as poor as a knight errant used to be in real life. This instance, together with the burgess's giving directions and following the knight, enunciates a new but very specific role for the rising bourgeoisie not only in romance but in society too. Both the burgess and his wife help and are at the service of the knight. Thus, the economic and political power of the bourgeoisie is acknowledged, but should be placed at the nobility's disposal. In fact, the treatment of the bourgeoisie under James IV presents several ideological correspondences with their new proposed role in the romance. On the one hand, individually some of them saw great advancement in society and as a group they were obviously present in trade negotiations. On the other, they were pressurised to remain as members of the Third Estate, thus limiting their power. In short, "they were tolerated rather than respected" (Nicholson 1977: 452–53).

Fin'amors

From the mid eleventh century, the troubadours developed many different conceptualisations of *fin'amors* (uninspiredly translated/adapted as "courtly love"). With the later appearance of *romans courtois* such as those by Chrétien de Troyes, intertextual references between troubadour poetry and romances started to occur. *Fin'amors* was probably the single most important borrowing from the troubadours in the composition of romances. It acted as a moving force for the hero to accomplish his knightly feats. As the genre spread all over Europe, however, some literary traditions such as the Anglo-Norman, the English, the Castilian, and the Scottish generally opted to concentrate on elements other than the tribulations of *fin'amors*. In *Eger and Grime*, the love affair between Eger and Winliane is supposedly central to the plot. The separation of the lovers could have been the perfect excuse for the author to elaborate on the nature of love through Eger's suffering, as *fin'amors* generally focuses on lack and absence rather than on fulfilment (Kay 1990: 217). However, as in the vast majority of Scottish romances, heroic deeds of arms take priority over long psychological disquisitions on love. The path of action taken for Eger to recover his honour, not Winliane's love, is at the core of the narrative.

This is not the only love affair in *Eger and Grime*. Had the author wanted to develop *fin'amors*, he would have had another chance with Grime and Lillias. On his way to fight Gray-Steel, Grime also spends a night at Lillias's castle. As he has changed his armour for that of Eger (another unequivocal sign of their doubleness), Lillias at first thinks that it is Eger. Their interchangeability is further demonstrated when the only way for Lillias to distinguish the two knights is by Grime not lacking his little finger. When she flies into a temper, it is Grime's command of rhetoric (ll.1261–358) that first calms Lillias and then persuades her to grow an interest in him. As in his cunning plan to save Eger, Grime's language becomes more important than his dexterity with weapons. The text seems to insinuate that the power of the word may be more significant than the power of sword, another example of *Eger and Grime* transformative and inquiring approach to the genre.

The author, however, does not take advantage of this situation to expand on the feelings of either Grime or Lillias. Indeed, when Lillias finally submits to Grime, the language of feudal interchange predominates, leaving no room for the idealisation of *fin'amors*.[2] Lillias tells Grime that her father will give him any reward. Grime does not want

---

[2] In *Squyer Meldrum*, Sir David Lindsay's approach to *fin'amors* is also very realistic. As Felicity Riddy points out Lindsay deals with the tension between sexual desire and courtly idealism in a humorous manner (Riddy 1974: 32–33).

anything but her hand (1.1950). Yet Lillias points out the financial implications of marrying:

"Yea, then," she says, "it may well be;
If it be so, so it likes me!
For he that hath my marriage,
Shall have my father's heritage" (ll.1951–54)

This undermines any kind of amorous aura. The notion of the landless knight whose feats of arms are rewarded with the love of an heiress, paralleling Eger and Winliane, is devoid of any courtly ornamentation. With such a detached attitude towards the precepts of *fin'amors*, the poem unmasks the functional nature of many late medieval romances. Even where courtly language and conventions were maintained, romance's initially subversive character against feudal laws and religious dogma as seen in troubadour poetry was tamed within the acceptable and non-transgressive bond of matrimony. *Eger and Grime's* uncompromised realism evinces an ironic twist, elucidating the inadequacy of idealistic representations of social realities.

Even when Grime is away from Lillias and something reminds him of her, the language deployed hardly resembles that of *fin'amors*:

When he [Grime] heard tell of Galias,
Then thought he on of Lilias,
That was ay worthy, ware and wise,
And joyned full of great gentrice. (ll.2279–82)

Compared to the long psychological disquisitions of Occitan and French authors when the lovers are apart, the mere four lines of Grime's *amor de lonh* may seem poor and clumsy. The association between "Galias" and "Lillias" sounds rather forced and openly unsophisticated, whereas the adjectives deployed to praise her are excessively conventional. The narrator appears to be more interested in the alliterative sonority of "worthy, ware and wise" than in a more convincing and definite courtly devotion. Indeed, a knight could be described in the same way and no-one would tell the difference. Nevertheless, this apparent narrative clumsiness could certainly be intentional. *Eger and Grime*'s narrative is skilfully woven with numerous subtle devices, such as Eger reporting his ill-fate in the first person, parallel actions and intricate meanings. The previous treatment of the love story between Grime and Lillias suggests an ironic approach to love (let alone *fin'amors*), so much so that, after this brief reference to Lillias, the following lines immediately turn to celebrate the magnificence of the food served! The sudden shift from the elevated appetites of the heart to the mundane ones of the body could not be more revealing.

Resolution

By the end of the romance, the major themes such as the supernatural, realism and the transgression of courtly and knightly norms come together. Experimentation with the narrative and topical limits of the genre pushes the text to its very limits. After a series of adventures, Grime fights and defeats Gray-Steel. To win the combat, the author makes use of a typical element of romance: a special sword like Arthur's Excalibur in Arthurian romances. Grime claims:

Had we it [the sword] now in borrowing,
It might make us some comforting:
We must now have it, ere we gang,
With other weapons good and strang. (ll.807–10)

Grime, however, does not attach the typical magical attributes to the special weapon. The redefinition of the motif coheres with his realistic vision of the world. His allusion to getting hold of "other weapons" operates as a distrustful comment on the supernatural as a whole, dissociating himself from Eger, Winliane and the margins of romance. Faris similarly concludes that the import and function of the sword can be understood in a rather ironic manner, whose real value is closer to fabliaux or *Don Quixote* than to *romans courtois* (Faris 1981: 98).

As in most Scottish romances, the makar prioritises battle scenes over courtly etiquette. 115 lines are devoted to the combat between Grime and Gray-Steel; yet, although the sword is mentioned, its use does not justify or explain Grime's victory. Why, therefore, did the better knight Eger not manage to vanquish Gray-Steel, whereas

Grime, a less prominent warrior, did kill their supernatural foe?
Grime's role answers this seeming paradox. Grime is only superior to
Eger in the understanding of the real world beyond the courtly ideal.
Eger needed to lose his fight in order to gain a new and more realistic
perception of warfare. Grime, on the other hard, already knew how to
cope with harsh reality. Hence, in his mediating role, his taming of
nature through the killing of Gray-Steel appears to bridge the discord
between the real and the ideal, since the instigator of this tension was
the supernatural. It also serves to recover the balance between *amor*
and *militia*.

Grime's final mediation consists of bringing Eger and Winliane
back together. Again, owing to her commitment to idealism, chivalric
and courtly vows prevent Winliane from forgetting about Eger's
defeat even if he has recovered his honour. Grime's non-chivalric arts
are required to reconcile love with the feudal institution of marriage.
He must resort to the ambiguous duality and intercheagability with
Eger again. Using his cunning once more, Grime tells Winliane that
Eger is now in love with Lillias. This forces Winliane to forget about
her pride and accept Eger again, whilst Grime will end up with Lillias.

Ideally, this seems the perfect conclusion to the romance, and in
fact this is where the Percy version of the romance finishes. Even so,
it reads like a forced conclusion not devoid of irony. Such an ending,
if considered unproblematically, is far from congruous with the
inquisitive and challenging nature of *Eger and Grime*. While on a
basic level Grime and Lillias "deserve" to be together, the union of
Eger and Winliane is much more difficult to justify. Eger has learned
about the limitations of the courtly ideal; however, his marriage to
Winliane has been led by deceit. As for Winliane, she finally ignores
her own pride and accepts Eger as his future husband, but only
because she thinks Eger has avenged himself on Gray-Steel and fears
to lose him. But she has learnt nothing since she is certainly attached
to the courtly ideal.

In the longer version, the author does problematise the outcome
of these issues to the extent that the ending is as shocking as it is
fascinating. The real hero of the romance, Grime, dies. His death can
be interpreted according to one of the favourite *topoi* of late medieval
European literature in general and late medieval Scottish literature in

particular: the *topos* of the wheel of fortune. The hero, after shortly enjoying the pleasures of life, perishes, reminding the audience of the mutability of earthly happiness. Nonetheless, the internal logic of the text enacts a more ironic formulation. Out of the five main characters, Grime is the only one who does not conform to romance ideals. He is brought in to solve the tensions caused by too chivalric promises. Once the desirable ending is attained, he is no longer necessary in a world to which he does not belong. Therefore, the narrator ironically eliminates him.

Grime's death also brings about a series of astonishing consequences. In the absence of Grime, the fragile correspondences between the domain of romance and realism begin to teeter. Out of remorse, Eger confesses to his wife what really happened. Winliane cannot come to terms with it and enters a nunnery. The further irony of this passage is enlightening: anchored in the realm of courtly ideals, she cannot cope with Eger's lie. As a romance heroine, to become a nun is the only way out she can imagine. At this point, the story seems to acquire a more redemptive tone as Eger decides to go on a crusade. Eger, who has been unable to fight for most of the romance, performs the most meaningful act a knight can carry out: preserving the Christian faith against the heathen. Allegorically and morally, this should serve for him to expiate his sins. However, by the end of the fifteenth century, crusades had partly or completely lost their originally idealised significance. Therefore their atoning import for a sinful knight could no longer function in the real world, but only in literature. By going on a crusade, Eger renounces any kind of realism to become ultimately absorbed in the domain of fiction. His learning process is nullified, taking him farther back than at the beginning of the story. He ironically *dis-learns* all he has been taught about the real world. His is a *dis-learning* involution, which is validated by his later marriage to Lillias. While the wedding rounds off the doubleness of the four characters, it also conveys his final renunciation of reality, regressing not only to the realm of romance, but to the magic world of Lillias.

Conclusion

From the mid-twelfth century romances had evolved in many different ways all over Europe. *Eger and Grime* examines and problematises the health and possibilities of the genre in late fifteenth-century Scotland. It destabilises the mechanisms and *topoi* of romance by confronting them with reality. Archetypal valiant knights such as Eger no longer offer an answer to the new conflicts, but an innovative proto-renaissance hero, Grime, with resourcefulness beyond chivalric standards, emerges. The peripheral bourgeoisie is also given a role in a fresh reformulation of romance, even if it is still at the service of the nobility. Within its detached and ironic construction, *Eger and Grime* does not propose conclusive solutions to the questions it posits. What it does suggest is that, with the absence of the new hero, Grime, romance collapses, becoming a self-reflective genre with characters too obsessed with their own impossible ideals. *Eger and Grime* becomes a consciously self-parodic meta-romance, seriously analysing and questioning its own nature.

Bibliography

Caldwell, James Ralston (ed.) 1933. *Eger and Grime: A Parallel-Text Edition of the Percy and the Huntington-Laing Versions of the Romance*. [Harvard Studies in Comparative Literature 9.]. Cambridge, Mass.: Harvard.

Dixon, T. and J. Balfour Paul (eds). 1877. *Accounts of the Lord High Treasurer of Scotland*. Volume 1. Edinburgh: General Register House.

Evans, Deanna Delmar. 2001. "Re-evaluating the Case for a Scottish *Eger and Grime*" in Caie, Graham et al. (eds) *The European Sun: Proceedings of the Seventh International Conference on Medieval and Renaissance Scottish Language and Literature*. Glasgow: Tuckwell Press. 276–87.

Faris, David E. 1981. "The Art of Adventure in the Middle English Romance: *Ywain and Gawain, Eger and Grime*" in *Studia Neophilologica* 53: 91–100.

Fellows, Jennifer. 1993. *Of Love and Chivalry: An Anthology of Middle English Romance*. London: J.M. Dent & Sons.

Hasler, Antony J. 2000. "Romance and its discontents in *Eger and Grime*" in Putter, Ad and Jane Gilbert (eds) *The Spirit of Medieval English Popular Romance*. Harlow: Longman. 200–18.

Jack, R.D.S and. P.A.T. Rozendaal (eds). 1997. *The Mercat Anthology of Early Scottish Literature 1375–1707*. Edinburgh: Mercat Press.

Kay, Sarah. 1990. "Desire and Subjectivity" in Gaunt, Simon and Sarah Kay (eds) *The Troubadours: An Introduction*. Cambridge: Cambridge University Press.

Laing, David (ed.) [1822] 1895. *Early Popular Poetry of Scotland and the Northern Border*. 2 vols. London: Reeves and Turner.

Mapstone, Sally. 1991. "Was There a Court Literature in Fifteenth-Century Scotland?" in *Studies in Scottish Literature* 26: 410–22.

Mohl, Ruth. 1933. *The Three Estates in Medieval and Renaissance Literature*. New York: Columbia University Press.

Nicholson, Ranald. 1974. *Scotland: The Later Middle Ages* [The Edinburgh History of Scotland, Volume 2]. Edinburgh: Oliver & Boyd.

Ramsey, Lee C. 1983. *Chivalric Romances: Popular Literature in Medieval England*. Bloomington: Indiana University Press.

Riddy, Felicity. 1974. "*Squyer Meldrum* and the Romance of Chivalry" in *The Yearbook of English Studies* 4: 26–36.

Tanner, Roland. 2001. *The Late Medieval Scottish Parliament: Politics and the Three Estates, 1424–1488* [Scottish Historical Review Monographs Series no. 12.]. East Linton: Tuckwell.

Van Duzee, Mabel. 1963. *A Medieval Romance of Friendship: Eger and Grime* [Selected Papers in Literature and Criticism no. 2.]. New York: Burt Franklin.

"Verbs, mongrels, participles and hybrids": Sir Thomas Urquhart of Cromarty's Universal Language

John Corbett

Sir Thomas Urquhart of Cromarty's extravagantly comic proposal for a universal language is viewed in the context of more earnest deliberations on the nature of a perfect language, in the 17th century and before. Urquhart's apparently eccentric notions are shown to have respectable counterparts in the linguistic literature of the time, while his insights and obsessions are linked to his status as a bi-dialectal Scottish royalist, imprisoned by Cromwell in republican England.
Keywords: Thomas Urquhart of Cromarty, George Dalgarno, Ramon Llull, Marin Mersenne, universal language.

The circumstances leading to the composition of Sir Thomas Urquhart's proposal for a Universal Language are well-known (and rehearsed, for example, in Craik 1993 and Jack and Lyall eds 1983) but they bear repeating. Urquhart, a member of the Scottish gentry, educated at Aberdeen University, spent some time as a young man at the court of Charles I, where he produced some minor poetry, *Apollo and the Muses* (c.1640) and *Epigrams, divine and moral* (1641), followed by a curious dissertation on trigonometry, the wilfully obscure *The Trissotetras* (1645). After Charles' execution, Urquhart fought with the Scottish forces against Cromwell's army at the Battle of Worcester in 1651; the author was among four thousand prisoners taken to London, where he was imprisoned in Windsor Castle. To secure his release, he began a programme of writing and publishing, designed to convince Parliament that he possessed sufficient "merits and services" to be allowed to win his liberty and keep possession of his lands. After producing *Pantochronocanoun* (1652), a genealogy that traced his family lineage back to Adam, Urquhart wrote *Ekskubalauron* (or *The Jewel*, 1653), which begins with a proposal for a Universal Language before shifting into a history of eminent Scots that climaxes with the narrative of the Admirable Crichton. The Universal Language is reprinted with some fairly minor alterations in *Logopandecteision* (1653), an extended diatribe against various creditors who were threatening to possess Urquhart's family lands.

Finally, Urquhart begins, but does not finish, translating *Gargantua and Pantagruel* (1653), an English version of Rabelais that is still unsurpassed. Urquhart's productivity during this period is astonishing, and gives some credibility to his assertion that some of the published work is based on papers written before and subsequently lost at the Battle of Worcester. Urquhart certainly claims that amongst the lost papers was a more fully worked-out description of his Universal Language.

In the introduction to their edition of *The Jewel* (1983: 26), Jack and Lyall treat Urquhart's proposal as a linguistic parallel to his treatise on trigonometry, namely a display of "hyperbolic rhetoric" predicated on an arcane topic. Yet there is a paradox here that the editors acknowledge: the exaggeration in Urquhart's scheme for a Universal Language is clear and must be deliberate; yet there is reason to believe that Urquhart presented his scheme in some seriousness to his captors as something that he could achieve and that would be of benefit to the Commonwealth of Britain. Beneath the florid rhetoric of *The Trissotetras* there is evidently substantial familiarity and engagement with trigonometry; how much of his Universal Language is exuberant invention, and how much lies in serious linguistic scholarship?

In 134 propositions, Urquhart sketches the characteristics for a new language "which never hitherto hath been so much as thought about by any" (Jack and Lyall eds 1983: 71). Among the main features of the Universal Language are the following:

- a universal alphabet (a Character) in which no letters will be lacking;
- each letter in the universal alphabet will be individually meaningful;
- these letters will make up words, in which the letter, monosyllable, and polysyllables will all add to the meaning of the word in a systematic manner;
- all meanings will be reduced to 250 "prime radices" or semantic primitives, represented by particular basic forms;
- complex meanings will be generated by adding further elements to these roots, up to a maximum of 7 syllables;
- the meanings of all words, existing and future, will therefore be immediately transparent to the user;
- the universal language will encompass all other existing and future languages;
- the rigorously systematic nature of the relationship between linguistic form and semantic content will aid in the understanding of various categories and systems, e.g. astronomy, botany, optics, trades, military hierarchies (from commander to footsoldier), mathematics, time and geography. For example, in astronomy "by the

single word alone which represents the star, you shall know the magnitude together with the longitude and latitude, both in degrees and minutes, of the star that is expressed by it" (proposition 101);

- the language will be both regular and copious, each noun having 4 numbers (singular, dual, the mystifying "redual" and plural), 10 cases, 11 genders (of which five are spelled out: man, woman, god, goddess, and beast/inanimate thing), whilst each verb has 10 tenses, 7 moods, and 4 voices. Noun-verb agreement further ensures that the form of the verb changes when the number, case or gender of the noun is changed (propositions 79–86, and 115);
- the lexicon will have a great "variety of diction" which will include at least 10 near-synonyms for each vocabulary item; an added feature is that words and their antonyms will share the same letters, the initial and final letter being identical and the only variation being in the sequence of the medial ones (propositions 87–92);
- words will have meaning when read both backwards and forwards; indeed any combination of letters will be meaningful, thus leading to the notable "facility [...] in making of anagrams" (proposition 93);
- the language will be aesthetically pleasing, having a flexible metrical system ("it trotteth easily" – proposition 96), there is a tremendous scope for rhyme, so great a scope, in fact, that translations from all other languages will be able to preserve their original metre and rhyme in the universal language (proposition 97);
- the universal language will be marvellously endowed with pithy proverbs, excellent maxims or aphorisms, and logical propositions and syllogisms (propositions 129–33);
- the universal language will be easily acquired – a boy of ten will be able to learn it in 3 months – because there are many "facilitations for the memory" that enable speedy learning (proposition 127).

Urquhart's proposals have been variously viewed by modern scholars. Eco (1995: 204) mentions it in passing as a "sort of polygraphy", that is, an artificially-designed perfect language that synthesises natural languages into a single pattern by assigning letters to fundamental concepts that can be translated into all other languages. Steiner (1992: 210) suggests that Urquhart's notion of a "Grammatical Arithmetician" anticipates "modern symbolic logic and computer languages". Urquhart also enjoys honourable, if brief, mention in Knowlson (1975: 37, 73 and *passim*); however, McClure (1978: 138) notes that "it is extremely difficult to determine Urquhart's attitude to his alleged Universal Language" and Cram and Maat (2001: 7) note that "many of Urquhart's claims are too extravagant to be credible". Urquhart certainly shares with Rabelais a taste for nonsense languages such as Puzzlatory and Buffoonish (cf. Corbett 1999: 91). However, it is equally clear that Urquhart's proposals are part of a rekindling of interest in the long tradition of European and English endeavours to create a perfect language. Eco (1995) traces the ebb and flow of interest in universal language from the Babel myth, through Dante to Esperanto. The peak of interest in devising a new and perfect language that occurs in the 17th century clearly coincides with the decline in the use of Latin as a *lingua franca* and the lack of a vernacular candidate to take its place. However, a consideration of the writers working in this area shows that they were inspired by a complex array of motivations. Among those who proposed or even worked out universal language systems in England around Urquhart's time were:

- Jan Amos Komensky (Comenius): *Pansophiae Christianae liber III*, 1639–40; *Orbis sensualium pictis quadrilinguis,* 1658; *Via lucis,* 1668 [possibly circulating in manuscript, at least in part, from around 1641 – see Salmon 1966; and Eco 1995: 215];
- Francis Lodowick: *A Common Writing,* 1647; *Ground-work of Foundation Laid (or so Intended) for the Framing of a New Perfect Language and a Universal Common Writing,* 1652;
- John Webster: *Academiarum examen,* 1654, which occasioned Seth Ward's response: *Vindiciae academiarum,* 1654;
- Cave Beck: *The universal character,* 1657;
- George Dalgarno: *Ars signorum,* 1661;
- John Wilkins: *Mercury,* 1641; *Essay towards a Real Character, and a Philosophical Language,* 1668.

This resurgence of interest in universal languages cannot be ascribed to a single cause. As Salmon (1966: 381) indicates, the reasons were many:

They include certain treatments of lexis for language-learning, the development of shorthand in England, the interest in codes, ciphers and methods of communication at a distance engendered by the Civil War and the long-standing fascination, which reached its peak in the seventeenth century, of the methods of organising knowledge devised by Lullism and the Caballah.

Urquhart's universal language touches on most of these topics at some point: his language will be easy to learn, it will have a new and concise alphabet, and it is tempting to read into the passing mention of his language's facility in classifying military ranks an allusion to the use of codes and ciphers in the Civil War.

Much of this renewed interest was stimulated by Francis Bacon – Eco credits him with being the "first European scholar to speak of a 'universal character'" in his *De dignitate et augmentis scientiarum [The advancement of learning]*, 1623 (Eco 1999: 83). However, others point to a less obvious but greater continental influence, Marin Mersenne, a French priest who corresponded with Descartes about a universal language in 1629 and published a section on the topic in his extended treatise on the voice, song and music, *Harmonie Universelle*, in 1636 (cf. Salmon 1966: 388–94; Knowles 1975: 66–72; Craik 1993: 98–108). Mersenne conceived of an alphabet whose characters would denote basic concepts that could be combined to express an infinitely broad range of complex ideas. Appropriately, Mersenne's consideration of a perfect language follows a discussion of the causes of laughter: "de rire & d'où vient les ris" (Mersenne [1636] 1963: 61).

However, the sources of Urquhart's universal language extend far beyond Bacon and Mersenne – among the scholars Urquhart mentions in passing (proposition 26) is the Catalan mystic Ramón Llull, known also as Raymond Lull or Lully (1232–1316). Llull was a Franciscan philosopher who became interested in devising a universal form of communication for the express purpose of converting Muslims to Christianity. In various publications (Bonner ed. 1985; see also Eco 1995: 53–54), he works out a system of combining six sets of nine entities:

- nine absolute principles (Goodness, Greatness, Eternity, etc);
- nine relative principles (Difference, Concordance, Contrariness, etc);
- nine questions (where, what, of what, etc);
- nine subjects (God, angel, heaven, etc);
- nine virtues (justice, prudence, courage, etc) ;
- and nine vices (greed, envy, pride, etc).

Each of the nine entities in the six sets is reduced to a single letter of the alphabet (BCDEFGHIK), and then, with the aid of four "figures", all possible combinations of the entities is considered. When combining the entities, the letter T is used to switch from one figure to another, eg BCTC should be read as "goodness" (B) + "greatness" (C) and therefore "concordance" (C), or, "goodness concords with greatness". In Llull's *Ars magna*, reprinted in Strasbourg in 1598, there are pages of such combinations. The combinations allowed by the figures were supposed to be self-evidently true: the *ars combinatoria* can be thought of as a machine for generating transparent truths. Llull devised his art as a means of convincing infidels of the precepts of Christianity; apparently he died in the attempt to demonstrate his figures to them (Eco 1995: 53–54).

Llull's books were not confined to the shelves of a few esoteric cabbalists in Europe: a copy of his *Ars magna* is listed in the library catalogue of William Drummond of Hawthornden (MacDonald 1971: 157). Other works by Llull were known in Scotland too – Sir Gilbert Hay's *Buke of Knychthede* has its origin in Llull's Catalan treatise *Libre de Caballeria*, probably via a French translation (Lyall 1988: 168). Of course, Llull's *Ars magna* is not a plan for a complete language; its vocabulary has only 54 items, and the point is to discover a means of combining these items systematically in such a way as the resulting propositions were transparently true and therefore persuasive. However, several of the principles behind the art of combining influenced later language planners, including Mersenne and Urquhart:

- experience can be reduced to discrete concepts ("prime radices");
- these concepts can be expressed by individual letters (a universal character);
- complex concepts can be articulated by combining individual characters.

Neither Mersenne nor Urquhart gives us any specific examples of a universal character or how the discrete concepts would actually combine. But some idea can be gleaned from the near-contemporary work of George Dalgarno and John Wilkins who both proposed more fully worked-out schemes. Dalgarno has 1068 "radical words" that can be combined in "compound words" (McClure 1978; Cram and Maat eds 2001). Dalgarno, like Urquhart, was an Aberdonian. In his late thirties, he moved south to become a schoolteacher in Oxford and, according to his autobiographical writings, he then began taking an interest in language planning (Cram and Maat eds 2001: 1). Dalgarno was aware of Urquhart's work, and he took it seriously enough to suggest in a letter that he expected Urquhart to produce a fuller version (Cram and Maat eds 2001: 7).

　　　Dalgarno's classification of the animal kingdom uses the following characters:

N (physical being)
γ (uncleft hoof)
k (terrestrial, as opposed to aerial or aquatic)

This combination gives the radical Nγk for all four-footed animals with uncleft hooves. Further letters, "a", "γ", "e" and "o", distinguish four species, thus:

Nγka (elephant)
Nγkγ (horse)
Nγke (ass)
Nγko (mule)

Words for utensils are signified by the radical *fren,* which is found in the combinations:

frenneis (fren, "utensil" + neis, "mouth" = spoon),
frenpraf (fren, "utensil" + praf, "drink" = cup)
frenirem (fren, "utensil" + i-rem, "urine" = chamber-pot).

Dalgarno's language has been variously discussed (see Cram and Maat eds 2001; McClure 1978; Eco 1995: 228–37); here it is sufficient to note the similarity in some of Dalgarno's principles to those of Llull, Mersenne and Urquhart – the universal language is a combination of characters representing discrete concepts. The systematicity should facilitate memorisation and swift acquisition.

　　　Urquhart's language, though at first sight extravagant and eccentric, indeed shows considerable familiarity with previous and contemporary linguistic scholarship. However, characteristically, Urquhart makes claims well beyond the bounds of Llull's truth-generator or Dalgarno's universal language; for example, Urquhart's combinations of letters will make sense read backwards as well as forwards, they will be both concise and comprehensive, and they will allow a flexibility in metre so that works translated into them will be able to maintain both the original metre and rhyme. As McClure observes

(1978: 141) "It is difficult to base any conjecture on the fascinating patchwork of sense and nonsense that represents Urquhart's extant linguistic writing". The internal contradictions and posturings in Urquhart's scheme are so obviously wild that it is difficult for most readers to take him seriously; however, there is still enough sense there for contemporary readers such as Dalgarno to recognise a fellow worker in the field of language planning.

Of all Urquhart's sources and influences mentioned above, the *éminence grise* behind Urquhart's universal language, the philosopher whose ideas he most often borrows and most fantastically elaborates upon, has been shown conclusively to be the French priest, Marin Mersenne (Craik 1993: 85–111). Salmon (1966: 388–89) argues that Mersenne's speculations on the possibilities and nature of a universal language, which he at one point conceives of as musical, "using the octave as a universal character", strongly influenced a group of Englishmen, including Samuel Hartlib, the patron of both Francis Lodowick and George Dalgarno. Craik (1993: 92) goes so far as to suggest that whilst writing his universal language, Urquhart had a copy of Mersenne's *Harmonie Universelle* at his side and, certainly, details and images from Mersenne's book crop up in Urquhart. A version of Llull's *ars combinatoria* is realised by Mersenne as tables that give, in principle, 38 billion pronounceable permutations of an alphabet of 19 consonants and 10 vowels. Of this vast number of permutations, Mersenne observes:

il ne faut que 46 charactères pour exprimer le nombre des grains de sable qui rempliroient toute la solidité du firmament, c'est a dire tout le monde qui nous est connu. (Mersenne, [1636] 1963: 73; quoted in Craik 1993: 104)

This passage finds an echo in Urquhart, when he is specifically discussing how the concision of his Universal Language will aid arithmeticians:

this language affordeth so concise words for numbering, that the figure for setting down whereof, would require in vulgar arithmetick, more figures in a row than there might be grains of sand containable from the center of the earth to the highest heavens, is in it expressed by two letters. (*The Jewel,* proposition 98; Jack and Lyall eds 1983: 76)

Although occasional echoes are evident, Urquhart's proposals for a Universal Language are not a translation or even much of a direct elaboration of Mersenne. The latter spends much time combining vowels and consonants in tables designed to show the potential limits of expression; he worries about Adam not having enough time (even during the 930 years of his lifetime) to name all the species and things in the world and articulate their properties; and he muses on the "natural" affinity of particular sounds with the objects they signify, thus: "*m* signifie ce qui est grand, comme les Machines, & plusieurs autres choses semblables" (Mersenne [1636] 1963: 76). Although Craik makes a strong case for Urquhart's familiarity with Mersenne, he acknowledges that Urquhart's invention leaves his sources "far behind" (cf. Craik 1995: 108).

An issue seldom discussed in relation to Urquhart's language is the light it casts on the language attitudes of a bi-dialectal, Royalist Scot writing specifically for an English Republican readership. There are passing allusions in *The Jewel* to the mixed nature of both language and nationality:

Eleventhly, verbs, mongrels, participles and hybrids have all of them ten tenses besides the present, which number no other language is able to attain to. (Jack and Lyall eds 1983: 74)

This is, on the face of it, just another example of Urquhart's hyperbole: he claims for his language an unparalleled 11 tenses (the present plus ten others) and applies this constraint to all verb forms (including participles), roots as well as compounds, and borrowings (which, I take it, are the "mongrels" and "hybrids"). Urquhart's view of language must be coloured by his status as a sometime Scots speaker who nevertheless writes in an English peppered with Greek and Latin neologisms. In Chapter VI of the translation of *Pantagruel,* Urquhart transforms Rabelais' provincial student from Limoges into an over-aureate Aberdonian, whose everyday speech is a parody of Urquhart's most ornate written prose, until Pantagruel shakes him warmly by the throat and forces him to talk in his natural Doric. The Limousin is an obvious and ironic self-portrait, by a man not usually credited with talent for self-deprecation (cf. Corbett 1999: 91–4). Nevertheless, Urquhart was evidently keenly aware of the extreme variation in styles

between broad Scots speech and high-style English prose. A knowledge of linguistic hybridity leads to an implicit challenge to narrow
conceptions of national identity, as in proposition 21 of *The Jewel*:

> The French, Spanish and Italians are but dialects of the Latine, as the English is of the
> Saxon tongue, though with this difference that the mixture of Latine with the Gaulish,
> Moresco and Gotish tongues make up the three first languages; but the meer qualifi-
> cation of the Saxon with the old British frameth not the English to the full, for that, by
> this promiscuous and ubiquitary borrowing, it consisteth almost of all languages,
> which I speak not of in dispraise thereof, although I may with confidence aver, that
> were all the four aforesaid languages stript of what is not originally their own, we
> should not be able with them all in any part of the world to purchase so much as our
> breakfast in a market. (Jack and Lyall eds 1983: 65)

Urquhart's linguistic internationalism is a far cry from the
patriotic raising of the Scots vernacular to the royally-sanctioned
medium of literary communication that we find in James VI's *Reulis
and Cautelis*. Jack and Lyall (1983: 35) observe – a few, possibly
covert scotticisms notwithstanding –

> [...] it must be emphasised that it is *English* in which *The Jewel* was written. Proud
> Scot though Urquhart was, there are few traces of his origins in his language, and
> throughout his works he proves how far English had supplanted Scots as the medium
> of serious writing in Scotland.

This observation demands some qualification. Episodes in *The Jewel*
and elsewhere show that Urquhart presents himself as a largely un-
ashamed mongrel: a Scot in a United Kingdom speaking and writing
varieties of a language whose various registers represent its disunited
history. A slightly Scots-inflected written English is what readers
might expect of a Scottish courtier, born after the Union of the
Crowns, composing works published in London for an audience that
consists most urgently of his gaolers, especially the Lord General,
Oliver Cromwell, and his Commonwealth Parliament. What remains
surprising is the extravagant high style of English that Urquhart
consistently adopts from *The Trissotetras* through the Rabelais
translations. In some respects Urquhart's English style is the ultimate
development of the latinate Scots prose of such 16th century Scots
historians as John Leslie, Bishop of Ross, whose *Historie of Scotland*

is a sequence of elegantly-balanced periods. The elegance of Leslie can be better viewed against the more colloquial plain style of Robert Lindsay of Pitscottie's *Historie and Cronikles of Scotland* (see, for example, the excerpts of each in Jack ed. 1971). Despite exceptions like George Buchanan and John Knox himself, there is a tendency, in prose as much as in architecture, to associate the baroque style of the seventeenth centuries with the Catholic or Episcopalian cause, while reformed and puritan writing is unadorned and plain. A preference for a plain style was expressed by several of the language planners too – Dalgarno commented that "Rhetoricall flourishes of words doe often obscure best literature" (cited in Salmon 1966: 387). While Urquhart *claims* his style is unadorned, it evidently is not. His claims have consequently been interpreted as a "modesty topos" (Jack and Lyall eds 1983: 17–18) that serves a double purpose:

It establishes that, in fact, he *can* be even more of a virtuoso than he has already proved, and it draws attention to the importance of his message, this time in the context of the decorum which is appropriate to his theme. He has properly chosen as high a style for his theme as is consistent with conveying it clearly: he has denied his rhetorical skill while doubly displaying it.

Modesty *topos* notwithstanding, in retrospect, at least, the choice of an extravagant high style to extol the virtues of a simple universal language to a puritan Council seems tactless, and may be part of the reason why Urquhart is sometimes seen as unself-aware (cf. Craik 1993). However, there are other problems in considering Urquhart's prose style as "decorous". His aureate prose may conform to a courtly sense of decorum in some respects, if we were to take the linguistic claims of *The Jewel* seriously, but the ultra-extravagant nature of much of his writing tips it into parody and so subverts the clear, hierarchical categories that govern decorous literature. If you do not know whether a text is satirical comedy or learned treatise, how can you know if the language used to express it is appropriate to its purpose? As noted above, sense and nonsense in *The Jewel* are notoriously difficult to distinguish. Jack and Lyall's argument that the "jewel" is really the wit with which the impossible language is proposed is itself a witty means of solving the puzzle of how seriously we are meant to take Urquhart, but I do not find it entirely convincing.

As in *The Trissotetras,* there is too much sense entangled with the nonsense to dismiss the universal language completely. However, this form of hybridity is one of the peculiar pleasures that *The Jewel* affords the modern reader: Urquhart's presentation of reality is simultaneously serious and surreal. His gift of exaggerated veracity reveals the absurdity of intellectual endeavour even while he delights in it.

Urquhart finds his modern literary counterpart in Alasdair Gray, whose short story "Logopandocy" in the collection *Unlikely Stories, Mostly* purports to be Urquhart's secret diary. Gray recounts a dialogue between Urquhart and John Milton,

the late Protector Cromwell's Latin secretary, which neatly unfolds a scheme to repair the divided Nature of Man by rationally reintegering Gods Gift of Tongues to Adam by a verboradical appliancing of Nepers logarythms to the grammar of an Asiatick people, thought to be the lost tribe of Israel, whose language predates the Babylonic Cataclysm. (Gray 1983: 137)

Like Urquhart's proposal, Gray's pastiche combines the various elements of seventeenth-century language planning: the cabbalists' desire to recover the Edenic language, Bacon and Mersenne's interest in hieroglyphs and Chinese characters, and Comenius' desire to reintegrate a common humanity, lately divided by religious strife. Gray's application of Napier's logarithms to an Asian language pays a double homage to Urquhart, as the mathematical grammarian who takes pleasure in Llull's *ars combinatoria* and its successors, and as the "grammatical Arithmetician" who devised *The Trissotetras.* Gray's temporary assumption of Urquhart's persona also rescues the earlier writer from the charge of solitary eccentricity: for three centuries his aristocratic, arcane, baroque, quintessentially *written* style has found few followers in a modern Scottish literary tradition that has appealed primarily to folklore and orality. "Logopandocy" gracefully acknowledges that Gray's own learned and mongrel brand of post-modernism has at least one eloquent antecedent in Scottish literary history.

Bibliography

Bonner, Anthony (ed. and tr.) 1985. *Selected Works of Ramon Llull (1232–1316)* Vols. 1&2. Princeton, N.J.: Princeton University Press

Corbett, John. 1999. *Written in the Language of the Scottish Nation: A History of Literary Translation into Scots.* Clevedon: Multilingual Matters.

Craik, R.J. 1993. *Sir Thomas Urquhart of Cromarty (1611–1660): Adventurer, Polymath and Translator of Rabelais.* Lampeter: Mellen Research University Press.

Cram, David and Jaap Maat (eds). 2001. *George Dalgarno on Universal Language.* Oxford: Oxford University Press.

Eco, Umberto. 1995. *The Search for the Perfect Language* (tr. James Fentress). Oxford UK and Cambridge USA: Blackwell.

—. 1999. *Serendipities: Language and Lunacy* (tr. William Weaver). London: Phoenix.

Gray, Alasdair. 1983. "Logopandocy" in *Unlikely Stories, Mostly.* London: Penguin. 134–96.

Jack, R.D.S. (ed.) 1971. *Scottish Prose: 1550–1700.* London: Calder and Boyars.

—. and R.J. Lyall (eds). 1983. *The Jewel, by Sir Thomas Urquhart of Cromarty.* Edinburgh: Scottish Academic Press and the Association for Scottish Literary Studies.

Knowlson, James. 1975. *Universal Language Schemes in England and France 1600–1800.* Toronto and Buffalo: University of Toronto Press.

Lyall, R.J. 1988. "Vernacular Prose before the Reformation" in Jack, R.D.S. (ed.) *The History of Scottish Literature: Volume 1, Origins to 1660.* Aberdeen: Aberdeen University Press.

MacDonald, R.H. (ed.) 1971. *The Library of William Drummond of Hawthornden.* Edinburgh: Edinburgh University Press.

McClure, J. Derrick. 1978. "The 'Universal Languages' of Thomas Urquhart and George Dalgarno" in Blanchot, Jean-Jacques and Claude Graf (eds) *Actes du 2e Colloque de Langue et de Litterature Ecossaises (Moyen Age et Renaissance).* Strasbourg: Université de Strasbourg. 133–47.

Mersenne, Marin. [1636] 1963. *Harmonie Universelle contenant La Théorie et la Pratique de la Musique, Vol. II: Traitez De la Voix et Des Chants.* Paris: Centre National de la Recherche Scientifique.

Salmon, Vivian. 1966. "Language Planning in Seventeenth-Century England; its context and aims" in Bazell, C.E. et al. (eds) *In Memory of J.R. Firth.* London: Longmans. 370–97.

Steiner, George. 1992. *After Babel: Aspects of Language and Translation* 2nd edition. Oxford: Oxford University Press.

Love and Chastity: Political Performance in Scottish, French and English Courts of 1560s

Sarah Carpenter

In 1564–65 the royal courts of France, Scotland and England all saw performances of debates between Love and Chastity. The similarities between these shows testify to the shared European diplomatic language of courtly performance; the differences reveal the subtlety with which performance might be used to intervene in politics.
Keywords: Performance; Sixteenth Century; Scotland; France; England; Love; Chastity; audience; courtly; diplomacy.

This paper begins from an interesting coincidence. In the single year between the Shrovetides of 1564 and 1565 the royal courts in Scotland, France and England were all entertained by performances involving debates between Love and Chastity. On the very same evening, Shrove Sunday 13 February 1564, the courts of France and of Scotland each witnessed Italianate musical *intermèdes* which set Amor against the greater power of Chastity. One year later, on Shrove Tuesday 1565, Elizabeth I and her court watched a comedy in which a debate over the respective merits of marriage and chastity was determined in favour of Marriage.[1] There is no evidence that this coincidence was deliberate, although the close links – and tensions – between the three countries and their rulers might suggest that it was not entirely fortuitous. At this moment marriage was also, to a greater or lesser extent, a live topical issue for all three monarchs. Planned or not, the falling together of the three shows is a revealing one that can teach us much about the rich and subtle uses of sixteenth century court performance.

Exploration of these three very specific events confirms a much broader truth: that we should be suspicious of ostensible content as the prime key to understanding the meaning of such court performances. Although apparently focused on the same subject, the three shows

---

[1] For records of the three performances see Graham and McAllister 1979: 24–5, 75; Ronsard 1948: 13: 218–21; Bain 1900: 2: 41, 47; Keith 1845: 2: 220; Hume 1892: 1: 404.

carried significantly different meanings for their first audiences, and engaged them in those meanings in very different ways. The limited significance of definable content is of course true of all forms of writing; but live performance, especially of this occasional kind, is especially acutely and obviously determined by factors beyond overt subject-matter. The production auspices and patronage, the political and social context, the identity of the performers, the different and often multiple audiences, as well as the production and performance styles will all influence meaning at least as much as the topic or text of the performance. As Roger Chartier reminds us, "when the 'same' text is apprehended through very different mechanisms of representation, it is no longer the same" (Chartier 1995: 2). Report of the subject matter of these shows suggests sameness; but it is in the conditions of representation and performance that we can rediscover their difference. By exploring these material contexts we can "take [these] works back to the situations that led to their production, that dictated their forms, and, for that reason, shaped their intelligibility" (Chartier 1995: 2). In Scotland, in particular, we can recover enough of this specific context to unravel some of the rich semantic layering of an apparently insignificant entertainment.

This is not to suggest that similarity is not an important aspect of the three performances. In fact, the popularity of this particular motif confirms how fully courtly performances of the later sixteenth century had developed an internationally shared European language, recognisable and active in all three courts. These three courts, famously, were headed by three female monarchs: Mary Stuart, Catherine de Medici (Queen mother of the 14-year-old Charles IX), and Elizabeth I. Like the performances they watched, the three queens were on the one hand bound together by their common, if contested status as women rulers, yet on the other differentiated by their individual political preoccupations and styles of rule. Comparison between both shows and Queens allows us to explore the shared language of courtly performance, but also the differing management of patronage and theatrical organisation at the three courts. Perhaps most interesting is the range of political purposes and modes of political intervention that could be served by such court performances.

Recognition of the international nature of sixteenth century court performance culture is of course not new: much influential work through recent decades from Sydney Anglo (1969), to Gordon Kipling (1977), to Roy Strong (1984) has demonstrated this in many areas of public show. But by the mid-sixteenth century we find this internationalism confirmed in increasing detail, both by the coincidence of visual and theatrical motifs, and by personal connections between particular individuals (designers, performers, courtiers) and their contacts. To take one example from the 1560s: we find a figure of *Discord*, characterised (as later in Ripa's *Iconologia,* 1611: 120–21) as a woman with wild hair accoutred with snakes, appearing across the three national boundaries. Discord features in devices for masks designed for a proposed meeting between Mary Stuart and Elizabeth I at Nottingham in 1562 (Chambers and Greg 1908), reappearing in almost identical guise wearing "Curling [...] Heare made of Black silk" in 1572 performances mounted by the English court for the French marshal Montmorency (Feuillerat 1908: 157–58). The same figure, this time with a snaky collar, is found on a triumphal arch welcoming Charles IX to Lyon in 1564, where he was visited by English diplomats arriving to invest him with him the Order of the Garter (Graham and McAllister 1979: 88, 193, and App VI). Finally, Discord is illustrated in a design for a masking costume by Primaticcio, the Italian court designer for the French royal family, which included for a significant period the Scottish Mary Stuart, in the mid-sixteenth century (Hall 1975–76: 353–54; Aldovini 2004: 134, 136). Another Primaticcio design, for a Foolish Virgin, may similarly testify to this international cross-fertilisation. According to JTB Hall, the design may have been influenced by an English court performance (Hall 1975–76: 372–73). He cites the French commentator Brantôme who tells us of a 1561 Elizabethan disguising of the wise and foolish virgins which especially impressed the French visitors for whom it was presented, the Constable Montmorency and François de Lorraine (Brantôme 1859a: 4: 127). The interconnections between designers, motifs and audiences are plain.

As this also suggests, court performances in all countries were watched, often performed, and at times specifically devised by some of the most powerful figures in the land. Equally, they were often reported on to home governments by diplomats and foreign ambassadors: much of our evidence for courtly performance culture comes from diplomatic reports. These were not always trivial entertainments presented to passive spectators as pastimes to fill the moment. Performance, in all its verbal and non-verbal aspects, could be deliberately addressed to one's national and courtly neighbours as well as to one's own court. However apparently slight or decorative a show and its overt subject matter, the court context and the international conventions of performance could turn these entertainments into one of the languages of diplomacy. In each of the three Love and Chastity performances, in Scotland, France and England, we are able to decipher a diplomatic intention.

Although the three performances all arise from the same common background, it is from their local contexts and inflection that each acquired its most telling meanings. Catherine de Medici, although a Queen Mother rather than a monarch in her own right, was the oldest and most experienced of the three queens, and her Love/Chastity debate was part of the most elaborate and spectacular of the three entertainments. Catherine took an active interest in courtly performance and its political uses throughout her life (Brantôme, 1859b: 10: 30–110; Prunières 1914: 34–57; Hall 1975–76: 359–61; Ruegger 1991: 145–62). The 1564 debate between Love and Chastity fell during celebrations at Fontainebleau which initiated the magnificent two-year Royal Tour of France which Catherine arranged for the young Charles IX in the wake of the first War of Religion (Graham and McAllister 1979). The young king was to travel through his realm, ceremoniously greeted by spectacular and triumphant shows and entertainments designed to enact his glorious relationship with the towns and cities of France. The moment was of serious political significance to the monarchy. Since the unexpected death of Henri II in 1559 France had been ruled briefly by the 15-year-old François II, followed in 1560 by his 10-year-old brother Charles. The serious tensions apparent among the advisors and regents of these immature boy kings were intensified by the eruption of religious dissent in the first War of Religion in 1562 (Knecht 1989). The Royal Tour attempted to address this long period of unrest, the Shrovetide celebrations at Fontainebleau marking the first stage of reconciliation of the conflicting nobility.

Catherine's acknowledged policy, throughout her reign as Queen Mother, seems to have been to use spectacle to reassure and unite the country, asserting security, splendour and harmony in the face of conflict or threat. Ruegger in fact traces back to at least 1554 "ce phenomène de vie des spectacles comme conjuration des menaces politiques", pointing to an elaborate "mascarade dansée" prepared for Henri II of the nymphs of waters, forests and fields asserting natural harmony (Ruegger 1991: 152–53). This was performed at a moment when the peace with England was in fact not at all secure but under threat. A similar pattern is suggested in 1560 during the brief reign of her eldest son François II, when Catherine arranged for the young king and his wife Mary, Queen of Scots to be received at the chateau of Chenonceaux by a spectacular *triomphe* involving figures of *Renomée, Victoire* and Pallas (Dimier 1900: 185–86). The pageants of this glorious entry suggest peaceful and splendid success; yet for the participants its very absence of direct comment must have tacitly addressed the violent tensions of the immediate political situation. The King was traveling to Chenonceaux from Amboise where barely two weeks earlier threats of Protestant uprising along with tensions and disaffection among the nobility had led to the "conspiracy of Amboise" resulting in a bloodily suppressed attack on the court (Frieda 2005: 155–57). The celebratory entry asserting glorious security is tonally strikingly at odds with the internecine violence of the preceding days.

Catherine herself openly acknowledged the value of entertainment in the art of peaceful rule. In a letter cited by Hall she observed to the young Charles IX how "j'ay ouy dire au Roy vostre grand père qu'il fallout deux choses pour vivre en repos avec les François et qu'ils aimassent leur Roy: les tenir joyeux, et occuper à quelque exercise" [I told the King your grandfather that two things were needed to live in peace with the French and for them to love their King: to keep them happy, and to occupy them with some activity] (la Ferriere 1880–97: 2: 92; cited in Hall 1975–76: 360). The poet Ronsard explicitly noted that the 1564 festivities at Fontainebleau were designed to draw together the factions among the nobility after another period of internal strife: "joindre et unir d'avantage par tel artifice de plaisir, noz Princes de France" [to bring together our Princes of France and unite them to advantage by some pleasurable spectacle] (Ronsard 1948: 13: 35–36). Another contemporary, Brantôme, asserts a foreign as well as domestic purpose here. Defending Catherine after her death against charges of superfluous and wasteful expenditure he claimed she saw such magnificent performance as demonstrating that "la France ne s'estoit si totalement ruynée et pauvre, à cause des guerres passées, come il l'estimoit" [France was not so wholly devastated and poor, because of the recent wars, as it was thought] (Brantôme 1859b: 10: 73).

The elaborate spectacles at Fontainebleau involved a wide variety of events sponsored, by command of the Queen, by a number of the most important nobles. These ranged from romance combats and games, to a water battle, a fête champetre, dance and mask performances, and drama. The Queen herself provided "une comedie sur le subject de la belle Genievre de l'Arioste" (Brantôme 1859b: 10: 73), an Italian story drawn from the *Orlando Furioso* but set in Scotland. For the interludes of the comedy Ronsard wrote two Italianate *intermèdes*, the *Trophé d'Amour* and the *Trophé de la Chasteté* (Ronsard 1948: 13: 218–21). So in this case the Love/Chastity debate formed just one tiny strand in a much more elaborate and spectacular festivity which was designed to delight the French nobility, to reflect to them their own modern magnificence, and to draw them into political unity.

The *Trophés* themselves may in fact seem dwarfed by the overall extent and duration of the entertainments. Ronsard's texts present self-defining neo-platonic sung speeches, first for Amor presented as an "enfant nud" with bow and arrow and possibly with a train of attendants representing "Joy, Youth and Idleness" (for music see Ruegger 1991: 153 n34). He asserts his power over all the world and his contrarious nature enclosing sweet and bitter, frailty and power, blindness and sight. In the second *Trophé* Chastity enters in a Chariot of Triumph, bearing an impenetrable shield of "constance and perseverance", with the infant Amor now bound and captive at the wheels. The motif is clearly drawn from Petrarch's *Trionfi*. Not only do the verses echo the language and sentiments of the *Trionfo d'Amore* and *Trionfo della Pudicizia*, but the implied characterisation and spectacle reflect many of the fifteenth and sixteenth century illustrations of the *Trionfi* (Petrarca 1984; see also Petrarca 1971: 28–71).

Politically, the specific production auspices of this show are crucial: in such court performances topical meaning is carried in the choice of who devises, who performs and who witnesses the performance as much as in its subject matter which is here both familiar and conventional. In terms of patronage it appears that Catherine de Medici took a highly active role, not only in the general initiation of courtly festivity but in the detail of the performances themselves. Speaking of spectacles that followed later in the Royal Tour, Brantôme comments, "et nottez que toutes ses inventions ne venaient d'autre boutique ny d'autre esprit que de la royne; car elle y estoit maistresse et fort inventive en toutes choses" [and notice that all these inventions came from no other store or imagination than from the queen, for she was mistress and very inventive in everything] (Brantôme 1859b: 10: 76). The comedy of "la belle Genievre", drawn from her native Italy with interventions specially commissioned from the revered court poet Ronsard, seems likely to reflect Catherine's own choices and intentions. While the *Trophés* as printed may now seem blandly ephemeral occasional pieces, they carried direct inspiration from the highest political authority as well as the cultural authority of Ronsard's poetic status. The performers in the piece equally mark its significance for the court: Brantôme tells us that it was performed by Diane de France (natural daughter of Henri II, later to be Duchess of Angoulême) and the "plus honnetes et belles princesses, et dames et filles de sa court" (Brantôme 1859b: 10: 73). The Sieur Mauvissière de Castelnau also played an important role in the tragicomedy, as well as delivering Ronsard's defence of tragedy at its close (Castelnau 1621: 303–4; Ronsard 1948: 13: 212–14). He left Fontainebleau directly after the celebrations on a diplomatic mission to the English court, thus making first hand comment on the performance available in England before he rejoined the French court at Bar-le-Duc, bringing Charles the offer of the Order of the Garter from Elizabeth (Castelnau 1621: 303). The festival was plainly a talking point. Castelnau remembered the *magnifiques festins* vividly and thought them worthy of record in his memoirs even though he claims to refer to them "en passant" as a relief from "discours plus serieux". The show was plainly the active production of the most important and influential figures of the court.

It is clear that the meaning of this show for its first audience lay in the splendour of the events as a whole, their inspiration from the highest authorities, and the involvement of the members of the court both as performers and as the intended audience, all of which were more important than the specific theatrical content. The subject matter is superficially a-political: Castelnau comments on the "gentiles et agreables inuentions pour l'amour & pour les armes" [noble and pleasing inventions of love and of arms] which accompanied the neo-Platonic focus of the Love-Chastity debate. Yet paradoxically this was itself probably a deliberately political ploy. Catherine was concerned to defuse political tension and engage the conflicting nobles in a harmonious joint display of cultural sophistication. One uncontentious ground on which they might be able to act in concert was the splendour of Renaissance spectacular display. The apparently trivial, decorative performance can thus be seen as carrying a carefully calculated political role in dissolving or concealing conflict, asserting harmony and displaying confident modern magnificence to a court and a nation unsettled by internal and violent tensions.

There are powerful links between the French and Scottish performances. But when we move to the entertainment enacted on the same evening at the court of Scotland, the specific content of the debate becomes far more significant (Carpenter 2003). The event itself, its style and auspices are remarkably similar to its French counterpart – although on a radically reduced scale befitting the poorer country and local context. The English agent, Thomas Randolph, describes at some length in a dispatch to the English Secretary Cecil an elaborate Shrove Sunday banquet with three courses, each introduced by music and pageantry: like Ronsard's *intermèdes* these sung episodes featured Eros and Chastity, but then finally added the figure of Mutual Love to conclude the entertainment. Eros was represented by "blind Cupid", Chastity by "a fayer yonge maid", while Mutual Love was presented by "a younge childe, set forth unto tyme" (Keith 1845: 2: 220). Each was accompanied by sung lyrics. The power of Love was celebrated in

Italian verses, earlier assumed to be by an unnamed local poet, probably David Rizzio (Robertson 1863: lxxxiii; Ford 1982: 107). In fact, as Ronnie Jack has pointed out, these are verses taken directly from Petrarch's *Trionfo d'Amore*, I: 76–87 (Jack pers. comm.). Chastity was then praised as "blandi domitrix amoris" in Latin stanzas composed, as were those for Mutual Love, by the eminent scholar George Buchanan (Buchanan 1725: 2: 409–10, 418; tr. Ford 1982: 139, 159). The final episode, the "younge childe [...] like unto tyme", appears to recall Petrarch's *Trionfo del Tempo*, though in fact the verses allude more obviously to themes expressed in the *Trionfo dell'Eternità*, the last in the series. It seems clear that the whole entertainment was specifically located in the context of the Petrarchan source, suggesting that for the deviser of the entertainment, if not the audience, the allusion was an active strand of its meaning. Superficially then, the Scottish shows are closely analogous in form and style to the Fontainebleau *intermèdes*. The verses, though not identical, are drawn from a closely familiar and common pool of courtly and Petrarchan discourse, sung by or about very similarly characterised personifications. But the moment of the Scottish performance was dynamically informed, not this time by a broad agenda of domestic peace-making, but by a very specific international political context which turns the conventional and decorative entertainment with its canonical source-text into an eloquent and multi-layered diplomatic statement.

Shrovetide 1564 fell in the middle of a protracted and oblique negotiation between Elizabeth I and Mary about the latter's plans for marriage. Mary had been seeking appropriate royal suitors across Europe, the names of Don Carlos, heir to Philip II of Spain, the Archduke Charles, brother to the Emperor, and the boy king Charles IX of France all tentatively mentioned. Elizabeth had insisted on their unacceptability to England, leaving Mary profoundly frustrated (Fraser 1969: Chapter 12; Bain 1898–1900: 2: 30). At the end of December 1563, Randolph, under orders from Elizabeth, began to hint more openly of the advantages of an English match. The dispatch of 21 February in which Randolph describes the entertainment is largely given over to reflection on the Queen's possible marriage. He presents his account of the banquet and its shows in that context, revealing the performance as a specific intervention into the debate with England over the marriage. This is confirmed by the texts. After the celebrations of Love and of Chastity, Mutual Love resolves the debate with an explicit statement of harmony. But this is not a generalised harmony in the arena of amorous love but an explicit statement about the two Queens:

Rerum supremus terminus
Ut astra terris misceat,
Regina Scota diligent
Anglam, Angla Scotam diliget. (Keith 1845: 2: 220)

[Though the final end of the universe confounds heaven with earth, the Queen of Scots will love the English Queen, the English Queen the Queen of Scots.]

The familiar allegorical and neo-platonic debate has resolved into a specific political statement about the relationship of the two monarchs and their nations.

Obviously for the Scottish court the traditional opposition of Love and Chastity was not incidental but carefully chosen when negotiations for marriage were so topical. The dominance given to Chastity over Love, although familiar from Petrarch and identical to Ronsard's *Trophés*, may well also be a courtly compliment to Elizabeth and a deprecation of Mary's commitment to marriage. But it is the final assertion of mutual love that shifts the foregoing debate firmly from the general to the particular, from decorative entertainment to political statement. Even so, the obliqueness characteristic of such allegorical courtly discourse is in this case not unambiguous: although the pageantry plainly emphasises compliment and harmony, it is not clear whether the show signals that Mary will follow Elizabeth's wishes in her marriage; or simply that her choice of husband, whoever it may be, cannot impair their friendship. While the dominant tone is conciliatory, the performance might be interpreted either as a gesture of compliance, or as an assertion of amicable independence.[2]

In this case in particular, the political meaning is bound up and multiplied in complex issues relating to audience. To understand the semantics of the performance, we need to identify the various layers of audience the show addressed. The immediate spectators were the Scottish nobles, as Randolph tells us that "the Queen dined privately with the chief lords and ladies", although he also refers to the audience as upwards of 300. So the statement was first addressed to the Scottish court, asserting to its mixed and frequently conflicting political inclinations Mary's own determination at this point in her reign to maintain close amity with England (for allegiances among Mary's nobility, see Donaldson 1983). The public performance of this amity is clearly an important statement in Mary's relationship with her own court: Randolph tells us that "My Sovereign [Elizabeth] was drunk unto openly, not one of 300 persons or more, but heard the words spoken and saw the cups pass between" (Bain 1898–1900: 2: 47). He signals to Cecil the importance of Mary's use of performance to declare to her nobility her own continuing pro-English stance. Beyond this immediate and internal audience, however, the entertainment deliberately singled out Randolph himself as a spectator. He was, he reports, "placed 'at the lordes table' that [the Queen] might speak with me". After the show Mary called him over and told him that the feelings expressed towards Elizabeth were "more in heart than in outward show". Clearly she wished to impress the political meaning of the performance personally on the English diplomat, making the show a signal to the English court and government as well as the Scottish. Yet the spectacle was also aimed a specific English spectator beyond Randolph himself. For Mary then produced what were clearly pre-prepared copies of the verses "which she gave me in my hand, '(the self same that were sung)' and willed me to do with them as I liked. I trust your honour [Cecil] will present them to the Queen's majesty". The debate and its resolution were

---

[2] Randolph's dispatch confirms this ambivalence: before describing the banquet he complains of Mary's contradictory views of marriage and reports to Cecil "I can neither assure her majesty of any good to insue of my labours, nor am I willing to put her out of hope" (Bain 1898–1900: 2: 46).

intended for Elizabeth's personal reception; although absent from the performance she becomes one of its key spectators.

We have here an overt recognition of the subtle power of performance as a reception mode. The simple complimentary verses of the text might easily have been sent directly to Elizabeth, as had indeed happened before (e.g. Bain 1898–1900: 1: 637). The indirect course Mary took via Randolph on this occasion suggests that she wanted Elizabeth to recognise and appreciate the performance context, rather than just the verses themselves. The theatrical *enactment* of amity to Elizabeth before the Scottish court was itself a significant part of the mask's political implication, a means for Mary to emphasise not just her own feelings but her political relationship with her nobles. The English queen is cast as the proxy audience not just of the performance itself, but of the Scottish court watching and hearing it. Elizabeth must be the spectator of the interlude as a play within a play, transforming what might appear just a courtly compliment into a complex diplomatic statement.

Both the mode and the auspices of the French and Scottish entertainments are remarkably similar: Renaissance Italianate spec-tacular pageantry, personally initiated by the queens, performed to audiences of high-ranking nobles and designed to affect their political relationship with their sovereign. Given Mary's own upbringing in France and active participation in French courtly culture this is not surprising. The remarkable co-incidence of the form and delivery, and even of the Petrarchan verses in which the theme is expressed, may be no more than that: there is no indication of direct communication between the two courts on this event, and Mary's personal relations with Catherine were by this time not close (e.g. Bain 1898–1900: 2: 60). According to Randolph, however, Catherine de Medici knew of the complications of Mary's marriage plans and Elizabeth's inten-tions, and only three weeks before this entertainment had tried to intervene: he told Elizabeth that "the Quene mother [Catherine de Medici] altogether mislykinge your majesties intente, perswadethe with the Cardinal of Guise to hinder the same" (Bain 1898–1900: 2: 37). Mary, he said, had also received a letter in which Catherine, alluding to a proposed meeting between Mary and Elizabeth, had "wished herself the third person of the three queens to be at the interview this next summer". It is therefore not impossible that the two performances were even more closely linked than they appear, in spite of their very different inflections as tools of diplomacy. The episode demonstrates peculiarly sharply the intimacy of Scottish courtly links with both France and England, yet the asserted independence of diplomatic stance within that closeness of culture and communication.

The performance at Elizabeth's court a year later, superficially similar again, reveals an entirely different conjunction of court, politics and performance. We hear from the Spanish ambassador Guzman de Silva that he was invited to a Shrove Tuesday entertainment at Whitehall (Hume 1892: 1: 404; Doran 1995: 264). After a joust and tourney, he attended

[...] the representation of a comedy in English. The plot was founded on the question of marriage, discussed between Juno and Diana, Juno advocating marriage and Diana chastity. Juno gave the verdict in favour of matrimony. The Queen turned to me and said "This is all against me".

Although it shares a topic with the previous year's French and Scottish entertainments, it is clear that this performance is not in the Petrarchan style of allegorical pageant derived from the *Trionfi*. This is a narrative debate comedy of a kind that seems to have been common at the early Elizabethan court. A few months later Guzman de Silva reports on another court comedy: "I should not have understood much of it if the Queen had not interpreted, as she told me she would do. They generally deal with marriages in the comedies" (Hume 1892: 1: 367). But the visual style of the show seems to resemble the earlier events. While no text survives, the Revels accounts record substantial payments for work on machinery, props and costumes for the play and the masks that followed, including "charetts for the goddesses [...] the hevens and clowds" (Feuillerat 1908: 117). Spectacular neo-classical entries unite the three shows.

In spite of the involvement of the Revels office in its material production, the drama itself seems not to have originated in the Revels. It was performed by the "Gentillmenne of the Innes of Court" and may have been organised by the Earl of Leicester to present to the Queen, as he had done several times before (McCoy 1989: 42). Although by this time Elizabeth was actually offering Leicester as a

husband for Mary, his suit to his own queen was still active and this
play might seem a lighter version of the mask accompanying the play
of *Gorboduc* which had urged his claims to her hand in 1561 (Axton
1970). Elizabeth's notorious tolerance of Leicester's courtship may
colour the apparently affectionate irony with which she remarked to
De Silva on the play's message. Doran argues persuasively that
Leicester was unlikely to have been the patron (Doran 1995: 264), and
a match for Elizabeth with the Archduke Charles of Austria was also
under open discussion at the time, which in spite of Leicester's own
opposition might equally have provided the context for the
performance and the persuasion towards marriage (Doran 1996: 73–
78). But it remains clear that the play was presented to the Queen by
the players of Grey's Inn rather than originating in the Court.

While Leicester was in an especially privileged position, it seems
a feature of Elizabeth's court that entertainment and spectacular
performance was as likely to be provided for her by her nobles –
either on her progresses to their estates or in the royal palaces – as to
be initiated by the royal household (Wilson 1980: 1–60). Although
Elizabeth took great pleasure in both dance and other kinds of
performance, she apparently arranged, partly for economic reasons, to
be a recipient more often than an instigator. While we have evidence
of her participation in masks and responses to shows offered to her
(see, for example, Hume 1892: 1: 71; Brown 1864: 7: 11, 101;
Melville 1827: 125; Nelson 1989: 242–43), she does not appear to
have had the active personal engagement of Catherine de Medici and
Mary Stuart in the design and deliberate use of court performance.

This contrast has a significant effect on the nature and
possibilities of the political dialogue the English entertainments present. The 1565 play shared its topic, and its neo-classical magnificent
style, with the earlier French and Scottish examples. But as a fully
developed spoken drama it clearly depended much more on debate
and the development of argument: as Da Silva records, "many things
[…] passed on both sides in defence of the respective arguments".
This is quite different from the emblematic and largely visual
oppositions and resolutions of the French and Scottish Petrarchan
entertainments. Even more crucially, perhaps, its prime audience
seems to have been neither the court nor the foreign ambassadors, but

the Queen herself. Elizabeth certainly interpreted it as designed – however playfully, with whatever royal sanction – to persuade *her*: "This is all against me". In 1565 she was 31, still marriageable although getting older. Public opinion in the court, parliament and beyond was still urgent that she should marry and produce a stable succession to the throne. It was Elizabeth's own ambivalence, her asserted reluctance for marriage and value for single life which frustrated movement. This performance addressed and sought to influence the Queen, casting her as the audience, rather than the author or patron of the event. But as Jessica Winston argues, in so doing it also asserted the right of other bodies, in this case the Inns of Court, to hold a view on the Queen's actions and decisions and to share those views publicly (Winston 2005). While Elizabeth is in one sense the crucial spectator, with the play designed to persuade her alone, it is also addressed beyond her as a contribution to the debate that was taking place around her, in and beyond the court: "the performers [become] during the performance legitimate contributors to a discussion about matters of state" (Winston 2005: 26). Like the Scottish performance, this was a show which addressed and engaged a number of different and distinct audiences.

Broadly, however, the 1565 English version of the Love/Chastity debate shows performance used as a means to influence the monarch rather than vice versa. Throughout her reign Elizabeth clearly accepted court performance as a valid means through which political issues could be explored. *Gorboduc*, presented in 1561, had debated questions of the succession, a play of Orestes in 1567 addressed the issues raised by the murder of Darnley, husband of Mary Queen of Scots (Carpenter 2003: 224–25). Her coronation procession, and court masks at various times raised questions of religious debate. Elizabeth appears to have sanctioned courtly performance as an arena for public discussion, even if it was a controlled and sometimes censored one. The famous dynamism of public theatre during her reign may owe something to this acceptance of performance as a forum for serious topical debate.

These three performances of 1564–65 show us three courts, led by three queens, each witnessing enacted debates between Love and Chastity. All are presented in high Renaissance neo-classical terms, sharing imagery, language and spectacle. Cultural, political and personal connections between the courts emphasise the shared performance language and all three courts show a sophisticated awareness in France, Scotland and England of the possibilities of intervention through performance in the political process. Yet what these performances also reveal are the differences, both profound and subtle, in the courtly exploitation of such shows. In the arena of court performance it is clear that subject matter and style are relatively minor elements in the generation of meaning: political circumstances, the authorising patron, the performers, the nature of the audience – or the overlapping audiences – addressed are all equally crucial in determining what and how a sixteenth century court performance might mean. The court of Scotland may have had fewer material resources, but it showed itself both equal and independent among the courts of Europe in its subtle exploitation of the politics of performance.

Bibliography

Aldovini, Laura et al. 2004. *Primatice: Maître de Fontainebleau*. Paris: Réunion des Musées Nationaux.

Anglo, Sydney. 1969. *Spectacle, Pageantry and Early Tudor Policy*. Oxford: Clarendon Press.

Axton, Marie. 1970. "Robert Dudley and the Inner Temple Revels" in *The Historical Review* 13 (3): 365–378.

Bain, J. (ed.) 1898–1900. *Calendar of the State Papers relating to Scotland and Mary, Queen of Scots 1547–1603*. Edinburgh: HM General Register House.

Bourdeilles, Pierre de, Seigneur de Brantôme. 1859a. "Le Roy Henry II" in *Oeuvres Complètes* (ed. Prosper Mérimée). Vol. 4. Paris: Plon.

—. 1859b. "Catherine de Medicis" in *Oeuvres Complètes* (ed. Prosper Mérimée). Vol. 10. Paris: Plon.

Brown, Rawdon (ed.) 1864. *Calendar of State Papers: Venetian*. London: Public Record Office.

Buchanan, George. 1725. *Opera Omnia* (ed. T. Ruddiman and P. Burmann). Leiden: Johannem Arnoldum Langerak.

Carpenter, Sarah. 2003. "Performing Diplomacies: the 1560s Court Entertainments of Mary Queen of Scots" in *Scottish Historical Review* 82 (2): 194–225.

Castelnau, Michel de. 1621. *Mémoires*. Paris: Chappelet.

Chambers, E. K. and W.W. Greg (eds). 1908. "Dramatic Records from the Lansdowne Manuscripts" in *Malone Society Collections*. Vol. 2. Oxford: Oxford University Press.

Chartier, Roger. 1995. *Forms and Meanings: Texts, Performances and Audiences from Codex to Computer*. Philadelphia: University of Pennsylvania Press.

Dimier, Louis. 1900. *Le Primatice: Peintre, Sculpteur et Architecte des Rois de France*. Paris: Ernest LeRoux.

Donaldson, Gordon. 1983. *All the Queen's Men: Power and Politics in Mary Stewart's Scotland*. London: Batsford.

Doran, Susan. 1995. "Juno versus Diana: the Treatment of Elizabeth I's Marriage in Plays and Entertainments, 1561–1581" in *The Historical Journal* 38: 257–274.

—. 1996. *Monarchy and Matrimony: the Courtships of Elizabeth I*. London: Routledge.

Feuillerat, Albert (ed.) 1908. *Documents relating to the Office of the Revels in the time of Queen Elizabeth*. Louvain: A Uystpruyst.

Ford, Philip J. 1982. *George Buchanan: Prince of Poets*. Aberdeen: Aberdeen University Press.

Fraser, Antonia. 1969. *Mary Queen of Scots*. London: Weidenfeld and Nicolson.

Frieda, Léonie. 2005. *Catherine de Medici*. London: Phoenix.

Graham, V.E. and W. McAllister Johnson (eds). 1979. *The Royal Tour of France by Charles IX and Catherine de' Medici: Festivals and Entries, 1564–6*. Toronto: University of Toronto Press.

Hall, J. 1975–76. "Primaticcio and Court Festivals" in *Bulletin of the John Rylands Library* 58: 353–77.

Hume, Martin A.S. (ed.) 1892. *Calendar of Letters and State Papers: Spanish, Vol. 1, 1558–1567*. London: Public Record Office.

Keith, Robert. 1845. *The History of the Affairs of Church and State in Scotland*. Edinburgh: Spottiswoode Society.

Kipling, Gordon. 1977. *The Triumph of Honour: Burgundian Origins of the Elizabethan Renaissance*. The Hague: Leiden University Press.

Knecht, R.J. 1989. *The French Wars of Religion, 1559–1598*. London: Longman.

la Ferriere, H de (ed.) 1880–97. *Lettres de Catherine de Médicis*. Paris.

McCoy, Richard. 1989. *The Rites of Knighthood: the literature and politics of Elizabethan chivalry*. Berkeley: University of California Press.

Melville, James. 1827. *Sir James Melville's Memoirs* (ed. T. Thomson). Edinburgh: Bannatyne Club.

Nelson, Alan H. (ed.) 1989. *Records of Early English Drama: Cambridge*. Toronto: University of Toronto Press.

Petrarca, Francesco. 1971. *Lord Morley's "Tryumphes of Fraunces Petrarcke"* (ed. D.D. Carnicelli). Cambridge, Mass: Harvard University Press.

—. 1984. *Trionfi* (ed. Guido Bezzola). Milan: Rizzoli

Prunières, Henry. 1914. *Le Ballet de Cour en France*. Paris: H. Laurens.

Ripa, Cesare. [1611] 1976. *Iconologia*. (ed. Stephen Orgel). New York and London: Garland.

Robertson, Joseph (ed.) 1863. *Inuentaires de la Royne Descosse Douairiere de France*. Edinburgh: Bannatyne Club.

Ronsard, Pierre de. 1948. *Oeuvres Complètes* (ed. Paul Laumonier). Paris: Didier.

Ruegger, E. 1991. "De Grace Dieu à Circé: le ballet de cour au XVIe siècle et son livret" in *Théâtre et Spectacles Hier et Aujourd'hui: Moyen Age et Renaissance*. Paris: Éditions du CTHS. 145–62.

Strong, Roy. 1984. *Art and Power: Renaissance Festivals 1450–1650*. Woodbridge: Boydell.

Wilson, Jean. 1980. *Entertainments for Elizabeth I*. Woodbridge: Brewer.

Winston, Jessica. 2005. "Expanding the Political Nation: *Gorboduc* at the Inns of Court" in *Early Theatre* 8(1): 11–34.

Drummond and the Meaning of Beauty

Sarah M. Dunnigan

This essay explores representations of beauty primarily in the secular, but with reference also to the sacred, poetry of William Drummond of Hawthornden. It argues for their significant aesthetic, philosophical, and spiritual import in understanding more fully the nature of human love and the comprehension of the divine in his work. Such manifestations of beauty are shown to be rooted in the Petrarchan love tradition and in Italian Neoplatonic thought. Beauty appears as a philosophical and spiritual ideal, and as a Baroque aesthetic, but one which does not entirely command the emotional and psychological assent of Drummond's lover. Instead, the persistence of sensual beauty points to the impossibility of renunciation, to love's enduring power, and to the complexity of an amatory sequence which is often perceived as out of joint with European and English love poetry of the period.
Keywords: Renaissance love; Renaissance beauty; Petrarch; Petrarchanism; Neo-platonism; pastoral; myth; Baroque

Beauty is everywhere present in the poetry of William Drummond of Hawthornden (1585–1649). It is manifest in a variety of different ways and in a diversity of kinds, just as in Renaissance culture itself – a culture in which "artistic purpose and commitment to beauty are defining characteristics" (Cropper 1999: 1). Despite the persuasive assertion that beauty "whether we try to define it or not, should maintain its recalcitrance and go its own way" (Donoghue 2003: 11), definitions of "the beautiful" are contingent on the particular aesthetic and philosophical languages of historical period. In Renaissance thought, beauty is irreducible to a single concept: not merely physical, it can also embrace "beautiful habits of the soul and beautiful cognitions" (Kristeller 1961: 167), and encompass ideas of aesthetic form, proportion, and concord (cf. Hendrix 2004). Mirroring the different contexts out of which it emerges, Drummond's poetry offers many illustrations and invocations of beauty and "the beautiful": whether in its variety of rhetorical figures and tropes; in descriptions of physical beauty (especially of the beloved woman, miraculous and humbling; or of nature, precious and consoling); or in attempted descriptions of God's wonder and divine creation in which the impossibility of ever sufficiently representing His beautiful forms challenges the meaning of beauty itself.

These particular verbal textures and imaginative impulses towards "the beautiful" have perhaps played a large part in shaping the popular critical perception of Drummond as an especially floriate Petrarchan, a fully-fledged Neoplatonic, or a proto-Romantic writer (cf. Fogle 1952; Wallerstein 1933; Ward 1894). Despite this last characterisation, Drummond's poetry is often perceived as somehow artistically and culturally belated; the consequence of untimely Petrarchism and Neoplatonism. By 1616, when Drummond's collection of love poems was first fully published, the European fashion for conventionally Petrarchan or Neoplatonic sequences appears to have fallen into steep decline; most criticism places Drummond at the very end of European amatory tradition, and at the near-conclusion of an already belated and fragmentary Scottish erotic tradition. However, as R.D.S. Jack has frequently pointed out, the chronological and critical landscape of Renaissance Scottish literature has often been tendentiously mapped out (cf. Jack 1997). Within the period, it should be remembered that French-influenced and Italianate-inspired tendencies and movements within the period might be the result of delicate political and cultural alliances rather than of any supposed cultural recalcitrance. And, as Edwin Morgan emphasises, Drummond "has suffered at various times from different prejudices, both literary and political" (Morgan 1990: 56). So, although this essay takes as a principal point of analysis the *end* of Drummond's love sequence of 1616, it does not argue for Drummond as a poet of cultural "finality" or "ends". In focussing on beauty in his amatory poetry, it suggests that it is an ideal of substantial physical, spiritual, and imaginative import which, while acknowledged in previous discussions of his Neo-Platonism (cf. especially Dorangeon 1988), has not been the subject of sustained analysis. Though Drummond's love poetry closely approaches the ideals and contradictions of beauty found in conventional portrayals of Petrarchan and Neoplatonic eros, the essay proposes that it does not present the conventionally transcendental and all-encompassing resolution which Petrarchan and Neoplatonic narrative sequences usually achieve. Exploration of beauty's meaning in Drummond's work reveals not simply its allusion and debt to traditional erotic and philosophical concepts but a new and different relationship between beauty, love, and loss in his poetry, emerging out of the apparent reluctance of the love sequence of *Poems Amorous, Funerall, Diuine, Pastorall in Sonnets, Songs, Sextains, Madrigals* (1616) to relinquish a hold upon the sensuous and the beautiful. This new understanding of beauty's ambiguity in the secular poetry sheds light on how beauty is represented in Drummond's sacred poetry: the ways in which its rhetorical, emotional, and philosophical meanings differ from, and yet are also analogous to, its profane counterpart.

Beauty, the beloved, and Petrarchan pastoral

Drummond's love poetry is perhaps best viewed as a palimpsest: an original creation which conceals the direct sources and implicit inspirations which underpin it. Michael Spiller comments that "half the love-poets of Renaissance Europe wander about in his lines" (Spiller 1992: 185), while Simone Dorangeon observes that his poetry distils "la mémoire culturelle de son temps" (Dorangeon 1988: 268). Drummond's poet-lover aptly confesses that "I first beganne to reade, then Love to write" (MacDonald 1976: 8; I.i.6).[1] In that opening sonnet, the desire is imposed on him by a smiling god of love as penitence for his literary artifice; as experiential atonement for knowing love only through words interpreted and created. Drummond's precise translations, allusions, and borrowings from Italian, French, and Spanish writers have been traced extensively in the work of L.E. Kastner, R.H. MacDonald, and R.D.S. Jack. Consequently, this essay chooses a far broader conceptual and comparative focus, and uses two sources, Petrarch's *Rime sparse*, or the *Canzoniere*, and the later writings of the Neoplatonic love tradition, through which to crystallise Drummond's philosophy of beauty. (Whilst for the purposes of this essay, Petrarchism and Neoplatonism are treated separately, their interconnectedness should be acknowledged. The philosophical continuity between Petrarchan and Neoplatonic thought is frequently

---

[1] Unless otherwise stated, all further references to Drummond's poetry will be to this edition and will appear in parentheses as reference to part, sonnet number, and line number(s).

observed [cf. Kristeller 1988: 64]. In literary terms, too, the profane-sacred love sequences of Renaissance poets ostensibly moulded by Florentine Neoplatonic doctrine also recall in part the transcendent eros of *stilnovisti* poetry, and of Dante and Petrarch [Robb 1935: 177–79]).

Drummond's response to Petrarch is best understood against the general backdrop of both European and Scottish Petrarchan reception. As William J. Kennedy has amply demonstrated, European Renaissance responses to the *Rime* were formed and bounded by the varying aesthetic, intellectual, and cultural preoccupations and sympathies of commentators and creative poets from the late fifteenth century onwards (cf. Kennedy 1994). In particular, secular reimaginings of Petrarch rapidly acquired what Kennedy calls a "protonationalist density" (cf. Kennedy 2003): whether manifest in the prolific commentaries and expositions of the *Rime sparse*, or in rhetorical and conceptual imitations of either the sequence or individual sonnets, they shared the same goal of vernacular revival and of national artistic reinvention. In Scotland, the first sustained importation of Petrarchan models occurs in the 1580s under the aegis of James VI (cf. Jack 1968; 1972; 1976; 1988) where the particular cultural and political impulses which shaped the courtly literature of his reign strongly reflect the "nationalistic" spirit of Petrarchan interpretation in France. James's desire to strengthen and consolidate the artistic and political vigour of the Scots language means that the creation of love poetry at his court has a relatively free artistic rein. Simultaneously, his own political anxieties, and the desire to distance himself from the turbulence of his mother Mary's reign, means that love poetry in particular comes freighted with its own ideological burden. While Italianate models of love poetry are pursued by many writers at his court, James himself seemed to eschew the tradition of Petrarchan eros, returning to French amatory sources which, although predominant in Scottish courtly literature of the earlier sixteenth century and in Mary's reign, are moulded to fit the king's protestantised sensibility. Consequently, it is fair to say that Petrarchan love, even in the period of the Jacobean high renaissance, rarely exerted absolute influence. For both political and religious reasons, then, Petrarchan love is seldom the source of "straightforward" imitation; despite its obvious Petrarchan debts, William Fowler's *Tarantula of Love*, for example, is replete with anxiety regarding the Catholic resolution of the object of Petrarch's love (cf. Dunnigan 2002).

It is striking, therefore, that well over twenty years after this Petrarchan movement, Drummond's *Poems* should outwardly seem the most faithful monument to its tradition in Renaissance Scotland. This is immediately witnessed in the twofold division of the sequence into parts which are only numerically titled (First and Second Parts) but which evoke the division *in vive* and *in morte*, editorially imposed on Petrarch's collection after his death. As in the *Rime sparse*, where the drama of Laura's death happens "beyond" the immediate drama of the sequence, so in Drummond's *Poems Amatory*, Auristella's death occurs for the reader in the imaginative interstice between Parts One and Two, announced in the rhetorically charged, apocalyptic tones of Part Two's first sonnet: "Of mortall Glorie ô soone darkned Raye! [...] / *Death* hath thy Temple raz'd, *Loves* Empire foylde, / The World of Honour, Worth, and Sweetnesse spoylde" (II.i.1, 13–14). Consequently, this second part explores the *Rime*'s elegiac and philosophical import. Indeed, as this essay will argue, it is this memorial theme of mourning and remembrance which emerges most sharply through the manifestations of beauty in Part Two. More generally, Drummond's sequence displays the rhetorical patterns of conceit, hyperbole, and oxymoron familiar to the Petrarchist tradition ("Faire is my Yoke, though grievous bee my Paines, / Sweet are my Wounds, although they deeply smart" (I.iv.1–2; cf. Wallerstein)) yet which, as early as the 1540s in France, were perceived to have "ossified" the tradition, provoking the "anti-Petrarchist" responses of Du Bellay, Ronsard, and others (Clements 1941: 16–19). Yet Drummond's love poems rarely seem to rework or critique, in Joel Fineman's phrase, the "foregrounded rhetoricity of Petrarchist manner" (Fineman 1986: 323). There is a case for suggesting that Drummond simply found the intrinsic aesthetic beauty of Petrarchan language sufficient in itself; but there is another vein of Petrarchism on which Drummond draws and in which ideas of the beautiful are differently manifest. As Elizabeth Cropper remarks:

the lyric poetry of Petrarch is [...] of the utmost importance for the understanding of concepts of beauty and its representation in the Renaissance, for the poet invokes a special relationship between love and the imagination [...] the capacity of the imagination to reconfigure the beloved at any time or place is fundamental to his poetry and its images (Cropper 1999: 4).

In imitating the *Rime's* pantheistic impulses, much of Drummond's Part One focuses on the lover's imperfect but powerful imaginative conjurations of Auristella; their "place" is in nature, and in the natural created forms which both conceal and unveil her beauty.

In Petrarch's sequence, the natural landscape is mostly a beneficent sign: a manifestation of divine creation, abundant proof of God's beauty. Here, Petrarch encounters the beautiful Laura, seemingly semi-divine herself, a creation as exquisite and ephemeral as the beautiful forms which surround her (see, for example, *Rime* 121, 125, 160, 162; cf. Sturm-Maddox 1999: 56–57).[2] Within the verdant beauty of the Vaucluse landscape, Petrarch seeks refuge; it offers consolations which are both emotional and physical. Yet often, and as if in reflection of nature's transformative powers, Laura too shows herself capable of metamorphosis, a tiger in "forma d'angel" (*Rime* 152). Drummond's sequence, both in individual sonnets and sustained through the songs and madrigals interwoven throughout both parts, is fully alert to the complex, significatory power of nature of the Petrarchan source. His *Songs* manifests both the erotic and elegiac strains of beauty in Petrarchan pastoral as well as being suffused with allusions to, and echoes of, the classical pastoral traditions, which inform Petrarch. Occasionally, nature's beauty falls short of Auristella's:

Faire are the *Meads*, the *Woods*, the *Flouds* are faire,
Faire looketh *Ceres* with her yellow Haire,
And *Apples* Queene when *Rose*-cheekt Shee doth smile.
That Heaven, and Earth, and Seas are faire is true,
Yet true that all not please so much as you. (I.xxxviii.10–14)

---

[2] References to Petrarch's *Rime-sparse* will appear throughout this essay as references to sonnet numbers in the Durling edition (Durling 1976).

But more often Drummond's pastoral offers self-contained allegories, painterly and eroticised mythological vignettes which dramatise the different forms of visual and sensual beauty which overwhelm the lover:

A Mirtle great with birth, from whose rent wombe
Three naked Nymphes *more white than snow foorth come.*
For Nymphes they seem'd, about their heavenly Faces
In Waves of Gold did flow their curling Tresses,
About each Arme, their Armes more white than milke,
Each weare a blushing Armelet of silke […]
But scarce the grove their naked Beauties graced,
And on the amorous Verdure had not traced,
When to the Floud they ran, the Floud in Robes
Of curling Christall to brests Ivorie Globes
Who wrapt them all about, yet seem'd take pleasure
To showe warme Snowes throughout her liquid Azure. (I.Song i.85–90, 95–100)

Drummond's lover seeks the solitary woody exile which, throughout the *Rime,* symbolises but also assuages Petrarch's pain (cf. *Rime* 169; 176):

All desolate I haunt the fearfull Woods
When I should give my selfe to rest at Night […]
Ende these my Dayes Endwellers of the Woods,
Take this my Life yee deepe and raging Floods,
Sunne never rise to cleare mee with thy Light,
Horror *and* Darknesse *keepe a lasting* Night […] (I.Sextain.i.17–18; 31–4)

Unlike the insentient Auristella, nature offers sympathy (cf. I.xv). The landscape, mostly beautiful though at times fearful, is even inscribed with his pain ("Enamell'd Banke, whose shining Gravell beares / These sad Characters of my Miseries" [I.xvi.3–4]). Yet the beauties of nature and Auristella are also inextricably linked. The *locus amoenus* of Song ii is marred by her absence ("*The Clouds bespangle with bright Gold their Blew: / Here is the pleasant Place, / And ev'ry thing, save* Her, *who all should grace*" [I.Song ii.45–47]). Auristella herself is embraced by and enfolded within the landscape (Petrarch's Italian rivers are transposed into the River Forth which cradles "the Boat that *Earths Perfections* doth containe" [I.xxxix.4]) as nature metonymically represents Auristella and her unrequited lover. Throughout Part One, Auristella's beauty is both aligned with nature's and surpasses it. Imagistic conceits blend the descriptive litanies of the female *blason* with an inventory of the landscape's bejewelled colours and textures. The natural and the artificial coalesce:

Your pure and burnish'd Gold, your Diamonds fine,
Snow-passing Ivorie that the Eye delights:
Nor *Seas* of those deare Wares are in you found,
Vaunt not, rich Pearle, red Corrall, which doe stirre
A fond desire in Fooles to plunge your Ground;
Those all (more faire) are to bee had in Her:
Pearle, Ivorie, Corrall, Diamond, Sunnes, Gold,
Teeth, Necke, Lips, Heart, Eyes, Haire, are to behold. (I.vi.7–14)

Perhaps most significantly of all, Auristella's beauty remains immutable. In this, it transcends nature's which is always subject to change (cf. I.xvii.13): "She whose faire flowrs no *Autumne* makes decay, / Whose Hue celestiall, earthly Hues doth staine" (I.xlii.1–2). Her departure denudes places of their beauty: "Deflourish'd *Mead* where is your heavenly Hue?" (I.xlv.9). The paradisiacal aspect of nature is only revealed or restored through Auristella's presence; the landscape is made beautiful by either her presence or immanence within it.

The First Part, therefore, delineates worlds, both external and interior, which are predominantly visual and sensual: physical and mythological landscapes where the beautiful form of Auristella, and the rich visual surfaces of a landscape which oscillates from the locally topographical to the eclectically mythographical, sensually charge and frustrate Drummond's lover. Beauty's power is perpetually mirrored in and magnified through Auristella, and the beautiful physical and mythological worlds through which she moves in the lover's imagination. In this, Drummond's lover recalls Petrarch who, until Laura's death, worships only external form; like the *Rime*, *Poems* evokes "one of the most pervasive themes of *dolce stil* poetry, that of a lady whose beauty dazzles or blinds a lover who cannot prevent himself from returning again and again to her presence" (Sturm-Maddox 1985: 45). Yet this absorption within beauty is not wholly unqualified. Auristella binds and circumvents the lover's intellect and imagination, confining him to contemplation not of "that vaste Heaven" or "any other *Worlds*" or of "Sprights, or Bodies, contrare-Wayes in Skie" (I.v.1, 2, 7). Drummond's lover, transposed into a semi-classical, pastoral figure, wanders a landscape which, in Part One, Song I, bears the visual memory of the pantheon of gods, goddesses, nymphs, and shepherds, which once traversed its streams, caves, and mountains. It inspires in the lover, "ravish'd" by the collective impress of physical beauty and mythological ghosts, the sensual, quasi-mystical vision of female beauty which suggests a loss of innocence, a "fall" into knowledge that hints at beauty's potentially corruptive powers:

I, who yet humane weaknesse did not know [...]
Did cast, and drowne mine Eyes in sweet Delight.
What wondrous Thing is this that Beautie's *named*
And never knowne in all my flying Dayes [...]
O precious Sight! which none doth els descrie
Except the burning Sunne, and quivering I.
And yet O deare bought Sight! O would for ever
I might enjoy you, or had joy'd you never! (I.Song i.137, 142–5, 151–52)

Beauty, mourning, and Neoplatonism

Only in the retrospectively clarifying light of The Second Part do such allusions to deceptive "false Gleames" (I. Madrigall ix.9), of "Minde that contains / A Power all Power of *Senses* to controule" (I.xiii.11–12), prepare the reader for this section's Petrarchan renunciation of beauty. The true ethical and spiritual meaning of beauty is only apparent *in morte* after the deaths of Laura and Auristella. Through the sinuous and complex revelations and self-chastisements of Petrarch's lover in the last third of the sequence, Laura's mortal feminine beauty is portrayed as the sin which has distracted Petrarch from loving God, the Creator rather than the created form. Called to remembrance of the "true path", or "true image", he has been made "forgetful" through beguilement by Laura's beauty (cf. *Rime* 126). Renunciation of his former physical love of Laura will enable him to find redemption (*salute*), and to perceive and emulate "the ways" through which Laura, transformed in death, "knows" God (*Rime* 343). In the *Rime*, and in the *Trionfo della castita* (of *I Trionfi*), Laura is reincarnate in visionary form, descending to earth from her heavenly realm to offer consolation to her bereaved and spiritually desolate lover:

Quando il soave mio fido conforto
Per dar riposo a la mia vita stanca
Ponsi del letto in su la sponda manca
Con quel suo dolce ragionare accorto,
Tutto di pièta et di paura smorto
Dico: "Onde vien tu ora, o felice alma?"

[When my gentle, faithful comforter, to give repose to my weary life, sits on the left side of my bed, with that sweet, skilful talk of hers, all pale with anguish and fear, I say, "Where do you come from now, O happy soul?"] (*Rime* 359; Durling ed. and tr. 1976: 556–57)

The Second Part unfolds with a lament for Auristella's vanished beauty – "That living Snow, those crimson Roses bright, / Those Pearles, those Rubies, which did breede Desire, / Those Lockes of Gold [...]" (II.ii.5–7) –which echoes Petrarch's elegies for a world deprived of beauty (cf. *Rime* 338). Similarly, Petrarch's estrangement from "il mondo errante" (*Rime* 350) find echo in Drummond's frequent condemnations of life's illusory temporality, its "Slumber [...] of fearfull Dreames" (II.v.8), and "Aire"-like fragility (cf. Madrigall i). In the culminative narrative of Song ii, Auristella returns as a Petrarchan *donna angelicata* to convince Drummond's grieving lover that there is no need to mourn: she has been taken from "this filthie Stage of Care" (II.Song ii.63; cf. *Rime* 359: 12–22) to be resurrected in a heaven where beauty is immutable:

It hath an Earth, as hath this World of yours,
With Creatures peopled, stor'd with Trees and Flowrs,
It hath a Sea, like Saphire Girdle cast,
Which decketh of harmonious Shores the Waste,
It hath pure Fire, it hath delicious Aire,
Moone, Sunne, and Starres, Heavens wonderfully faire:
But there Flowrs doe not fade, Trees grow not olde,

The Creatures doe not die through Heat nor Colde [...]
Dayes make no Months, but ever-blooming Mayes. (I.Song ii.123–30, 136)

In Drummond, the consolation of eternal life, of divine redemptive grace attained by renouncing, in Petrarch's phrase, "passati tempi" (*Rime* 365), is largely translated through the language of beauty in Song ii. Auristella's speech implores that the lover come to a realisation of Petrarchan *errore,* and discover the "utili oneste" (virtuous paths", *Rime* 360) which lead to God. It does so by portraying the divine beauty which awaits him in terms which are predominantly aesthetic and visual but which also convey the aural and sensory beauty of heaven too. Though such beauty can only be experienced by dying ("thou art dead, / And still shalt bee, till thou be like mee made" [II.Song ii.105–6]), its glory can nonetheless be visually and sensorily comprehended. Despite the analogous language of description, this is "correct" beauty, as opposed to its earlier wrongful kind. Where the lover was once consumed by sensual beauty, now he is instructed by its former embodiment, Auristella, to turn his "gaze" to "that only Faire" (MacDonald 1976: 71; 211). Illusionistic beauty has been replaced by authentically beautiful forms. In his religious sequence and elsewhere, the language of physical, natural beauty makes manifest God's beneficent, creative presence, an aspect of Drummond's sensuous mysticism to which this essay later returns. Yet the shared impulse behind these ideas of spiritual beauty derives from Neoplatonic thought. Petrarch and Petrarchism deeply mould the rhetorical and spiritual contours of Drummond's 1616 love sequence but arguably its philosophy of beauty is also substantially indebted to Italian Renaissance Neoplatonism.

The catalogue of Drummond's library amply attests his interest in both Platonic and Neoplatonic thought (MacDonald 1971: 81–83). However, his prose treatise, *A Cypresse Grove*, published in 1623, usefully exemplifies the tenets of Renaissance Neoplatonism that most preoccupied him. Essentially a meditation on death, through which "Images [are] limned in [his] Minde" (MacDonald 1976: 165), Drummond comes to an awareness of the inconstant, mutable nature of earthly "Matter, like a still-flowing and ebbing Sea" (MacDonald 1976: 149) which in turn highlights the delusional nature of human desire: "a Circle of idle Travells, and Laboures (like *Penelopes* Taske) unprofitablie renewed. Some time wee are in a Chase after a fading Beautie" (MacDonald 1976: 152). The soul, fettered within its bodily prison (cf. MacDonald 1976: 161), evokes the Platonic notion of the soul's imprisonment within the body as in an oyster shell. Apostrophising the soul, Drummond portrays the orthodox Platonic separation of soul from body, before their "long wished and generall Reunion" (MacDonald 1976: 170), as a departure "from this mortall Bride, thy Bodie; sith it is but for a tyme, and such a tyme, as shee shall not care for, nor feele any thing in, nor thou have much neede of her?" (MacDonald 1976: 163). The concept of beauty has a pivotal role to play in this philosophical awareness. The soul itself is perceived as a beautiful object:

thou art so wonderfull a Beautie, and so beautifull a Wonder, that if but once thou couldst be gazed upon by bodily Eyes, every heart would be inflamed with thy love, and ravished from all servile basenesse and earthlie desires. (MacDonald 1976: 162)

God Himself is the "onlie essentiall and true Beauty, deserving alone all love and admiration, by which the Creatures are onely in so much faire and excellent, as they participate of his Beauty" (MacDonald 1976: 169). The divine and cosmological principle of beauty animates the world.

While this treatise represents his fullest exposition, and synthesis of, the Neoplatonic philosophical issues which underpin his work as a whole, his love poetry is informed in particular by the body of Neoplatonic thought derived from the commentaries, or the *trattato d'amore,* of late fifteenth and early sixteenth-century Florentine writers, which appeared with the development of the formal academies in Renaissance Italy (cf. Kristeller 1961; 1965). Marsilio Ficino's *De Amore* or the *Commentary on Plato's Symposium on Love,* was one of the most influential of the *cinquecento* tradition. In his major philosophical work, an exposition and interpretation of Plato's *Symposium*, he produced a three fold distinction of love, founded on a hierarchy which ascends from bestial or voluptuous desire to human or active love, and culminating in the supreme form of divine or contemplative love. This is the template for the ascension from sensual to spiritual desire which underpins the Neoplatonic love tradition of Renaissance poetry. In this process which expounds the "mysteries of love" (Plato quoted in Hofstadter and Kuhns 1964: 75), the concept of beauty plays a key part. It is through the perception of different forms of beauty that the lover achieves spiritual ascension. In the Second Oration of Ficino, where the influence of Plotinus can especially be seen, it is also the power of beauty which engenders love. In the Fourth Oration that beauty is now defined as incorporeal (e.g. Ficino 1548: 72b–74a). In Mario Equicola's encyclopaedic *Libro di natura d'Amore*, love is portrayed as the desire to have, use, and enjoy that which is considered beautiful; the desire to create beauty is itself called love (cf. Ficino 1548: II.16). Pico della Mirandola's commentary on the *Canzone del Amor Divino* of the Florentine Platonist, Girolamo Benivieni, follows Ficino's exposition of the interrelationship between love and beauty. Beauty may be either physical or intellectual (cf. Pico: II.10). The power of love — and love is always of something beautiful — is to awaken in us the dormant desire of the soul for that divine or "intellectual" beauty which bodily desire has oppressed. Love, in Benivieni's poem, "has the meaning of the desire and attraction of all things towards ideal beauty" (Robb 1935: 60). In the reconstruction of the Platonic ladder of love, the soul comes to know beauty universally, enabled to see the image of ideal beauty imparted by the intellect (Robb 1935: 61). The idealised image of the beloved elevates itself "di grado in grado" until finally revelatory of the divine source of beauty. The soul ascends via contemplation to that perfect beauty, striving for union with the divine. In Bembo's famous oration in Castiglione's *Il Cortegiano* (and also in his own *Gli Asolani*), the ladder of love has sensation as its lower part and understanding as the uppermost rung. The lover's contemplative imagination is led from adoration of one individual beautiful body to admire the universal beauty which is to be discovered in all bodies. In ascending the ladder of love from particular to "bellezza uniuersale", the lover's soul is enflamed with desire for "unione della bellezza" (Castiglione 1541: 190a–191b, 190b, 192b).

The Neoplatonism of Drummond's love sequence, and the philosophy of beauty it thereby entails, is clearly indebted to the Florentine Neoplatonists. The Second Part is rich in Neoplatonic tropes, metaphors, and allusions which delineate a clear path for his love's apotheosis. Auristella's death is announced by the desolation of particular archetypes, personified abstractions which, if not strictly Platonic Forms, still imply that Auristella incarnates their single and pure form:

Let *Beautie* now be blubbred Cheekes with Teares,
Let widow'd *Musicke* only roare, and plaine,
Poore *Vertue* get thee Wings, and mount the Spheares,
And let thine only Name on Earth remaine (II.i.9–12).

Borrowing the celebration of light as the most beautiful earthly form (Ficino's "Lume del Sole"; Ficino 1548: 212), a radiance most approximate to God's resplendent light, Auristella is insistently described in illuminatory ways: she "Now makes more radiant Heavens eternall Day" (II.i.8) when absorbed into the true and eternal light of the divine.

Of all the Platonic Forms or Ideas which she incarnates or resembles, Beauty is the most significant. Auristella's death deprives the earthly world itself of its capacity to be beautiful: "A litle Space of Earth my Love doth bound, / That Beautie which did raise it to the Skie, / Turn'd in neglected Dust, now low doth lie" (II.iii.5–7); "For if they would such Beautie bring on Earth, / they should be forc'd againe to make Her breath" (II.ii.13–14). The separation between lover and beloved is imagined as absolute and unbreachable. In Sonnet vii, the lover construes himself, left to mourn on earth, as "(a Shadow) yet to stay" (II.vii.7), a term evoking associations of the Platonic shadow world. Song i's resumption of Part One's separate pastoral narrative, in which the shepherd Damon laments at his beloved's graveside, echoes The Second Part's comprehensive theme of lost Platonic Forms: "Perfections Mirrour" is now shattered, and the natural earth has returned to a desolate and wintry state: "Winter is fallen in our May, / Turn'd is in Night our Day" (II.Song i.87–8). Auristella is the link which binds, in Plotinus's words, "beauty here and beauty There" (Hofstadter and Kuhns eds 1964: 143). In Sonnet viii, the extended apostrophe to the Lute which parallels Sonnet xxviii in Part One, the instrument rededicates itself to lamenting Auristella's death, "Like widow'd Turtle"; "orphan'd" and without purpose, the lute can only

fall silent "Sith that deare Voyce which did thy Sounds approve [...] /
Is reft from Earth *to tune those Spheares above*" (II.viii.5; 7).

These Neoplatonic echoes culminate in the two sonnets (xii and
xiii) which precede Song ii. In the first, Auristella's uniqueness is
again proclaimed as the star which once shone brightly "in this blacke
Age" (II.xii.5). The rhetorical questions of its third quatrain re-
emphasise her incarnation as the absolute Form of Beauty:

Who more shall vaunt true Beautie here to see?
What hope doth more in any Heart remaine,
That such Perfections shall his *Reason* raine?
If Beautie with thee borne too died with thee? (II.xii.9–12).

Sonnet xiii is constructed as if in answer:

Sith it hath pleas'd that First and *onelie Faire*
To take that Beautie to himselfe again,
Which in *this World of Sense* not to remaine,
But to amaze, was sent, and home repaire,
The Love which to that Beautie I did beare
(Made pure of mortall Spots which did it staine,
And endless, which even *Death* cannot impaire)
I place on him who will it not disdaine.
No shining Eyes, no Lockes of curling Gold,
No blushing Roses on a virgine Face,
No outward Show, no, nor no inward Grace,
Shall Force hereafter have my Thoughts to hold:
Love heere on Earth hudge Stormes of care doe tosse,
But plac'd above, exempted is from Losse. (II.xiii.1–14)

God, Himself imagined as supremely beautiful, has temporarily
loaned Auristella to earth, "this World of Sense". The lover pledges
adoration of "him who will it not disdaine", entering into a state of
love which is pure and immaculate. Replete with echoes of Petrarch's
renunciatory poems, the sonnet also implies that the topmost rung of
the Platonic ladder of love has been successfully scaled. Not only is
divine love, the *bellezza intelligible,* "Made pure of mortall Spots"
(Sonnet xiii) but is shown to be eternal, unlike human love which is
transient and therefore imperfect (cf. Bembo in Castiglione 1541:
183bff).

The tenaciousness of beauty

In the final Song of The Second Part, the imagistically elaborate dream vision invoking, as suggested earlier, Laura's consolatory return (in the *Rime* but also the *Trionfo della castita*), Drummond's Neoplatonic exaltation of spiritual love at the expense of profane finds its fullest expression. Marrying the conventions of courtly allegorical vision with Christian consolation, the Song also interprets earthly forms as lesser, impermanent reflections of Ideal, or divine, Forms. Heaven, portrayed in its immaculate perfection, and immured to change, is unimaginably beautiful: *"There is a World, a World of perfect Blisse, / Pure, immateriall, bright, more farre from this [...]"* (II.Song ii.117–18). Auristella's visionary return, then, echoes Laura's but her speech more closely recalls the conventional Neoplatonic exposition of spiritual beauty, consoling and inspiring, than it does Laura's serene chastisements in canzone 359. Though Auristella urges Drummond's lover to renounce the love *"which reacheth but to Dust"* (II.Song ii.197), she seeks to comfort him with the knowledge that everything beautiful on earth is an imperfect, shadowy representation of the perfect divine Forms which she has witnessed in heaven, just as Equicola's treatise urges that the beauty known through our senses awakens in us a recollection of the Beauty that "our souls have known in Heaven" (cf. II.ch. 8).

> *If once thou on that* only Faire *couldst gaze,*
> *What Flames of Love would hee within thee raise?*
> *In what a mazing Maze would it thee bring,*
> *To heare but once that Quire celestiall sing?*
> *The fairest Shapes on which thy Love did sease,*
> *Which earst did breede Delight, then would displease,*
> *Then Discords hoarse were Earths enticing Sounds,*
> *All Musicke but a Noyse which Sense confounds.* (II.Song ii.211–18)

As in Neoplatonic doctrine, material beauty is loved insofar as it induces knowledge of the perfect incorporeal beauty which resides in the divine intellect. It inspires the soul's yearning for union with this superior intellectual and divine beauty which is urged to break free from devotion to any flawed corporeal beauty.

And in our Beautie, his us made admire,
If wee seeme faire? ô thinke how faire is Hee,
Of whose Fairnesse, shadowes, Steps we bee,
No Shadow can compare it with the Face,
No Step with that deare Foot which did it trace. (II.Song ii.230–4)

The *summum bonum* of "Happinesse", Auristella firmly announces, cannot be attained by love of mortal things, by "Sense", or "false Pleasures Might" (II.Song ii.236, 237).

The conclusion to Auristella's long consolation, and to the sequence as a whole, is brief:

Heere did shee pause, and with a milde Aspect
Did towards mee those lamping Twinnes direct:
The wonted Rayes I knew, and thrice essay'd
To answere make, thrice faultring Tongue it stay'd.
And while upon that Face I fed my Sight,
Mee thought shee vanish'd up in Titans *Light,*
Who guilding with his Rayes each Hill and Plaine,
Seem'd to have brought the Gold-smiths World again. (II.Song ii.241–48)

Despite its brevity, several points are worthy of note. Auristella's vision, though in part lovingly and familiarly rendered, makes him inarticulate; while moral and philosophical in import, it is also sensuously intense (cf. "I fed my Sight"). And her consolation, unlike Laura's, remains unanswered. The return of a golden age, that ideal of edenic innocence and beauty which forms a significant imagistic and conceptual strand in both parts of Drummond's sequence, suggests an optimistic end, promising a redemption or transcendence beyond the sequence's final imaginative contours. Yet the verb, "Seem'd", (line 248 in the extract above), when foregrounded at the beginning of the final sentence, evokes, if not entirely doubt, an element of pro-visionality or of fragile irresolution. It might be suggested that, even if this final song seems outwardly to declare that the only bulwark against sorrow is to transform the object of perception from beauty of body to beauty of soul, to turn from the finite and imperfect beauty of earth to the thereby incomprehensible and infinite beauties of heaven, this is a curiously irresolute phrasing. The sequence's eight-line con-clusion, however brief, is therefore arguably sufficient to question the

completion or totality of the otherwise apparently seamless Neoplatonic transformation. Where ostensibly Song ii portrays the material world as inferior to the divine world, illuminated and changeless,
of which the earthly realm is a shadow, it fails to convince wholly that
Drummond's lover, in other ways pursuing a conventionally
Petrarchan and Neoplatonic fate, submits his soul to divine love. That
the sequence should end with apparent hesitation between imminent
spiritual apotheosis and the survival of the beautiful and earthly reflects what Simone Dorangeon perceives in the 1616 sequence as "une
étrange dialectique entre, d'une part, la jouissance visuelle, la
tentation de l'hédonisme et, d'autre part, le repli vers une région
secrète où tout est silence et méditation" (Dorangeon 1988: 271). It
suggests that Auristella's beautiful form still holds the lover captive
("upon that Face I fed my Sight"), and that contemplation of "beauty
absolute" (Plato, quoted in Hofstadter and Kuhns 1964: 76) remains
elusive, perhaps unwanted.

   I shall return to the implications of the sequence's seeming
refusal entirely to negate beauty's power but it is illuminating to compare briefly Song ii with the more securely deployed Christian
Neoplatonism of Drummond's later religious poetry. His religious
sequence of 1623, *Flowres of Sion or Spiritual Poemes* (reprinted in
1630), which, as R.D.S. Jack has demonstrated is deeply influenced
by the poet Marino, begins, like *A Cypresse Grove*, as a meditation on
transience and death. It becomes both contemplation, and enactment
of, Christ's life in the sequence's central section, and concluding in
celebration of God's eternal love, and of the spiritual and philosophical purposiveness of a universe whose meaning and perfection, according to Neoplatonic cosmology, has finally been revealed. Beauty
has an interesting role to play in this process. In the early sonnets of
the sequence, beauty's delusional powers are wholly condemned:

Once did this World to mee seeme sweete and faire,
While Sense light Mindes prospective keept blind,
Now like imagin'd Landskip in the Aire,
And weeping Raine-bowes, her best Joyes I finde (iv.9–12)

I found all but a Rose hedg'd with a Bryer,
A nought, a thought, a show of golden Dreames. (v.7–8)

But sillie wee, (like foolish Children) rest
Well pleas'd with coloured Velame, Leaves of Gold,
Faire dangling Ribbones, leaving what is best [...] (vi.9–11)

And yet despite this *vanitas* theme, praise of God is frequently manifest through a language which fuses spiritual rapture and sensuous
beauty without apparent theological contradiction or emotional tension:

Not to be Beauties Thrall,
All fruitless Love to flie,
Yet loving still a Love transcending all.
  A Love which while it burnes
The Soule with fairest Beames,
In that uncreated Sunne the Soule it turnes,
And makes such Beautie prove,
That (if Sense saw her Gleames?)
All lookers on would pine and die for love.
                              (Hymne iv.94–6)

Arguably, Drummond's poetic, religious sensibility is deeply indebted
to that dominant strain of medieval mysticism which translates experience of the ineffable and spiritual through the sensuous and corporeal.
As much as Drummond's religious poetry strikes out against beauty's
flawed and corrupting powers, it too, through its painterly, imagistic
language and rhetorical forms, strongly retains, indeed exonerates, the
idea of the beautiful *per se*. In Sonnet xii, "For the Magdalene"
(MacDonald 1976: 94), based on one of Desportes's "Sonnets
spirituals", the former emblems of the Magdalene's beauty, "These
Lockes", have become themselves healingly redemptive. But, in
common with many literary and artistic representations of the *beata
peccatrix* in early seventeenth-century Catholic Europe (Haskins:
270–73), Drummond's sonnet delineates with fascinated precision,
their almost labyrinthine, Eve-like beauty:

Smooth-frizled Waves, sad Shelfes which shadow deepe,
Soule-stinging Serpents in gilt curles which creepe,
To touch thy sacred Feete doe now aspire. (xii.6–9)

In "An Hymne of the Passion", Drummond's narrative "I" acts as a witness to the crucifixion, urging us, as if spectators or viewers of its depiction in art, to contemplate "His Head bow'd to His brest, Lockes sadlie rent, / Like a cropt Rose that languishing doth fade" (Hymne 1.29–30); the dying Christ is portrayed as an emblem of beauty. In the sonnet which instructs the angels to behold Christ's agony on the cross, he does not flinch from the contemplation of suffering but, characteristically, in part transmutes it into an image of beauty: "Preserve this sacred Blood that Earth adornes, / Those liquid Roses gather off his Thornes" (xv.10–11). Aesthetic spectacle is the means by which to know Christ. In the Hymn on the Resurrection, nature's beauty is revivified when Christ rises (MacDonald 1976: 102); "flames of beautie" enkindle the "Bright Portalles of the Skie, / Emboss'd with sparkling Starres" (Hymne iii.16; 1–2).

Whether consciously evoking earlier mystical practice or not, Drummond's poetic spirituality is informed by an aesthetic and spiritual alertness to the power of beauty. Beauty is a means of unveiling the purpose and perfection of divine creation; and of awakening devotion within the reader by "stilling" moments of the Christological narrative into moments of visual contemplation: painterly meditations which both arrest and inspire the reader or spectator in their delineations of beauty, even at moments of extreme suffering and desolation. This sensitivity to the drama and physicality of beauty can perhaps be construed as another aspect of what David Atkinson has analysed as Drummond's Baroque sensibility (cf. Atkinson 1991: 394) which richly suffuses his work. In Drummond's religious poetry, then, beauty is a vital part of his spiritual poetics, and an important element of its aesthetic spectacle and illusionism. In a narrative world harnessed resolutely both to commemoration and celebration of God, physical beauty — the beauty of the world — ultimately attains a beneficent meaning, even as it also helps to express the dramatic and melancholic elements of Drummond's spiritual vision.

With this understanding of beauty's power in Drummond's sacred corpus, it is instructive finally to return to the end of *Poems* where, it has been argued, the sensual, rather than transfigured, beauty of Auristella remains (unlike Petrarch's efforts to perceive Laura with his "inward eye"), and where the Neoplatonic apotheosis is doubtfully embraced ("Seem'd"). The implications of beauty's endurance are suggestive. Whilst the debts to erotic and philosophical notions of beauty which have their roots in the *Rime* and in Neoplatonic inspired love poetry are amply attested, the apparent refusal of the sequence to realise their full potential implies that it seeks to raise questions about the Petrarchan narrative of "love and death", and of the Neoplatonic resolution which purports to answer vital questions. Why did the beloved die? What was the meaning of her death? What ethical and spiritual purpose does the bereaved lover's life now serve? These are questions which, as Castiglione's words are translated by Sir Thomas Hoby, are "shadowed with the darke night of earthlye matters" (Cox ed. 1994: 358). Drummond is therefore not "simply" an imitator. His particular evocation and reimagining of these two intertwined, Renaissance love traditions can ultimately be seen to foreground the subject of grief and mourning and, accordingly, becomes enmeshed in expressions of love-mourning that have roots in Petrarch (and in Dante's *La Vita Nuova* too, one might suggest).

The uncertainty with which Auristella's consolation is met may suggest the inadequacy or imperfection of the philosophical and spiritual comfort offered; it rejects the belief of *A Cypresse Grove* that "Death is best young; things farre and excellent [...]" (MacDonald 1976: 166). As suggested earlier, the rhetoric of the closing lines belies a fascination still with the physically beautiful, displaying resistance to the philosophical and spiritual devaluing of sensual or earthly beauty which the Neoplatonic narratives demand. Instead, it foregrounds the memory of beauty: the elegiac, memorialising power of Auristella's beauty which makes the remembrance of the beloved as she was, rather than her divine transmutation, most pervasive in the end. In this, it strongly echoes the recurring memories of Laura's beauty – "the most beautiful eyes and the brightest face that ever shone, and [...] the most beautiful hair, which made gold and the sun seem less beautiful" (*Rime* 348) – which interrupt Petrarch's renunciation of his *errore* before the final hymn to the Virgin: "it is evident in the *Rime* not only that the poet's early love for Laura is characterised by desire but also that the desire that continues unabated despite her negative response or her lack of response is not ended even by her death" (Sturm-Maddox 1985: 59). Whether the *Rime sparse* is finally convincing as a "record of human love wrongly directed" (Sturm-Maddox 1985: 132) is, of course, debateable; the persuasiveness of Petrarch's renunciation of Laura is open to question. In the context of Drummond's sequence, however, beauty's persistence ascribes equal validity to the earthly experience of love, however "fading" (MacDonald 1976: 152); and arguably this finally mitigates the "sense of ennui [...] rootlessness and a sense of missed opportunity" which has been perceived in the sequence, and helps to draw out its *carpe diem* motif: "the need to seize on each experience of life, even while one realises it has only momentary significance" (Atkinson 1986: 407).

In conclusion, then, this essay has sought to analyse the meaning of beauty in Drummond's love poetry, arguing that manifestations of "the beautiful" – which appear in nature, in art, in the feminine beloved, and in divinity itself – hold one key to a fuller understanding of interrelated ideas and themes in Drummond's art. Though Drummond's love poetry has been perceived as the twilight tradition of late Renaissance Scottish love poetry, R.D.S. Jack has argued that it exemplifies the defining "spiritually oriented Petrarchism" (Jack 1976: 806) of the Scottish Renaissance which pursues a philosophical and intellectual approach to the topic of love. Although this essay has argued that Drummond's engagement with Petrarchan and Neo-platonic philosophies are, in the end, purposefully imperfect, they re-main enduringly meaningful for the poet in a period which poetically often derided their belatedness: their supposedly anachronistic aesthetics and "worldview". Even if ultimately the end of *Songs* is inconclusive, undecided whether the eternal beauty of the spiritual world or the particular participatory beauty of individual bodies should claim the lover, it leaves open different philosophical, not least psychological, possibilities. It returns the reader to the theme of grief in Petrarch, and to perceive anew the persistence of love behind the philosophical and spiritual veil which insists that the Neoplatonic lover must forget "all that is known by the eyes, turning away for ever from the material beauty that once made his joy" (Plotinus, cited in Hofstadter and Kuhns eds 1964: 149). The human longing to see again the figure "cui veder m'è veder" [whose sight is taken from me] en-dures. And, in its "opulent and emotional" baroque style (Martin

1989: 30), Drummond's poetry reminds us of the meaningful consolations of the beauty of the world, and of love, while they last.

Bibliography

Alexandrakis, Aphrodite. 2004. "Plotinus, Marsillo Ficino, and Renaissance Art" in Cheney, Liana and John Hendrix (eds) *Neoplatonic Aesthetics: Music, Literature, and the Visual Arts*. New York: Peter Lang. 187–96.

Ames-Lewis, Francis and Mary Rogers (eds). 1999. *Concepts of Beauty in Renaissance Art*. Aldershot, Hants: Ashgate.

Atkinson, David W. 1986. "The Religious Voices of Drummond of Hawthornden" in *Studies in Scottish Literature* 21: 197–209

— . 1991. "William Drummond as a Baroque Poet" in *Studies in Scottish Literature* 26: 394–409.

Bembo, Pietro. 1515. *Gli Asolani*. Venice.

Carritt, E.F. 1931. *Philosophies of Beauty*. Oxford: Clarendon Press.

Castiglione, Baldesar. 1541. *Il Libro del Cortegiano del Conte Baldesar Castiglione*. Venice.

Cheney, Liana de Girolami and John Hendrix (eds). 2004. *Neoplatonic Aesthetics. Music, Literature, and the Visual Arts*. New York: Peter Lang.

Clements, Robert J. 1941. "Anti-Pétrarchism of the Pléiade" in *Modern Philology* 39(1): 15–21.

Cole, Alison. 1999. "The perception of beauty in landscape in the quattrocento" in Ames-Lewis and Rogers (eds) *Concepts of Beauty in Renaissance Art*. Aldershot, Hants: Ashgate. 28–43.

Cox, Elizabeth (ed. and trans.). 1994. *The Book of the Courtier*. London: J.M. Dent.

Cropper, Elizabeth. 1999. "Introduction" in Ames-Lewis and Rogers (eds) *Concepts of Beauty in Renaissance Art*. Aldershot, Hants: Ashgate. 1–11.

Donoghue, Denis. 2003. *Speaking of Beauty*. New Haven and London: Yale University Press.

Dorangeon, Simone. 1988. "William Drummond of Hawthornden: Mémoire et création" in Bellenger, Yvonne (ed.) *Le Sonnet à la Renaissance: des origines au Xviie siècle*. Paris: Aux Amateurs de Livres. 265–78.

Drummond, William. 1616. *Poems*. Edinburgh: Andro Hart.

Durling, Robert M. 1976. Trans. and ed. *Petrarch's Lyric Poems. The Rime Sparse and other Lyrics*. Cambridge, Mass.: Harvard University Press.

Eisenbichler, Konrad and Olga Zorzi Pugliese (eds) 1986. *Ficino and Renaissance Neoplatonism*. Ottawa: Dovehouse Editions Canada.

Ellrodt, Robert. 1960. *Neoplatonism in the Poetry of Spenser*. Geneva: Librairie E. Droz.

Equicola, Mario. 1536. *Libro di Natura d'Amore di Mario Equicola*. Venice.

Ficino, Marsilio. 1548. *Marsilio Ficino sopra lo amore o ver'convito di Platone*. Florence.

Fineman, Joel. 1986. *Shakespeare's Perjured Eye: the invention of poetic subjectivity in the sonnets*. Berkeley; London: University of California Press.

Fogle, F.R. 1952. *A Critical Study of William Drummond of Hawthornden*. New York: King's Crown Press.

Forster, Leonard. 1969. *The Icy Fire. Five Studies in European Petrarchism.* Cambridge: Cambridge University Press.

Haskins, Susan. 1994. *Mary Magdalen.* London: HarperCollins.

Hemsoll, David. "Beauty as an aesthetic and artistic ideal in late fifteenth-century Florence" in Ames-Lewis and Rogers (eds) *Concepts of Beauty in Renaissance Art.* Aldershot, Hants: Ashgate. 66–79.

Hendrix, John. 2004. "The Neoplatonic Aesthetics of Leon Battista Alberti" in Cheney and Hendrix (eds.). 133–86.

Hofstadter, Albert and Richard Kuhns (eds). 1964. *Philosophies of Art and Beauty. Selected Readings in Aesthetics from Plato to Heidegger.* Chicago: University of Chicago Press.

Jack, R.D.S. 1968–9. "Drummond: the major Scottish sources" in *Studies in Scottish Literature* 6: 36–46.

—. 1972. *The Italian Influence on Scottish Literature.* Edinburgh: Edinburgh University Press.

—. 1976. "Petrarch in English and Scottish Renaissance Literature" in *Modern Language Review* 7: 801–11.

Kastner, L.E. (ed.) 1913. *The Poetical Works of William Drummond of Hawthornden.* 2 vols. Edinburgh: Blackwood.

Kennedy, William J. 1994. *Authorising Petrarch.* Ithaca: Cornell University Press.

—. 2003. *The Site of Petrarchism. Early Modern National Sentiment in Italy, France, and England.* Baltimore and London: The Johns Hopkins University Press.

Kristeller, Paul Oskar. 1961. *Renaissance Thought. The Classic, Scholastic, and Humanist Strains.* New York: Harper Torchbooks.

—. 1965. *Renaissance Thought II. Papers on Humanism and the Arts.* New York: Harper Torchbooks.

MacDonald, Robert H. (ed.) 1976. *William Drummond of Hawthornden. Poems and Prose.* Edinburgh & London: Scottish Academic Press.

—. 1971. *The Library of Drummond of Hawthornden.* Edinburgh: Edinburgh University Press.

Martin, John Rupert. 1989. *Baroque.* Harmondsworth: Penguin.

Morgan, Edwin. 1990. "How Good a Poet is Drummond?" in *Crossing the Border.* Manchester: Carcanet. 56–66

Niccoli, Sandra (ed.) 1987. *Marsilio Ficino. El libro dell'amore.* Florence: Leo S. Olschki Editore.

Plato. 1937. *The Dialogues of Plato* (tr. Benjamin Jowett). 2 vols. New York: Random House.

Plotinus. *The Enneads* (tr. Stephen MacKenna). London: Faber and Faber Limited.

Robb, Nesca A. 1935. *Neo-Platonism of the Italian Renaissance.* London: George Allan and Unwin Ltd.

Sewter, A.C. 1972. *Baroque and Rococo Art.* London: Thames and Hudson.

Spiller, Michael. 1992. *The Development of the Sonnet.* London: Routledge.

Sturm-Maddox, Sara. 1985. *Petrarch's Metamorphoses: text and subtext in the Rime sparse.* Columbia: University of Missouri Press.

—. 1992. *Petrarch's Laurels.* University Park, Pa.: Pennsylvania State University Press.

—. 1999. *Ronsard, Petrarch and the Amours*. Gainesville: University Press of Florida.

Wallerstein, Ruth. 1933. "The Style of Drummond of Hawthornden in its relation to his Translators" in *Proceedings of the Modern Language Association* 48: 1089–2007.

Ward, W.C. (ed.) 1894. *The Poems of William Drummond of Hawthornden*. London: Lawrence and Bullen.

Warnke, J. 1972. *Versions of Baroque. European Literature in the Seventeenth Century*. New Haven: Yale University Press.

Yavneh, Naomi. 1993. "Images of Beauty in Tasso and Petrarch" in Turner, James Grantham (ed.) *Sexuality and Gender in Early Modern Europe*. Cambridge: Cambridge University Press. 133–57.

Thomas Ker of Redden's Trip to the Low Countries, 1620

John J. McGavin

An unpublished and unstudied travel journal, written to store information for social use, gives insight into the *spectacula* enjoyed by a Scots gentleman abroad, but also proves an unconscious witness to Prince Maurits of the Netherlands' preparations for war, and to high-level, if possibly opportunistic, British intelligence gathering.
Keywords: travel; Low Countries; Sir Robert Ker; Thomas Ker; William Drummond of Hawthornden; Prince Maurits; intelligence gathering; King Charles I; *spectacula*; visual aesthetic; ceremonial entry; relics; Thirty Years' War; Palatinate; painting; architecture; military strategy.

This study of a travel journal arose, perhaps surprisingly, from the project *Records of Early Drama: Scotland*, which aims to publish all Scottish records of drama, secular music, and ceremonial before the mid 1640s. The document's contribution to the records of Scottish drama might be thought indirect, since it tells us more about a Scot abroad than at home, but it nevertheless bears witness to the European dimension of Scottish cultural experience, and has the advantage of revealing in its author, as in other men of his class, a visual aesthetic which was indiscriminately theatrical and non-theatrical. In this re-spect it supports the modern sense that the dramatic shades into the purely spectacular, having affinities with what is neither textual nor mimetic. However, it is my hope that such features will emerge *en passant*, for the focus of this study is more on what the journal's author did not mention, and perhaps did not even notice. The search for drama records avoids positivism through constant revision of one's interpretative assumptions about what is said, and what omitted from the records (and why); what may have been originally implied; what might now be inferred; and what types of context are relevant to answer any of these questions. Nowhere are the disjunctions between original authorial outlook, the researcher's narrower interests, and a document's wider historical significance more challenging than in the case of this travel journal.

Thomas Ker, farmer of the lands of Redden, which lie in a bend of the River Tweed, was the third son of William Ker of Ancram Castle which lies near Jedburgh. When he went to the Low Countries in 1620, he was at least in his early thirties (his father having been murdered in 1590), and had the gentleman farmer's customary financial and social responsibilities. His knighthood was thirteen years in the future. Accompanied by his younger brother Andrew, he left Jedburgh on 10 April 1620. They took the North of England crossing from Shields, and arrived in Delfshaven on 22 April, after what was a fairly standard voyage of forty-eight hours. He returned on 7 August by the shorter Calais-Dover route and, after travelling through Kent, parted with another brother in London a couple of days later, returning to Scotland in the middle of August 1620. It was a round trip of about four months, some weeks of which were needed for actually getting there and back, one month of which was spent in the town of Spa, enjoying the waters and aristocratic company, just as the gentry would in Bath the following century, and two months of which were occupied in a substantial tour through different theological, cultural, and political regions: the southern and eastern provinces of the Dutch United Provinces; those parts of the Netherlands controlled by the Spanish Hapsburgs; the prince-bishopric of Liege, and the Electorate of Cologne.

Following his return, Thomas Ker wrote in French an account of the trip in his *Notebook*.[1] The choice of French for this may have been prompted by the quasi-academic nature of the task: when a schoolboy, Ker, like others of his rank, would have been heavily instructed in French and was expected to use it in ordinary discourse at school. But his choice may also reflect the predominance of French as the language used during many of the encounters abroad, and also therefore the language of any notes he took when travelling. French was the common language of international exchange in northern Europe, and Scottish-French was a recognised dialect of it (Bates [1911] 1987: 50). The *Notebook* shows him comfortably moving between Scots and French, especially in entries from earlier years. One cannot see the

---

[1] Quotations from the text in this *Notebook* will follow the spelling, punctuation, and diacritic choices of the original as far as possible. But the yogh symbol will be normalised to z, and the single dots which he uses diacritically have been omitted.

language chosen as implying a particular intended audience. Unlike the many seventeenth-century travellers who "had publication in mind before they packed their baggage" (Links 1980: 155), Ker probably did not expect his *Notebook* or the travel account in it to be read by anyone other than himself.

The account of his trip was probably based on notes taken en route, though his frequent use of the phrase "il me souuiene" [I recall] also indicates memorial reconstruction and, by implication, the opportunity for reflective shaping of the material. His stylistic homogeneity, even repetitiveness, bears this out, and *Notebook* entries written in exactly the same language and style, but for activities in the eighteen months following the trip, suggest that reconstruction may have taken place after some time. There appears to have been light correction during the making of the final version – insertion of commas, or of a plural "s"; an added note of the distance between two towns (for which he had left a space); an extra line of text inserted into the bottom margin to help the account flow. More substantially, he added a table of the names of his fellow visitors to Spa, placing this as an appendix, presumably to avoid compromising the paratactic style and episodic strategy of his preceding narrative, but also as a ready guide to the acquaintances he had made. He arranged them into groups, firstly by nationality, English before French, and then by visiting party, with some division by sex. In the case of the English, he seems also to have had a greater understanding of social hierarchy, or perhaps a greater concern to remember and represent it, than with the French. In the latter case, a "gentil Homme" called Mr Marfils precedes princes and counts, and the hapless Governor of Luxembourg ends the section of "grandes Dammes" because Ker only remembered him when he reached the governor's wife, Madame de Barlamounde. He seems the quintessential socially alert "sight-seer" for whom the names of gentry and aristocracy met en route either were at the time or became in retrospect just as worthy of record as the sights.

Journals were common at this time of increasing gentry travel, and it is therefore useful to consider what kind of traveller emerges from Ker's account, bearing in mind that the written record is only a selective and rhetoricised version, intended for a specific purpose. In its pages, Ker does not appear as a philosophiser; nor as a judge of

detail; nor as *overtly* engaged with the trip as self-education. He is not
a religious traveller. He sees things which are indicative of religious
observance, but does not comment on their wider significance, and he
does not seem particularly interested in Catholic forms, as was his
covenanting nephew, the Earl of Lothian, who first attended the Papal
Jubilee in Rome in 1625, and in later fragmentary travel notes commented on the colours of habit worn by the Marquis of Argyll's sis-
ters, who were nuns of different orders in Brussels (Ker c.1638–
c.1650). Still less does Thomas Ker play the part of a protestant hooli-
gan, damaging religious material, or quarrelling with papists. Like
other tourists he ascends buildings for a better view, though in his case
more for the spectacle than to permit comparisons between towns, as
was frequent (Mączak 1995: 255). He notes, as so many responsible
travellers did, the distances between places, and does so using the
more reliable continental measurement of "leagues" (Mączak 1995:
262). He does not talk about the nature of the countryside, but he
includes some geographical details which were of military significance, such as the strategic positioning of towns between rivers.
Unlike many travellers, he evinces no particular affection for the
people he meets and seems uncommitted to learning about their way
of life or, indeed, death. For example, when travelling from Tilmont to
Liege, he encounters rural poverty, but notes only its practical disa-
dvantage to the party: "vn meschant village ou nous ne poüuions
trouuer ny vin ny pain poür noüs ny nos chevaux" [a wretched hamlet
where we could neither find bread and wine for ourselves nor fodder
for our horses] (f.9[r]). Such narrative baldness need not imply lack of
sympathy; more likely it reflects the private nature of the account
itself. Ker sees no need to display emotion in the text because he expects no other reader; probably for the same reason he does not
pretend to greater experience or understanding than he has actually
acquired. But, on the evidence of his report alone, he is not what
might be called a "thoughtful" traveller (Mączak 1995: 291). Though
at times he records admiration, it is not always identifiable as his own,
and is sometimes obviously received wisdom. He notes, for example,
that a Jesuit church in Antwerp "est estimé le plus belle qui et en
Europe qui et tout basti cet á dire le piliees de Martre" [is reckoned the
most beautiful completed building in Europe, namely, the Pillars of

the Martyr church]. He includes dates, and is interested in the fact that people in the Hague date according to the French method, that is, employing the new style, common to Catholic Europe since 1582, which placed continental dates ten days ahead of those in Scotland or England (Cheyney [1945] 1995: 10–11). He specifies times of travel in relation to meals, thus indicating in which part of the day a journey between towns might be conducted. He gives the names of the Scots Brigade officers in Holland whom he encountered, and the names of taverns where his party stayed.

His work is clearly highly selective, but it is not self-conscious, let alone explicit, about the principles of selection, nor who helped him to form them, nor about the narrative structure within which he deployed the contents. The episodic sequence of the narrative prevails, with its recurring phrases, such as "et puis-apres" [and then afterwards], "le lendemain" [the next day], "nous sommes (or *avons*) arivé" [we arrived], "nous avons demuré" [we stayed], "nous fumes logé" [we were lodged], "nous sommes parti" [we left], obscuring potentially more significant divisions of the journey into time spent in Protestant Holland, the Catholic Low Countries, and Spa. Ker does not explicitly direct us to this division, focussing instead on the individual experiences which he chooses to record, and giving no sign of finding context interpretatively significant. Instead, the names of the places visited are placed in the margin in a layout suggestive of the functionality of court documents, where the names of the people involved in proceedings were similarly placed for quick retrieval. There is no sense of the journey having an authorial drive or dynamic, or being worked up to a conclusion. Things tend to happen "par cas fortuit" [by lucky chance] or "par bon fortüné" [by good fortune]. Without any stated motive or indeed much indication that there was a motive at all, parties meet by happy chance, stay together for a period of time, travel together, and at times diverge, only to meet up again. Ker does not think it necessary to record why he left Scotland to make the trip nor why it took the shape it did nor why it ended when it did. There is no indication that he chose his own tourist destinations or that he ever had his own plans which he was forced to change by circumstances. There is thus much which Ker does not feel the need to include – the corollary of his determinedly limited rhetorical palette and focussed subject matter. The value of the document for him as a *private* record undoubtedly lies behind such restrictions, but so do the special circumstances behind the trip itself, and possibly a genuine failure on Ker's part to appreciate some of what was happening. The meetings he describes to himself as fortuitous, for example, were unlikely to have been so, as we shall see. However, before discussing these gaps and silences in the account, I would like to spend some time on the positive: the visual experiences which contributed such a major part of his subject matter.

If one takes simply those events which would merit inclusion in a *Records of Early Drama* volume, Ker probably saw ceremonial entries at Tiel and Geertruidenberg, and certainly reports military musters there. The difference between the two types of event was not always great in Protestant Holland at this time. He sees another staged entry at Nijmegen, and notes that there was a magnificent reception with volleys of shot accompanying the entry. He goes into greater detail about the "grand reception" at Breda, commenting on the "feü de joy", presumably pyrotechnics; cannons firing from the ramparts; scholars making orations "avec belles inventions" which possibly implies a more theatrical than purely rhetorical inventiveness. After processing along the main street, the visiting party enter the Castle, where they witness further "Jeües et Inventions", which were probably staged plays, visual representations on the gateway, or tableaux by the local Chamber of Rhetoric; there is a "grand volie" [volley of firing] by the townsfolk and burgesses; and then a muster by the troops. Later in the trip, Ker goes from Brussels to Antwerp specifically to see the Kermes at Pentecost, though he makes no comment on its boorish jostling, unlike John Evelyn (Links 1980: 178). He further notes non-ceremonial recreations, such as dancing and music, which he enjoyed in Brussels. These would also appear in a records volume:

et püis-apres noüs avons passé le temps en allant chez les dammes en danssant en oyant musick tellement que me lorde & sa femme & mon frere ont eü grande cognoissançe parmy les dammes & dammoissells – et parce cett moyenne nous avons aresté dix joures oü quatorzè toute. (f.8[v])

[and then afterwards we passed the time visiting the ladies, dancing and hearing music, to such an extent that my lord and his wife, and my brother were well known among the ladies and young women – and in that fashion we stopped there for ten days or at most a fortnight.]

Ker's account, however, reveals an aesthetic of the visual which goes beyond the staged events. At its broadest, it encompasses the civic and architectural beauties of the towns of the region, viewed from ground level and above. He enjoys the general beauty and spaciousness of the town of Leiden, and views Nijmegen, Utrecht, Antwerp, Brussels, Cologne, Aalst, and Ostend. More locally, he appreciates specific buildings, fountains, and gardens: cathedrals (he mentions the 455 steps to the top of the cathedral at Utrecht); chapels, both an English one, where the nuns made music every Sunday, and Jesuit ones, noting especially the eighty pillars in the famed church at Antwerp. He looks at the house, gardens and convent of the Jesuits at Liege; the baths at Aachen; and the houses of Spanish and Dutch leaders, of the Bishop of Liege, and of a rich merchant (at that time in Spain). Ker uses the phrase "veu et reveü" [viewed and viewed again], suggesting that they went over these houses in detail, possibly to glean hints on domestic style and high fashion. Ker and his companions seem to be at the beginning of the house-visiting trend, which eventually led to Jane Austen's Elizabeth Bennett and her aunt and uncle meeting up with Mr d'Arcy when she toured his house and grounds during his supposed absence. Indeed, much cultural behaviour which we associate with the *wider* gentry of the eighteenth and nineteenth centuries seems adumbrated here, early in the seventeenth, on a trip which, as it turned out, was at a much higher aristocratic and state level than Thomas Ker could have achieved on his own.

Of specific sights, he mentions particularly the famous anatomy theatre at Leiden, giving a written account of the crowded and varied specimens which one sees in contemporary engravings, though it seems to be the flayed skin rather than the skeletons which attract his attention: "il estoit forçe Attomies, de toute sorts; hommes femmes; enfants; les hommes et femmes Escorche3 et leüres peaüx entier pendant lá et forçe espes de bestes" [there were a great many anatomical specimens of all sorts, men, women, children, the men and women disembowelled and their entire skins hanging there, along with many kinds of animal] (f.3[r]). Interestingly, he recognises, or is prompted

to recognise, the new naturalistic mode in painting, commenting on
the depiction "á vif" [to the life], of a duel between two sides of
twenty men. However, he remembers this "tragadie" not for its style
or painter (a common omission among culture-bibbers of this time),
but rather because it showed a M. Briotte killing a lieutenant and his
brother with two pistol shots. He also notes a room of Emperor
Charles VIII in s'Hertogenbosch, which offered sanctuary to anyone
regardless of the political seriousness of their crime. When he visits
Cologne, a city which appears to have had more holy bones in it per
square metre than any outside the Middle East (Mączak 1995: 224), an
interestingly nationalistic principle directs his tourism, perhaps now
taking the place of any religious views which would once have coloured relics: his brother particularly wants to see the tomb of John
Duns Scotus, and when Thomas sees the tomb of the 11,000 virgin
martyrs, he says that they had come from Rome with a queen who was
the daughter of a king of Scotland. This latter may mean that the story
of the virgins as told to the Kers, probably by a French-speaking guide
in Cologne, had been contaminated by a version of the French romance *La Fille á la Main Coupée*, a "Constance"-type story in which
the heroine marries the King of Scotland.[2] Possibly the guide told the
visiting Scots what he thought they would want to hear.

　　If we wish to understand Ker's motive for writing the travel
journal and, through that, its particular characteristics as a narrative,
we need to attend to its manuscript context and especially to the title
he gives it. The principle of inclusion, or of preservation in the small,
vellum-bound *Notebook* of eighty-three paper leaves, a further nine-
teen of which have been cut out, seems to have been that of the
memorandum. This is indeed the term Thomas Ker uses for the title of
his travel account: "Memorandum de mon woyage au Pay-bas d'Escos
en L'Ane 1620" [Memorandum of my voyage from Scotland to the
Low Countries in the year 1620]. He includes in the *Notebook* such
things as the names and dates of his children's births, with the state of
the moon at the time for the purpose of casting a horoscope; the date
of Elizabeth, his first wife's, death in childbed (1626), touchingly referred to on several occasions, and the naming of that "unhappy

---

[2] I am grateful to Philip Bennett of Edinburgh University for this suggestion.

dochtir", Elizabeth, whose birth killed her mother. That which is to be remembered would not necessarily be forgotten if no record were kept: it is also that which is thought worthy of memorial. He also includes details of the numbers, and names, of sheep and cattle which he had when he first started farming in his own right, money received and fruit trees planted. And he includes his trip of 1620.

Socially, Ker fits perfectly into that class of junior aristocracy which increasingly went abroad. Although he does not *explicitly* share their customary educational motive for travel, that is, acquisition of information not available at home (Bates [1911] 1987: 25), his use of the word *memorandum* for his account implies that he saw the enduring value of his experiences in at least a quasi-educational way. They were things which he felt he *should* remember. Though he does not say why, one can infer the reason. The location of the travel account among other personal written *memorabilia*, the use of French, which, however much a common tongue for Scots at school or on the continent, was not the normal language of Scottish publication, and Ker's highly idiosyncratic, if reasonably consistent, system of punctuation, with its numerous diacritic acute accents, cedillas, umlauts and ubiquitous dots – all these features signal a centripetal impulse in the "Memorandum" at odds with its emphasis on the external, the sights seen and people met. Strangely, this finds a parallel in his nephew Sir William Ker's fragmentary travel notes where, for no obvious reason, the writer occasionally chooses to spell words or phrases backwards! In both texts there is a guardedness, a sense that one is memorialising experience for a *personal* textual bank.

Perhaps more than the early-modern genre of travel writing, to which it obviously belongs, Ker's account reflects non-literary developments in Scottish culture: firstly, the massive proliferation of Scottish civic and aristocratic record keeping – receipts, retours, inhibitions, sasines, transfers, inventories of the furnishing and plenishing of houses, debts owed, accounts paid or partially paid, and so on. In particular, this is the period of extensive gentry estate accounts in which the income from lands is set out as the "Charge" (in the way that a battery is charged up) and the expenditure is detailed as the "Discharge". Secondly, this is also a time when gentry, gradually forced out of sepulchres in the kirk building, are again getting into

trouble with the kirk for purchasing tomb stones ("through stones")
for head and feet, and believing, by virtue of that demarcation of land,
that they own the ground occupied by their corpse. Whatever value
Ker's "Memorandum" might now have for historians of culture, or of
the Low countries, it seems to have been for him a sizeable "charge"
of personal data which might have future social currency, like sheep,
cattle, land, wives, and children. The travel account, so strong in positivist details of dating methods, names, places, distances, sights, gen-
erally-held opinions, numbers of companies of infantry, military and
aristocratic connections, yet so lacking in personal judgements, explicit discrimination, reflection, wonderment, political, religious, and
even family comment, held data which would give Ker a conversa-
tional credibility at his social level, or even a direct access to well-
placed contacts. He could be said to have acquired the land of his
experiences by marking it out in the "Memorandum" for future use. In
one sense, therefore, this *is* an educational enterprise, so long as one
understands education strictly in relation to social advantage: taken
together Ker's "Memorandum" and the *Notebook* in which it appears
constitute an account (in both narrative and financial senses), charged
up in the same way, and for the same reasons, as young men filled
their minds with Latin conjugations or their commonplace books with
famous sayings from Seneca, Cicero, and others. Ker had no need for
more than a spare, almost schematically functional, rhetoric in the service of such a document because this was learning with a purpose,
knowledge with bullet-pointable outcomes, a harvest of facts which
permitted disbursements in the realm of social discourse. Drummond
of Hawthornden knew the Ker brothers well. In one of his commonplace books, compiled in the decade before Thomas's journey, he
quotes from *The court of ciuil conuersation*, noting that the second
rule for a man in conversation is "to speake no thing affirmatiuely but
that himselfe hath seen" (Drummond n.d.a: f.349[r]). This indicates
the kind of context in which Ker would have expected to draw on his
"Memorandum". The document is thus a useful primary source for the
history of polite society.

Given such a positivist emphasis in the "Memorandum", it is
easy to forget what remains unstated and unexamined, some aspects of
which I mentioned earlier. But it is through chasing these up that the

account becomes a witness to more than either early-modern *spectacula* or Ker's own authorial intentions. Perhaps the best way of understanding this is to see Thomas's record of information gathered as simply the surface structure of the "Memorandum". We find a deeper value for the account if we attend to those features which Ker omits, or only bears silent witness to, that is, the occasion which gave rise to the journey; the precise course it took; the social and political level at which it was conducted, and the assistance which Thomas's party received as it progressed. The essentials of the journey appear to have owed nothing to Thomas, who merely reports what happened, without presuming to have his own plans or to comment on the reasons behind the plans of others.

Throughout the journal Thomas Ker mentions an anonymous brother, "mon frere", some two dozen times. This is not the brother Andrew who came from Scotland with him, and who leaves the party at one point to travel to Bohemia, disappearing at that point from the journal. But this unnamed brother seems to have been the person who directs Thomas and the others as to where, when, with whom, how, and how long, they will travel. He has dining rights at the very top of the political or social hierarchy: we see him waiting to accompany Prince Maurits, the Calvinist Stadt Holder of six of the seven United Provinces; dining with him and the burgomaster of Tiel; forming a party with the newly-arrived English aristocrat, Lord Purbeck, and his family. He stays with, and gives dinner to, the French princes of Syme and Pineau, and the Governor of Limbourg; he attends the wedding of the Duke d'Escot; and accompanies Lady Arundel when she arrives in Spa. He receives ready assistance from officers, aristocracy, and local dignitaries; can expect military escort at times; and, in the "highly ideological" environment of Catholic Antwerp (Israel 1995: 419),[3] as soon as he makes his presence known by passing through the streets, is immediately targeted by an official Jesuit guide. Ker writes, "nous rencontrasmes vn Anglois prestre qui ce appelloit pere Tempeŝt qui á bien attendü mon frere" [we met up with an English priest, by the

---

[3] It will be evident to any historian that this study could not have been made without the magisterial work on the Low Countries by Jonathan Israel (Israel 1995). My argument for the significance of the "Memorandum" depends on this work throughout.

name of Father Tempest, who waited attentively on my brother]
(f.7[r]). He finally spends eight days in Brussels, either out of friendship for, or at the request of, an English diplomatic team which has
come to the Spanish Netherlands to head off war in the Palatinate. On
his return home, he meets up with Sir Edward Sackfield and two or
three other gentlemen at Dover, and then dines with the Archbishop of
Canterbury. Thomas, who records all this without comment, accompanies him, respecting, and, as far as one can see, taking pleasure in
his brother's high level of connection, from which he also benefits,
though without receiving quite the same level, or degree, of intimate
access to the highest. At key moments, Thomas dines or stays nearby,
but elsewhere. For example, "mon frere et allé chez le Evesche et
souppé auec lüy et moy je souppé chez noüs" [my brother went to the
Bishop's house, and took supper with him, and I ate at our lodgings]
(f.15[v]). Thomas's brother may have been anonymous in the
"Memorandum", but he was far from being so in British or, indeed,
continental society.

"Mon frere" was Sir Robert Ker or Carr, and is not to be con-
fused with King James VI's favourite of the same name (who was,
nonetheless, a relative). Thomas's brother was forty-two at the time of
the trip to Holland. He was one of the aristocracy who had followed
James south, being knighted some time between 1602 and 1604. He
was appointed groom of the bedchamber to Prince Henry, and then
Gentleman of the Bedchamber to Prince Charles, a position he kept
when Charles became king (Paul 1904–14: 5: 452–87; Stevenson
2004: 1). In February 1620, he was forced into a duel by Charles
Maxwell, "that great Giant", whom he killed (Drummond 1711: 138
footnote). It appears that everyone regarded Ker as the innocent party,
and the dead man's relatives either agreed with this or felt it politic to
do so. Sir William Alexander writes from the court at Newmarket to
Drummond of Hawthornden, 7 February 1620:

I doubt not you have heard how Sir Robert Ker hath kill'd Charles Maxwell in
Combat, which was so much pressed upon him, and so well carried, that my Lord
Maxwell and the Gentleman's Brother who are here, and know all the circumstances
thereof, have very generously protested, that they shall never quarrel nor dislike him
for it. (Drummond 1711: 151)

After being exiled for six months, Robert was specially pardoned on 23 October 1620. He evidently spent that brief exile in the Low Countries, being joined there by his brothers in April. In a letter which, though undated, must have been written before 10 April 1620 when Thomas and Andrew left, Drummond of Hawthornden apologises to Sir Robert for his unstudied writing "I haue not had leasure to cover my purposes your Brothers departing being to mee so sudain & unespected" (Drummond n.d. c.: f.12[r]). If the "Memorandum" is accurate, Sir Robert returned with Thomas in mid-August at the end of his period of exile, though not exactly six months after leaving Britain (which Thomas records elsewhere in his *Notebook* as c. 1 April), and before any pardon was formally pronounced (October 1620). He was able to proceed quickly on his way and enjoy high level visits, having been intercepted at the sea port as he would have expected, being a man in public life. He later used the likelihood of his movements being known at sea ports to refuse a secret duel at Flushing (Drummond n.d. b.: f.185[v]). The importance of this period of exile lies in what Robert did, where he went, and in whose company, testimony to which is provided, as far as I know, solely by Thomas Ker's "Memorandum".

    After meeting up with Thomas and the others, Robert uncharacteristically waited for several weeks in the Hague without apparently touring, seeing sights or doing anything that Thomas found worth recording until, supposedly by chance, he met up with "his Excellency", who must have been Prince Maurits, though Thomas does not so name him. Maurits was to make a tour of the fortifications of the defensive ring towns between the United Provinces and the Spanish Netherlands. They therefore accompanied him from 3–20 May:

[…] et püis par cas fortuit son excellens êstoit poür fair vn visitation par toüte les fortifications qui appertinoit aux estats et noüs sommes allé avec lüy jüsques de commencement a lá fin de son voyage. (f.2[v])

[and then by fortunate chance his Excellency planned to go on a visitation of all the fortifications which belonged to the Estates, and we went with him right from the start to the end of his trip.]

Behind Thomas Ker's narrative of unexplained inactivity, chance meeting, and unmotivated accompanying of Maurits probably lies a more considered plan of action. Robert would have had many opportunities on the trip for gathering, and possibly sharing, information with Maurits, a man who preferred political communication with a few aristocratic companions to working with the established democratic institutions (Israel 1995: 452). What could be more natural for Maurits than to invite into his company the confidant of the English heir, in the hope that he could gain access to English court thinking beyond the official statements of ambassadors? And what could be more beneficial to Sir Robert, especially in exile, than to gain personal access to the leader of the neighbouring Protestant state, for Maurits's political and military intentions were the focus of international speculation at this time, not least because of his own continual, and successful, dissembling (Israel 1995: 471–73). Through Robert, Maurits's movements at a crucial time could be communicated and interpreted back in the British court.

Thomas's account gives the day-by-day sequence of Maurits's tour to Bodegraven, Buren, Tiel, Nijmegen, the family lands in Moers (north of Cologne), back to Nijmegen; then to inspect Grave. On 18 May he leaves Nijmegen by boat for Tiel, and lunches on board at the fort of Grave-de-Coeur; thence to Heusden, Geertruidenberg, and then to Breda, leaving there to return to the Hague. During this trip, Robert, with Thomas in tow, makes some brief detours to take in Leiden, Utrecht and Grave-Arnhem, the strategically significant town of Schenkenschans, and, when Maurits is at Heusden, the Spanish-held s'Hertogenbosch only a league away. They always return to Maurits or wait for him, and are not away from him for long, except when he visits his family lands for five or six days.

Maurits's choice of towns to visit would have suggested much about his political plans following his coup over Oldenbarneveldt in 1617–18, and would have indicated his concern for areas of strategic importance in any imminent conflict with the Hapsburgs. More informative even than the movements of the stadt-holder was the reception he got in his towns, the state of his defences in the ring, and his control over the military, and the townspeople. In Maurits's company, Robert Ker is able to observe all this. Accompanied by Thomas,

Robert also takes advantage of the proximity of Spanish-held towns to make excursions into Hapsburg-controlled areas not open to Maurits, and to observe their state of readiness. Immediately after Maurits leaves for the Hague, the Kers visit Spanish-held Antwerp, and find great difficulty getting entry to the castle because of the anxiety of the sentries. Thomas recalls one Spanish sergeant who was "extremement fasché contre noüs" [extremely angry with us]. In an unaccustomed surge of specialist vocabulary, Thomas lists the "counterscarps, bvlvarts, palassads, demy lunes, grand fousses" [...half-moon batteries, great ditches] which marked out Antwerp militarily, and there are several other moments when he observes, possibly prompted by Robert or their military companions, the strategic positioning of towns between rivers, or other features which would become significant in conflict. Robert saw, and Thomas reports, the staged ceremonial entries which Maurits employed as a standard tactic to control towns which he had been purging of his theological and political enemies. "The Prince's visitations marked the beginning of a new era in each town" (Israel 1995: 453). Thomas makes no comment on any of this, and one would not know from his account that there was such a thing as Arminianism or that Maurits's resurgent Calvinism was still engaged on a determined internal campaign to subjugate it. However, on one occasion in the journal, Thomas is perhaps an unknowing witness to Maurits's imperfect success in winning hearts and minds: he mentions that at Nijmegen, it was *particularly* the soldiers who provided Maurits's greeting, and that Maurits did not enter the town until he had seen a muster of twenty-two companies of infantry and four of cavalry. The description appears driven solely by admiration for what is grandiose, but may yet imply the *realpolitik* of the event, in which Maurits's entry was simply the exercise of military power by other means, and the two types of activity needed to be perceived together by a recalcitrant citizenry.

If anything was fortuitous, it was the timing of Robert's exile, for the Twelve Year Truce between the Provinces and Hapsburg Spain was coming to an end, and it was not known by either side, still less by surrounding countries, whether it would be renewed. Furthermore, James VI's son-in-law, Frederick, Elector of the Palatinate, had accepted the crown of Bohemia in 1619, against James's advice but with

the support of Prince Maurits, his uncle, who hoped thereby to turn
Spanish attention from the Netherlands into Germany. James's earlier
support for Maurits had been predicated on the mistaken view that
England would then be able to influence his foreign policy (Israel
1995: 469), and it was the ensuing war, the Thirty Years war, which
the English ambassadors were trying to prevent when Robert Ker
waited with them in Brussels. His stay in the Netherlands was thus
spent on the brink of catastrophic European conflict, partly in the
company of the very man who had precipitated it, and partly touring
the other areas which would soon be involved, and their different
military, aristocratic, national and political groups. For example, on
the way to Cologne, he and Thomas visit the town of Julich, strategically placed on the road to the Palatinate, and his contacts with the
Scots Guard there and elsewhere are close and at a high level, including dining with Sir Francis Henderson, brother of the commander of
one of the two Scots regiments. Sir Francis would later take command
by the personal order of Maurits, despite the post having been solic-
ited for the Earl of Buccleugh by King James himself (Ferguson:
1899–1901: 1: 232, 378).

Perhaps "mon frere" discussed what he saw with Maurits or with
the French princes who entertained him and were entertained by him,
but one imagines that the main eventual recipient of the information
gathered would have been James VI himself or the future King, Prince
Charles, in whose bedchamber Ker was a Gentleman. Sir James
Balfour reports that on the 10 April 1620 (coincidentally the same day
as Thomas and Andrew left Jedburgh for the continent) James I
handed over to Prince Charles, "the full adminstratione and
gouerniment of hes auen affaires […] [and he] was presented this day
to the counsaill, and by them allowed" (Balfour 1824–25: 2: 79). So
Sir Robert Ker would have been anxious to return to the Prince with a
gift of substantial foreign policy information for his master to use in
his new capacity as a member of council. He probably made prelimi-
nary communication of his findings through the English agent, whom
Robert and Thomas moved lodgings to be near, or Mr. Trumbell, or
the ambassadors, Sir Edward Conway and Sir Richard Weston, whom
he spent time with in Brussels. Eventually, however, he would have
made his information known fully in person, when he resumed his

place as an opinion-former and intimate in the royal family. His smooth return to England and the welcome he received may well have been predicated on the value of the information which he was to impart as much as on the established friendship of the prince. Drummond of Hawthornden wrote to Robert at the time of his departure that the court in losing him "hath loosed an Eie" (Drummond n.d. c.: f.10[r]). However commonplace a metaphor, Drummond's choice of it may have been fortuitously apt, reflecting not just Robert's importance to the body politic but his particular talents. Rather than losing an eye, the English court was benefiting from its gaze being turned in a more profitable direction. This is not exactly spying, since it is not covert, and not obviously employed to work against the interests of the person observed. Rather it is that gathering of information which can occur at a high social level in which every side hopes to gain from information shared, revealed, or even planted. The quality of the intelligence depends on physical proximity, that proximity depending in turn on social rank and connection. Sir Robert Ker's fellows in the court may have come to associate him with the affairs of the Low Countries, and with Maurits in particular, for we see the following train of thought in a 1625 letter of Lauderdale to Lord Yester:

ther was word last weik of the prince of Orange his deadlie seiknes, this day ther is advertisement cumes of his death, and of the Proclamatione of *Count Henrye*, wch I thinke is neither lyklie, nor necessar seing befoir he was both sworne, and resaved coniunct *with* him: your freindes heir ar all weill especiallie noble Sr Robert Ker to whoes kyndnes and courtesyes I can not tell yow how infinitlie I am bound (Hay 1620–32: f.4)

Whatever the value of Thomas's "Memorandum" to the records of early drama, it would therefore seem to be a significant document in the history of the Low Countries. It is also, without its author apparently being aware of the fact, the record of two Scottish brothers, each of whom saw an opportunity to "charge" up his resources with information useful for his own ends and social situation, one highly political, the other more casually urbane. Drummond wrote to Sir Robert after his return from exile that he had gained more from the calamity than he would if he had "like another Endymion […] sleeped away that swift course of [tym] Days in the embracementes of your

Mistresse the court" (Drummond n.d.c.: f.22[r]; fair copy f.35; Drummond 1711: 142, no.14). Robert might well have replied that he had hardly ever been out of court circles during the time he was abroad. Drummond's understanding of the consolations which Robert could have found during exile does reflect, in part, the substance of Thomas's "Memorandum" in that he mentions "the sight of so many statlie Townis and differing manners of Men, the conquest of such friendis abroad the tryall of those at home" as among the things which will have made his distressed situation more happy (Drummond n.d.c: f.22[r]). But he is also writing with the generic and rhetorical slant of someone who does not actually know how Robert spent his exile, and is imagining what any refined person would get from the experience. He thus fails to grasp a key feature of what Robert was doing with his time, and speaks instead from his own literary mind-set. Consequently, he is not wholly unlike the less expressive Thomas, who *did* know exactly where Robert had been, and may have had an inkling of what he was doing, but also set down a record which reflected instead his own private interests, in his case social rather than literary.

Thomas Ker became *Sir* Thomas on the occasion of King Charles I's coronation in Edinburgh in 1633. Sir James Balfour, who was made a baronet, wrote of this time,

For maney ages this kingdome had not seine a more glorious and staitly entrey, the streetts being all railled and sanded; the cheiffe places quher he passed wer sett outt with staitly triumphall arches, obeliskes, pictures, artificiall montains, adorned with choysse musicke, and diuersse otheres costly shewes. (Balfour 1824–25: 2: 196)

Drummond of Hawthornden, in whose house Sir Robert Ker had been a guest,[4] was among the pageant devisers, writing the speech of Caledonia; the Song of the Muses at Parnassus; and the speeches of the planets, opened and closed by Endymion, at the Horoscopical Pageant (Drummond 1711: 38–41). At the entry Thomas would have seen again John Duns Scotus, whose tomb he and Robert had visited when in Cologne, because the philosopher was depicted, with other

---

[4] Drummond had mused in his letter of 10 February 1620 on the possible prescience which led Robert to engrave on the window at Hawthornden the following: "Fraile Glasse thou beares this Name as well as I, / and none doth know in which it first shall dye" (Drummond n.d. c: f.7[r]).

past Scottish masters of learning, on the Mountain of Parnassus erected at the Salt Tron. He would also have seen the Scottish empire in America optimistically adumbrated by an American dressed in feathers, and with an olive-coloured mask. Drummond's account of the celebrations was rushed out by John Wreittoun the same year (Drummond 1633). But of all this, the soon-to-be-knighted Thomas was silent. There was no need for a memorandum of these new *spectacula*: he had reached his social apogee. But Thomas owed his elevation, as he had owed his guided trip through the sights and sounds of the Low Countries, and as we owe the wider significance of that journey, to the life and influence of his brother. Unnamed, if ubiquitous, in the "Memorandum", Sir Robert Ker, companion of King Charles since childhood and through the abortive Spanish match-making, Privy Councillor since 1631, friend of writers such as Drummond, Samuel Daniel and John Donne, Keeper of the Privy Purse, was also present with the King in Edinburgh in June 1633, being made 1st Earl of Ancram, when younger brother Thomas, as they say in such circles, "got his K".

In the encouraging letter sent to Robert via his brother at the time of exile in 1620, Drummond of Hawthornden had written, "You are born to act braue Parts on this Theatre of the world" (Drummond 1711: 142). Thomas's "Memorandum" is an obscure and inexplicit but unique testimony to one of those "braue" parts which his brother had played. But Sir Robert Ker's presence on the stage was to end tragically, with death abroad in extreme poverty as a consequence of the Civil War and the Protectorate, which had interrupted his pension and prevented his family from succouring him. Again, he was in exile, and again, it was to the Low Countries that he had gone, but that is a story known to us from sources other than his brother Thomas's "Memorandum".[5]

[5] This project is part of the *Records of Early English Drama* series. An edition of the "Memorandum" will appear in the *South-East Scotland* volume, which has been financially supported by the Modern Humanities Research Association and the Arts and Humanities Research Council of Great Britain. This help is most gratefully acknowledged. I am grateful also to the organisers of the conference, from which this volume derives, and to the participants, particularly Sarah Carpenter, Jamie Reid Baxter, Philip Bennett, and Greg Walker for their comments and additional points. I acknowledge particularly the kind assistance I received from Alastair Duke, who helped with the identification of places mentioned in the "Memorandum" and appropriate political terminology.

Bibliography

Balfour, Sir James, of Denmylne. 1824–25. *The Historical Works* (ed. J. Haig). 4 vols. Edinburgh: W. Aitchison.

Bates, E.S. [1911] 1987. *Touring in 1600: a Study in the Development of Travel as a Means of Education.* London: Century.

Cheyney, C.R. (ed.) [1945] 1995. *Handbook of Dates for Students of English History.* Cambridge: Cambridge University Press.

Drummond of Hawthornden. n.d. a. *Drummond's Miscellanies I.* Hawthornden MSS, vol. VII. National Library of Scotland MS 2059.

—. n.d. b. *Drummond's Miscellanies II.* Hawthornden MSS, vol. VIII. National Library of Scotland MS 2060.

—. n.d. c. *Letters amorous, complementall, consolatorie, informing, militarie, historicall.* Hawthornden MSS, vol IX. National Library of Scotland MS 2061.

—. 1633. *The entertainment of the high and mighty monarch Charles King of Great Britaine, France, and Ireland, into his auncient and royall city of Edinburgh, the fifteenth of Iune, 1633.* Edinburgh: John Wreittoun.

—. 1711. *The Works.* Edinburgh: James Watson.

Ferguson James, (ed.) 1899–1901. *Papers illustrating the history of the Scots Brigade in the Service of the United Netherlands 1572–1782* [Scottish History Society no. 32, 35, 38.]. 3 vols. Edinburgh: T and A Constable.

Hay, Marquis of Tweedale. 1620–1632. *Letters, papers.* National Library of Scotland MS 7002.

Israel, Jonathan. 1995. *The Dutch Republic: Its Rise, Greatness, and Fall 1477–1806.* Oxford: Clarendon.

Ker, Sir Thomas, of Redden.1620. "Memorandum" in *Notebook.* National Archives of Scotland GD40/15/57: 3–34.

Ker, Sir William, Earl of Lothian. 1625. "Sir William Ker of Ancram's Journey to Italy and back through France, 1625". National Library of Scotland MS 5785.

—. c.1638–c.1650. "Travel Notebook fragment". National Archives of Scotland GD40/15/58.

Links, J.G. 1980. *Travellers in Europe: Private Records of Journeys by the Great and the Forgotten from Horace to Pepys.* London: The Bodley Head.

Mączak, Antonio. 1995. *Travel in Early Modern Europe* (tr. Ursula Philips). Cambridge: Polity Press.

Paul, Sir James Balfour. 1904–14. *The Scots Peerage...Containing an Historical and Genealogical Account of the Nobility of that Kingdom.* 9 vols. Edinburgh: David Douglas.

Stevenson, David. 2004. "Ker, Robert, first earl of Ancram (1578–1654)" in H. C. G. Matthew and Brian Harrison (eds.) *Oxford Dictionary of National Biography.* Oxford: OUP. <http://www.oxforddnb.com/view/article/15457> . 29 October 2004.

Rutherford's Landscapes

David J. Parkinson

The literary affinities of the seventeenth-century Presbyterian apologist Samuel Rutherford emerge in his elaboration of some descriptive contrasts characteristic of late-medieval and early modern Scottish poetry. Significant connections appear between the interweaving of the earthly and heavenly in Scottish depictions of the pleasant place and the enfolding of the anti-secular and maternal in Rutherford's landscapes. At such junctures, Rutherford is participating in the shaping of a national literary canon, a project gaining momentum in seventeenth-century Scotland.
Keywords: Patrick Anderson; George Buchanan; James Caldwell; Geoffrey Chaucer; *The Complaynt of Scotland*; Gavin Douglas; Alexander Hume; Sir Patrick Hume; James VI; landscape; Sir David Lyndsay; Blessed Virgin Mary; Elizabeth Melville; James Melville; pastoral; Presbyterianism; Samuel Rutherford.

Despite ongoing renovations, a "historical Myth – that the Scottish consciousness was disastrously split by the Union with England" (Crawford 1979: 9) still obstructs our understanding of the literature written in Scotland between the two Unions of 1603 and 1707. By setting a limit in the study of Scottish literature (Jack 1997: x), this myth continues to serve a certain intellectual thrift, thanks to which, literary culture in seventeenth-century Scotland remains largely unexamined. Beyond the same few names – notably the "unrepresentative" Drummond, Ayton, and Urquhart (Gribben 2006: 66) – the century is labelled retrospective, even stagnant (Riddy 1988: 51; Spiller 1988: 143). Such a representation has become untenable: in seventeenth-century Scotland, literary affiliations and continuities may be experimental but are seldom arid or nostalgic; they indicate the cultivation of sustainable rich grounds rather than the stoic endurance of loss upon loss. Stocked with themes and genres that have not withered but rather grown increasingly accessible and multi-layered during the unfolding Reformation, Scottish literary culture broadens, gaining readers and writers across the political, social, regional, and religious landscape. The gravitational pull of the court having weakened with its removal to London, textual communities and individual literary identities proliferate at home (Mapstone 2005: 414). A penchant for thematic and stylistic juxtapositions distinguishes this culture; during the seventeenth century, this penchant tends to extremes, not only in the places where it might be expected – Sir Thomas Urquhart's version of Rabelais for example – but at least as much in Samuel Rutherford's gendered depictions of the self and the deity in the beautiful landscape. In his sometimes outrageous variations on the pleasant landscape, this Presbyterian writer is working out a coherent pattern of mutual accessibility between the divine and the human, one deeply rooted in Scottish literary tradition.[1]

In Scottish literary studies, admittedly, the seventeenth century is rarely considered in terms of continuity, health, or abundance: instead, it is taken to epitomise George Gregory Smith's whimsical "Caledonian antisyzygy", a coinage redolent more of pathology than literature (Chandler 1994: 218). Smith illustrates the clash of opposites implicit in the term: he produces two cultural villains, "the preaching and arguing Scot of the seventeenth century" and "the neoclassical Scot of the eighteenth" (Smith 1919: 37). Confronted with these decisive categories, the reader might be forgiven for forgetting Smith's preceding, subtle investigation of "that prevailing sense of movement, that energy and variety" in Scottish literature (34). Smith owes this emphasis on the dynamic to William Hazlitt's essay "On the Picturesque and Ideal"; the phenomenon of the picturesque, which Hazlitt investigates principally in the painting of landscape, involves "particular points or qualities of an object, projecting as it were beyond the middle line of beauty, and catching the eye of the spectator", and "may be considered as something like an excrescence on the face of nature. It runs imperceptibly into the fantastical and grotesque" (Hazlitt 1930–34: VIII: 317; cited in Smith 1919: 34). Hazlitt's picturesque encourages Smith to assign a definitive value to description in Scottish literature, in which the interplay of sudden contrasts and gradual emergences provides the occasions for inventiveness. In this context, *antisyzygy* refers less usefully to Jekyll and Hyde than to Samuel Johnson's definition of metaphysical wit as a "kind of *discordia concors*; a combination of dissimilar images, or discovery of occult resemblances in things apparently unlike" – and few would

---

[1] I am grateful to Heather Giles, Michael Cichon, and Jamie Reid Baxter, who showed me how to improve this essay.

hold that Johnson was commenting on a poet's psychology (1905: I: 20). During the age that Gregory Smith deprecated for preferring "preaching and arguing" to the cultivation of more exalted literary endeavour, the evidence exists for

the true feeling of Scottish literature, which at all periods has shown a readiness not only to accept the contrary moods more or less on equal terms, but to make the one blend imperceptibly into the other. (Smith 1919: 37)

Smith's best insights overcome his strictures: inadvertently perhaps, "all periods" encompass the seventeenth century. Such imperceptible blends of apparent opposites emerge memorably in the devotional and epistolary writing of one of the most notorious and outspoken among the "preaching and arguing" sort, the Presbyterian divine Samuel Rutherford.

Often vilified for stylistic excess and instability, the "thoroughly aggravating" Rutherford remains a villain of Scottish literary and historical studies (Todd 2002: 390, 103n): almost everyone, it seems, hates, regrets, or at least feels uncomfortable with his overblown style. Even his warmest advocates admit that he falls into "unconscious", extravagant poetry, "slatternly and down-at-the-heel English", "somewhat too full of ecstasy", suitable "only for old wives" (quoted in Coffey 1997 110; Whyte 1894: 9, 12; Bonar 1848: 24). Sectarian controversy in the guise of literary judgement, the old opinion has prevailed that Rutherford breaks decorum, his writing no more than

Nonsensick Raptures, the abuse of Mystick Divinity, in canting and compounded Vocables, oft-times stuffed with impertinent and base Similes and always with homely, course, and ridiculous Expressions, very unsuitable to the Gravity and Solemnity that becomes Divinity (Curate 1692: 22–23).

Rare indeed is the sense that the clotted, vivid, energetic writing he produced might be of particular interest now (Jack 1971: 41). At their most perceptive, recent critics note "how closely his enthusiasm is tied to his orthodoxy [...] [with] felicities drawn from country life [...] [and] all experience glinting with spiritual meaning" (Reid 1989: 339). The deeper affinities in Rutherford's writing evoke a significant ambivalence from modern readers: the author of a fine recent book cannot decide whether Rutherford's "'medievalism' may be taken as further evidence of his narrow scholasticism or as striking proof of the breadth of his sympathies" (Coffey 1997: 74). The castigation to which Rutherford has been subjected bears relation to the general disfavour under which seventeenth-century Scottish literature languishes. In particular, the apparent wildness, eccentricity, and lack of decorum of Rutherford's devotional style deserve to be located within Scottish literary culture and reconsidered as indications of, not naivety or decadence, but deep familiarity and artistry.

The variegated weave of Rutherford's style, exhibiting both erudition and "a raw, colloquial energy", was designed to "grab the attention of a congregation" and keep its hold on the common imagination (Coffey 1997: 110). From the late nineteenth-century perspective of the Kailyard novelists, devout working people continued to treasure such classics of religious discourse as a sustaining domestic comfort:

When the sheep were safe and his day's labour was over, [Lachlan the shepherd] read by the light of the fire and the "crusie" (oil-lamp) overhead, Witsius on the Covenants, or Rutherford's "Christ Dying", or Bunyan's "Grace Abounding", or Owen's "130th Psalm", while the collies slept at his feet, and Flora put the finishing stroke to some bit of rustic finery. (MacLaren 1894: 1)

The durability of Rutherford's appeal, like that of Sir David Lyndsay's *Works* or Hary's *Wallace*, guarantees the continued viability of the past. *Christ Dying* provides the nineteenth-century reader with access to its author's cultural heritage: deeply versed in the vernacular classics as well as the learned foundations of his national literature, Rutherford's style looks back as well as ahead. He demands to be considered in the context of the leading topics of earlier Scottish literature, in which the interplay of similarity and difference is closely bound up with a perennial literary topic: the allegorical garden of medieval poetry, embodying the contrast between "the fading flower of human glory and radiance" and "the evergreen leaf of the Tree of Life" (Robertson 1951: 30). With its emphasis on nurture and its dichotomy between spiritualised and fleshly femininity, the allegorical garden provides an intriguing instance of "older deep-structural form" of the sort that Fredric Jameson calls "immanently and intrinsically an ideology in its own right", to be "functionally reckoned into" subsequent, apparently transformed, genres and topics (Jameson 1981: 141). True to tradition, the Scottish literary landscape also involves a complex relation between nature and art: for instance, the "scattering of ornamental detail" redolent of "the decorative arts in general, and of heraldry in particular" in the gardens of Gavin Douglas's *Palice of Honour* (Lyall 2001: 74). Repeatedly, the garden of Scottish dream vision presents the protagonist, the dreamer, the narrator and the reader with a choice between earthly power and heavenly illumination. Occasionally, this choice becomes possible through an apparent merging of the opposed categories; sometimes, the depiction of the garden exposes "the dangers to which such sensuous language might be thought to lead" (Lyall 2001: 80). In Scotland as in late-medieval England or France, the deities who wield immediate authority over such landscapes tend to be female, or at least to have feminine characteristics: Fortune regnant in the "lusty plane" of *The Kingis Quair*, "the goddess whose hostility begins the poem, and whose favour must end it" (Spiller 1986: 22); Calliope and her nymph in *The Palice of Honour* (1501); Dame Remembrance in Lyndsay's *Dreme* (c.1526) and the "affligit lady Dame Scotia" in the anonymous *Complaynt of Scotland* (1549); the Church in James Melville's *Black Bastel* (1611). So prevalent in sixteenth-century Scottish writing is the feminine personification of the place or the nation that Edward Cowan identifies a genre of the "intangible mistress" (Cowan 1993: 537).

His poems reprinted in the 1550s and late 1570s, Gavin Douglas plays a continuing role in the articulation of the quest for refreshment and inspiration in the natural scene. His influence on the handling of landscape in Scottish literature extends well beyond the confines of the dream vision; one need only recall the high reputation of his prologues of natural description in the *Eneados*. The theme of life-determining choice in the pleasant place unfolds from the outset of that work, when, confronted by the sublime prospect of the great work, the translator must announce his cultural and ethical priorities. Repudiating Virgil's pagan inspiration in favour of contemplation of the Virgin, Douglas states his faith in an immanent source of inspiration:

Thou, Virgyn Moder and Madyn, be my muse,
That nevir yit na synfull lyst refus
Quhilk the besocht deuotly for supple.
Albeit my sang to thy hie maieste
Accordis nocht, yit condiscend to my write,
For the sweit liqour of thy pappis quhite
Fosterit that Prynce, that hevynly Orpheus,
Grond of all gude, our Saluyour Ihesus. (*Eneados* I prol. 460, 463–70)

The Virgin Mother's *vertu*-engendering "sweit liqour" subsumes the inimitably "scharp sugurate sang Virgiliane"(*Eneados* I. prol. 29) and offers the ostensibly humble, devout translator the prospect of ascent above his glorious pagan exemplar. Hailed by pagans and prophets – "our Sibill, Crystis moder deir, / Prechit by prophetis and Sibilla Cumane" – Mary embodies the crucial intersection between humility and authority:

Thou brocht the hevynly lynage in erd heir,
Moder of God, ay virgyne doith remane,
Restoring us the goldin warld agane. (*Eneados* VI prol. 14549)

Douglas's evocative statement contains an implicit rebuke to the ambitions of the more powerful among his Scottish readers as well as those of Virgil's characters. In Mary's restoration of the golden world, innocence nourishes harmony.

Though the theme of the restorative power of the natural scene has wide and sustained distribution in European culture (Curtius 1953: 195), it has been mistaken for a symptom of historical change. The great nineteenth-century historian Jacob Burckhardt identified the spontaneous delight in nature felt by Leon Battista Alberti, the quintessential Renaissance man, as a badge of his modernity (2004: 110). Given Boethius's emphasis on the harmonising, restorative properties of nature, one might broaden Burckhardt's interpretation: for Alberti's contemporaries, landscape affords the thoughtful viewer the scope to reflect far back and forward in time. Famously, the eleventh ode of the greatest Scottish humanist, George Buchanan, exhibits this temporal sweep:

[*Calendae Maiae*] glides effortlessly from the warm breezes of May-day to the Golden Age of earth's first spring and thence to the never-failing warmth of the Isles of the Blessed, to the soft breezes which gently stir the cypresses by the streams of Lethe, and finally, and triumphantly, to the warmth which will rouse and vitalise the souls of the dead [...] "Welcome, glory of the fleeting years; welcome, red-letter day, welcome, for you remind us of the spring-time of the world, and give us a glimpse of the life that is to come" (MacQueen 1988: 216).

John Durkan speculates that these lines may

have commemorated [Buchanan's] Easter communion after his temporary return to the faith; if so, they give a summary of salvation, a *speculum humanae salvationis*, of the pilgrimage of *homo viator* from paradise lost to paradise regained (Durkan 1962: 311; cf. Macfarlane 1981: 111, 114).

Whatever the exact biographical circumstances of composition, the poem memorably expresses a core value of early modern Scottish culture: seeking respite from pressing cares and responsibilities, the man of affairs encounters the natural scene as redolent of both early childhood and extreme old age (Brown 2000: 209–10). Expressing delight in natural beauty with its promise of salvation, Buchanan's ode also has the reputation for inspiriting its appreciative reader. In 1785, Hugh Blair warmly recalled a conversation with an "uncommonly bland and gay" Samuel Johnson twelve years earlier:

Dr [Johnson] expressed a very favourable opinion of Buchanan, and instantly repeated, from beginning to end, an ode of his, intituled *Calendae Maiae* (the eleventh in his *Miscellaneorum Liber*), beginning with these words, *Salvete sacris deliciis sacrae*, with which I had formerly been unacquainted; but upon perusing it, the praise which he bestowed upon it, as one of the happiest of Buchanan's poetical compositions, appeared to me very just. (Boswell 1936: 388)

For Durkan, Buchanan's eloquent landscape heals sectarian rifts; for Blair, it allays Johnson's anti-Scottish prejudices; and for the devoted Boswell, the preserver of the anecdote – who, in his own youth had connected "the pastoral register of Jacobite discourse" to his own desire for "simplicity and ease" (Loar 2004: 597) – it bridges the years accumulating between him and his deceased friend.

In the rendering of landscape, interwoven values had long diverted and challenged Scottish readers: Henryson's depiction of the

local countryside in his "simultaneously witty and serious" *Fables*
(Henryson 1981: xliii); Dunbar's interplay of the courtly and the
moral in the visionary scene of the *Goldyn Targe*. In later Scottish
poetry, the sense persists that earthly delight is applied like a thin
layer, the seductive garment that barely conceals a beautiful feminine
presence, a ghastly corpse, or – as in John Burel's *Passage of the
Pilgremer* – a demon (Schama 1995: 531–38; Reid Baxter 2000: 241–
42). At times, the stylistic contrasts become so stark that they flatten
genres into layers, one upon another. For instance, the Edinburgh
printer John Wreittoun published a solidly devotional treatise by the
Presbyterian minister James Caldwell under the enticing title *The
Countesse of Marres Arcadia* (1625). In an inversion of a common
publishing strategy, spiritual improvement takes the guise of a best-
seller – a businesslike variation on the pastoral "games with the
teasingly indistinct boundary between the sacred and the profane" that
became fashionable in sixteenth-century Europe (Schama 1995: 534).
The substance of Caldwell's book lies in territory foreign to Sidney's
pastoral-political romance; the connection between the title page and
the contents lies entirely in an introduction written by Patrick
Anderson, the physician to the Countess of Mar, Marie Stuart, daughter of Esmé, first Duke of Lennox, whom Anderson compliments thus:
"[A]s his Majestie long since, in his Booke of Poesies, called your
Noble Father the Phoenix of al the Nobility; so may the world esteeme
your Honour to be another elect Lydia of that same Noble qualitie"
(sig. *5v; Bawcutt 2000: 31; Brown 2000: 234; van Heijnsbergen and
Royan 2002: xviii–ix). Latterly physician to Charles I, Anderson is
remembered for his invention of a famous and best-selling pill, "the
first of a long line of proprietary remedies for disturbed British
digestions" (Corley 2004). Writing to a noblewoman with Catholic
antecedents, Anderson alludes to her late father's cultural ascendancy
at court and sugars with rural images the pill of Caldwell's meditations:

There is heere Musicke for the minde, Physick for a sicke soule; and Divine nourish-
ment to feede them both. Sir Philip Sidneys Arcadia hath manie faire and recreatiue
discourses for Ladies; a faire Field in deede to feede on, for young and fond Lovers.
The Countrie it selfe, is a fresh and pleasant Soile in the middle of Peloponesus, a

ground that floweth of manie delicates, fyne pasturages for flockes, and pleasant Rivers. But this is a spirituall Arcadia: it is your Honours litle Arcadia. (sig. *3r–v)

In duodecimo, the Countess's book is indeed a little Arcadia, a little sanctuary of consecrated ground encircled by a depraved world. The familiar bait of the *locus amoenus*, the pleasant place, stimulates the reader's longing for harmony in existence, a longing to be met, the editor, author and publisher hope, through earnest contemplation and practice of religion, both under royal authority. Diplomatically and advisedly, the physician gives secular form to the familiar relation between the soul and the garden. In effect, Anderson justifies the Arcadian packaging of Caldwell's treatise by recourse to the trope of "Paradise as the interior of the soul", a perennial feature of the persistent garden imagery in religious discourse, in Scotland as elsewhere (Pearsall and Salter 1973: 61).

Scottish poetry had long featured the masculine resolution of feminine resistance and initiative in the visionary scene. The Scottish version of Chaucer's *Parliament of Fowls* ends not with deferral of the formel eagle's choice but with a peacock settling the choice of a husband for her (Fradenburg 1991: 130; Boffey and Edwards 2005: 26). Over a century later, in *Ane Godlie Dreame* by Elizabeth Melville, Lady Culross, Christ rebukes the female dreamer for her "incontinent" rush to the pleasant prospect at the end of her journey (l.231). So decisive an arrival is after all the prerogative of sovereignty asserting its balance between discipline and nurture, so that, "in experiencing [feminine] innerness, masculinity will be refound" (Fradenburg 1991: 190). Thus the dawn of reformed kingship involves a secular transformation of Palm Sunday, the celebration of Christ's entry into Jerusalem, into a triumphal procession. This achievement takes visionary form in Sir Patrick Hume of Polwarth's *Promine* (1579), written to celebrate the first riding forth of James VI "[w]ith manlike maneris, maikles to behald" (l.22) to take his place as the virile but virginal ruler over a Scotland depicted as a dewily bejewelled paradise: instead of the strewing of blossomy boughs on Palm Sunday, the "[c]ristall croppis me thocht thay did Incline / In signe of homage to that Prince deuine" (ll.137–38). Over the landscapes of the nation, the church, and the soul, James assumes his ordained place; accordingly, Sir Patrick Hume, the king's "familiar seruitour" ascends the steps of royal favour (Mapstone 1999: 26–27).

To wrest the topic of the visionary landscape away from royal control, advocates of religious reform strengthened the medieval and European associations of the topic. For the reformer Alexander Hume – younger brother of the courtly Sir Patrick – making poetry, "prosecuted in my wraslings with the world" (cited in Dunnigan 2004), entailed a struggle to redefine nature in God's image. Thus his *Day Estivall* (*Hymnes and Sacred Songs*, 1599) centres upon spiritual choice. A survey of a harmonious fruitful world at midsummer, this poem earns praise for its writer's "courage to choose for a poetic subject exclusively a purely descriptive scene, and that a Scottish one" along with rebukes for his references to siestas and salad-oil (cited in MacDonald 1991: 15; Bawcutt and Riddy 1987: 291). The combination of the domestic with the exotic may indicate a desire to locate the immediate Scottish scene within a Europe that centres upon the Mediterranean; the evocatively hybrid rendering of space bespeaks a shared heritage (Bath 2003: 139). In Hume's poem, this sense, already intricately interconnected, is subtly reoriented through scriptural allusion, notably to the Psalms, but also re-grounded through allusion to stylised depictions of nature in earlier vernacular poetry, notably Dunbar's *Goldyn Targe* and Chaucer's *General Prologue* and *House of Fame* – "Natures clarks", the "tender crops", dew like "pearles", the farmers' favourite quaff of "reamand London beare", even the shepherds' pipes and "lilting horne" (ll.15, 57, 58, 147, 224; Bawcutt and Riddy 1987: 413–14). The occasion invites such gestures of affiliation and continuity. Especially perceptive is the recent comment that Hume "gives an idealised picture of the beauty and orderliness of God's creation, and the 'message' emerges with discretion, only becoming explicit at the very end" (MacDonald 1998: 89). Like Ronsard, who employed the myth of the Golden Age as "a way of expressing dissatisfaction with the present" (Armstrong 1968: 51), Hume contrasts the midsummer world of nature and simple labour against the vicissitudes of earthly rule: the "perfite light" of God has set the "shining Sun" as "a ruler ou'r the day", under whose "ardent course" today the world is revealed "poleist", "tranquill", "still and calme" (ll.1, 3, 8, 106, 25, 73, 214). This sacred course is emphatically

Nocht guided be na Phaeton,
Nor trained in a chyre,
Bot be the high and haly On,
Quhilk dois all where impire. (ll.109–12)

A masterfully guided sun shines upon a fertile land watered by fresh rivers that run smoothly into a calm and mighty sea: without Hume's insistence on divinity, the images would flow, as if naturally, toward royal encomium. In the discourse of James's kingship, the sea was an especially important emblem of royal power. In his inaugural speech to the English Parliament, James returned to this hallmark of his regime when he said,

For even as little brookes lose their names by their running and fall into great Riuers, and the very name and memorie of the great Riuers swallowed vp in the Ocean: so by the coniunction of diuers little Kingdomes in one, are all these priuate differences and questions swallowed vp. (James 1994: 269; Fleming 2002: 105)

Resisting the royal deployment of this emblem, Alexander Hume demurs. In "Of Gods Benefites Bestowed vpon Man", the poem immediately preceding *The Day Estivall* in *Hymnes and Sacred Songs*, he directs the reader to "Extoll the Lord, let ay his praise and glorie be renewed" because "Thy domicile and dwelling place Christ Jesus hes prepard, / Aboue quhilk, blis but end salbe thy last and best reward" (ll.242–44). The solstitial panorama in *The Day Estivall* sweeps aside mere kingship to prefigure that heavenly domicile.

In its resistance, Alexander Hume's great poem strikes medieval roots. Hume shows his followers, Rutherford among them, how the depiction of landscape can involve political revision but also literary continuity: his subordination of secular to eternal realities also recalls Douglas's. One source rarely identified for *The Day Estivall* is the Boethian lyric on which Chaucer drew, directly and indirectly, for the encomia of Love the narrator and protagonist utter in Book III of *Troilus and Criseyde* (*De consolatione philosophiae* II metrum viii; *Troilus and Criseyde* III.1–14, 1744–71; cf. Bath 2003: 96; Brown

2000: 210). In Boethius, in the prose immediately preceding that lyric, Philosophy offers a paradox:

> For bad fortune, I think, is more use to a man than good fortune. Good fortune always seems to bring happiness, but deceives you with her smiles, whereas bad fortune is always truthful because by changing she shows her true fickleness [...] So you are weeping over lost riches when you have really found the most precious of all riches – friends who are true friends. (Boethius 1998: 80–81)

This reversal of expectation leads Lady Philosophy to sing about the power of Love to harmonise nature. That adversity can produce enlightenment underlies the mindset of early seventeenth-century Scottish reform as articulated by Hume and, later, Rutherford. From the surface traces of its allusions to its coherently theocentric theme, *The Day Estivall* restates the durable connection in Scottish literature between a beautiful landscape and the revelation of the eternal in the ephemeral.

To unmask false friends and esteem the true in reformed Scotland is to insist on proprietorship of the old maternal categories of humility, freely flowing generosity, and protectiveness of the suppliant, all ransacked from medieval depictions of the Virgin Mary. Few Scottish writers pursue this quest further than Samuel Rutherford, whose rhetorical commitment is especially apparent in *Christ Dying and Drawing Sinners to Himself* (1647), published at the highwater mark of his political influence, and *Joshua Redivivus* (1664), the collection of his letters first published posthumously and clandestinely after the Restoration (Coffey 1997: 52–53). In each of these works, Rutherford works assiduously to domesticate crucial but forbiddingly abstract theological concepts:

> Election, as the cause and fountaine-grace, is the great mother, the wombe, the infinite spring, the bottomlesse ocean of all grace; and wee say, effects are more copiously and eminently in the cause than in themselves; as water is more in the element and fountaine, then in the streames; the tree more in the life, and sapp of life, then in the branches. (Rutherford 1647: 265)

In this symbolic landscape of sources, the body of God's foreknowledge and grace has a generative completeness and integrity that seems to presage Lacan's formulation of the ideal, fully realised identity an infant perceives at the mirror stage (Lacan 1972: 1–7). In reference to earthly existence at least, Rutherford forestalls the climactic predicament of this stage, namely that "imaginary narcissistic embrace" inhibiting the individual's access "to the symbolic realm" (Heller 1996: 395). After all, royalty had claimed a monopoly on that embrace, as, for instance, did King James in his deployment of the image of the encompassing sea as an emblem of his reign: as discussed above, James preferred his subjects to have access to the symbolic realm only vicariously, as spectators of his own triumphal progress. Rutherford, in opposition, depicts the secular sea as unable to quell the soul's individuality: "[B]e like to the fresh river, that keepeth its own fresh taste in the salt sea" (Rutherford 1664: 461). Just as the wayfaring Christian is buffeted but not dissolved in the tides of the world, so indeed the fragmentary but numinous signs of Christ's presence in creation preserve their identity by declaring their origin: "these chips, created leavings, small blossomes, daughters, and births of goodnesse and grace have streamed out from [Christ]" (Rutherford 1647: A4r–v). Again, Rutherford seems to anticipate a distinguished modern theorist: in an addendum to "On the Concept of History", Walter Benjamin remarks that the thoughtful historian "establishes a concept of the present as that of the here-and-now in which splinters of messianic time are shot through" (Benjamin 2005). In each of these cases, insight depends on recognising the separateness of identities even in the act of perceiving the relationships between them.

Some splinters evidently arouse a keener reaction than do others. Repudiating the authority of the book as a vehicle of divine truth, he offers the visionary prospect of immediate physical proximity: "it is little to see Christ in a book, as men doe the world in a card, they talke of Christ by the book & the tongue, & no more; but to come nigh Christ and hausse him, & embrace him, is another thing" (Rutherford 1664: 22). Rutherford's heaven is a "publike" but also intimate place, its immediacy making naught of "the heritage of perishing things" (Rutherford 1647: 188–89; Lynch 1992: 251). When recognised by faithful communicants, spiritual signs negate the threats and seductions of the world. Rutherford composes numerous variations on this theme: like a gardener feeding and pruning a vine, Christ fosters and strengthens the elect in this world (Bonar 1848: 80; Robertson 1951: 32; Pearsall and Salter 1973: 71). Seen athwart, however, the vision of the heavenly garden dwindles into the "the thorny hedge of daily grief, loss of children, weakness of body, iniquity of the time, uncertainty of estate, lack of worldly comfort, fear of God's anger" (Rutherford 1664: 428). Experience stains the soul so that it becomes "blacked with hell, lying amongst the pots, till Christ take us up, and wash, and lick the Leopard Spots off us" (Rutherford 1647: 250). Rutherford balances characteristically between the scriptural and the homely (Psalm 68:13; Jeremiah 13:23; Isaiah 11:6); with that verb *lick*, the image of a cat washing her kittens springs to mind unbidden. To trace the associations of this evocative passage further, for the common reader of the cheap reprints of vernacular classics circulating in seventeenth-century Scotland, Christ's maternal solicitude realises the final wish of Henryson's Cresseid, her "lustie lyre ouirspred with spottis blak", to walk with Diana "in waist woddis and wellis" (ll.339, 588; Lynch 1992: 260). The consoling force of Rutherford's natural imagery – like that of romance or folktale – strives to meet the deep old need for reassurance that the grimy, destitute self shall at last be revealed in its true glory (Allen 1964: 108–10).

This imagery epitomises the preference for "broken, heterogeneous figures" typical of medieval scriptural commentary (Reid 1989: 339; cf. Dove 2004: xvii), but it also brings the exegetical *Kulturkampf* of Kirk against Crown to a fever pitch:

[W]ee see [Christ] as hee is in report, and shadowed out to us in the Gospel, the Gospel is the Portraiture of the King, which hee sent to another Land to be seen by his Bride, but the Bride never seeth him as hee is, in his best Sabbath-Robe-Royall of immediate glory, till shee be married unto him: So Kings and Queens on earth wooe one another [...] To see Christ himselfe, the red and the white in his owne face, to heare himselfe speak, to see him as hee is, and in his robes of Majesty now at the right hand of God, is in thousand thousand degrees, more then all the pictured (if I may so speak) and shadowed fruition we have here. The Gospel is but the Bridegroome's Mirror and Looking-glasse, and our created Prospect: But O his owne immediate perfume, his mirrhe, the oyntments, and the smell that glory casteth in heaven, who can express? [...] O what delights he casteth forth from himselfe! The river of life is more than a sea of milk, wine and honey. To suck the brests of the consolations of Christ, and eat of the clusters that grow on that noble Vine Jesus Christ, and take them off the tree with your own hand, is a desireable and excellent thing [...] The Mediators hand wipes the foule face, and the teares off all the weeping strangers that come thither; hee layeth the head of a friend under his chin, between his brests. Joh. 14.3 Revel. 21.4 (Rutherford 1647: 288–89)

This passage commences with an allusion to Aarne-Thompson type 516, the folktale type in which the protagonist falls in love with a portrait; the Bride's love for Christ may be compared to the wooing of earthly sovereigns, but Rutherford leaves the reader in no doubt as to which love is more meaningful. The folktale, like the dimly perceived courtly protocol and like the imperfect witness of scripture itself, remains nothing more than a collection of shadowy images; to recognise the substance of the signifier in this life is to enjoy oral gratification, "the brests of the consolations". Rutherford threads a narrow path between distasteful extremes. On the one side, these are emphatically not the breasts of that "most tender and louing nourcing Father" the king (Holy Bible 1612: "To the Most High and Mightie Prince, Iames"; cf. Numbers 11:12, Isaiah 60:16, 49:23). On the other, the mammary aspect of the heavenly landscape has been necessarily transferred from the mediating, nurturing, regnant Virgin and bestowed upon the person of Christ, where it has become, at least notionally, safely available (Dove 2004: xxv, 9; Bynum 1981: 119; Coffey 1997: 93). In the trappings of maternity, patriarchal divinity assumes, unexpectedly, something of the qualities of Hazlitt's picturesque, "catching" the reader's least voluntary, intellectualised senses, and running into the "fantastical and grotesque" (Hazlitt 1930–34: VIII: 317). The landscape of trees, clusters, and consoling breasts embodies a confining authority in the guise of freely bestowed bliss. Allegories of transgendered corporeality are proliferating strategically in Rutherford's writings (cf. Bruce 1590: sig. B6r, B7v); in effect, he is working to stimulate an apprehension of divine substance by returning the reader to infancy – regression equals recognition.

Rutherford thus ceases to discriminate between an increasingly infantile self and the maternal presence it craves. Here the soul, which preserved its separate identity through all the torrent of Stuart discourse, dissolves into the sea of divine influence, which impels and absorbs its every motion. Like water, blood and the cycles of the moon, all human awareness alternates between high tides and low ebbs, fullness and exhaustion (Rutherford 1664: sig. B5):

[N]ow its full moon, againe no moon light at all, but a dark ecclipse [...] The beleever hath flowings of strong acts of faith, joy, love; supernatural passions of Grace arising to an high spring-tide, above the banks and ordinary coasts; and again, a low-ground ebbe. The condition in ebbings and flowings, in full manifestations and divine raptures of another world, when the wind bloweth right from heaven, and the breath of Jesus Christ's mouth, and of sad absence, runneth through the Song of Solomon, the Book of Psalmes, the Book of Job, as threeds through a web of silke, and veines that are the strings and spouts carrying bloud through all the body, lesse or more. (Rutherford 1647: 27–28)

This spasmodic alternation of energies dispels any thought of reading as a consoling, enlightening progress towards personal cultivation. Like the scenes of preternatural intimacy evoked in Rutherford's depictions of the joys of the elect in heaven, the scriptural page now conveys a sustenance that is both physical and spiritual in a pulse of presences and absences. With metaphysical complexity and energy, Rutherford merges the raptures and sadness of mutual spiritual experience into the tides and winds of this world and the next, Christ breathing and the believer experiencing flowings, with the woven threads of text. In its immediacy, each exchange is vivid and raw. Rutherford gives no place here to any conscious human agency: in all its dimensions, the whole significance of this intercourse depends on the believer's prior intimations, his or her openness to grace. In the mysterious passage of blood through its tracery of veins, the human body bears witness to the rightness of the relation and responds to a profound desire for knowledge (Sawday 1995: 180). A sanctuary no more, the book has become a mirror to creation from the perspective of eternity.

From this perspective, Rutherford's reader faces a revelatory choice. One's interpretation of "ebbings and flowings" manifests the state of one's soul. In a brilliant reorientation of the *locus amoenus* – a passage searchingly discussed by David Reid (1988: 194) – Rutherford depicts Gethsemane, where Christ suffered the withdrawal of vivifying "strong love". That ordeal prefigures human isolation:

[S]elfe-terrors are a hell carried about with the man in his bosome, hee cannot run from them. Oh! hee lieth down, and hell beddeth with him; hee sleepeth, and hell and hee dreame together; he riseth, and hell goeth to the fields with him; hee goes to his garden, there is hell. It is observable, a Garden is a Paradise by art; and Christ was as deep in the agonie and wrestlings of hell for our sins, in a garden, a place of pleasure, as on the crosse, a place of torment. The man goes to his table, O! hee dare not eat, hee hath no right to the creature; to eat is sin, and hell; so hell is in every dish: To live is sinne; he would fain chuse strangling; every act of breathing is sin and hell. Hee goes to Church; there is a dog as great as a mountaine before his eye: Here be terrors. But what, one or two terrors are not much, tho' too much to a soule spoyled of all comfort. (Rutherford 1647: 41–42)

Reid notes the "images crowded thick with visionary grotesqueness" and acknowledges that "someone who can write like that about wretchedness is an extraordinary force at least" (Reid 1989: 340–41). Arguably, Rutherford aims beyond mere force and wretchedness: in the shock of their juxtapositions and combinations, his scenes stage the recognition of one's spiritual condition in the character of one's perceptions. Experiencing guilt and fear as the withdrawal of the sustaining maternal presence of a loving God produces a hellish counter-presence, embodied climactically as a massive dog. Where Rutherford surpasses Bunyan – whose *Grace Abounding* also kept its place on the shepherd Lachlan's shelf (Lynch 1992: 259) – is precisely in his fraught dependency of experience upon identity. For Rutherford, as for Augustine, "what one learns […] is what one has in mind beforehand, although that knowledge may be tucked away in memory, far from conscious thought" (Stock 1995: 718). In his landscapes, rich in abrupt contrasts and "imperceptible blends" between the divine and the human, the feminine and the masculine, Rutherford initiates a crisis of self-recognition.

Bibliography

Aarne, Annti, and Stith Thompson. 1932–36. *Motif-Index of Folk-Literature*. 6 vols. Helsinki: Suomalainen Tiedeakatemia (Academia scientiarum fennica).

Allen, Dorena. 1964. "Orpheus and Orfeo: The Dead and the Taken" in *Medium Aevum* 33: 102–11.

Anderson, Patrick. 1623. "Epistle Dedicatorie" in Caldwell, James *The Countesse of Marres Arcadia*. Edinburgh: Wreittoun.

Armstrong, Elizabeth. 1968. *Ronsard and the Age of Gold*. Cambridge: Cambridge University Press.

Bath, Michael. 2003. *Renaissance Decorative Painting in Scotland*. Edinburgh: National Museums of Scotland.

Bawcutt, Priscilla, and Felicity Riddy (eds). 1987. *Longer Scottish Poems Volume One: 1375–1650*. Edinburgh: Scottish Academic Press.

Bawcutt, Priscilla. 2000. "'My Bright Buke': Women and Their Books in Medieval and Renaissance Scotland" in Wogan-Browne, J. et al. (eds) *Medieval Women: Text and Contexts in Late Medieval Britain: Essays for Felicity Riddy*. Turnhout: Brepols. 17–34.

Benjamin, Walter. 2005. "On the Concept of History" (tr. Dennis Redmond). <http://www.marxists.org/reference/archive/benjamin/1940/history.htm>. 12 June 2006.

The Bible [Geneva]. 1561. Geneva: s.n.

Boethius, Anicius Manlius Severinus. [1969] 1998. *The Consolation of Philosophy* (tr. V.E. Watts). London: Folio Society.

Boffey, Julia, and A.S.G. Edwards 2005. "Bodleian MS Arch. Selden. B. 24: The Genesis and Evolution of a Scottish Poetical Anthology" in Mapstone, Sally (ed.) *Older Scots Literature*. Edinburgh: Donald. 14–29.

Bonar, Rev. Andrew A. (ed.) 1848. *Letters of Samuel Rutherford With a Sketch of his Life and Biographical Notices of his Correspondents*. Edinburgh: Whyte.

Boswell, James. 1936. *The Journal of an Excursion to the Hebrides with Samuel Johnson, LL.D* (ed. F.A. Pottle and C.H. Bennett). Toronto: Macmillan.

Brown, Keith M. 2000. *Noble Society in Scotland: Wealth, Family and Culture from Reformation to Revolution*. Edinburgh: Edinburgh University Press.

Bruce, Robert. 1591. *Sermons vpon the Sacrament of the Lords Supper*. Edinburgh: Waldegrave.

Burckhardt, Jacob. 2004. *The Civilisation of the Renaissance in Italy: An Essay* (tr. S.G.C. Middlemore). London: Folio Society.

Bynum, Caroline Walker. 1982. *Jesus as Mother: Studies in the Spirituality of the High Middle Ages*. Berkeley: University of California Press.

Chandler, James. 1994. Review of *Devolving English Literature* by Robert Crawford (Oxford: Oxford University Press, 1992) in *Modern Philology* 92: 211–19.

Chaucer, Geoffrey. 1985. *The Riverside Chaucer*. (ed. L. D. Benson et al.). Boston: Houghton Mifflin.

Coffey, John. 1997. *Politics, Religion and the British Revolutions: The Mind of Samuel Rutherford*. Cambridge: Cambridge University Press.

Corley, T.A.B. 2004. "Anderson, Patrick (1579/80–c.1660)" in *The Oxford Dictionary of National Biography*. Oxford: Oxford University Press. <http://www.oxforddnb.com/view/article/495>. 5 June 2006.

Cowan, Edward J. 1993. "Mistress and Mother as Political Abstraction: The Apostrophic Poetry of James Graham, Marquis of Montrose, and William Lithgow" in Caie, Graham et al. (eds) *The European Sun: Proceedings of the Seventh International Conference on Medieval and Renaissance Scottish Language and Literature*. East Linton: Tuckwell. 534–44.

Crawford, Thomas. 1979. *Society and the Lyric: A Study of the Song Culture of Eighteenth-Century Scotland*. Edinburgh: Edinburgh University Press.

"Curate, Jacob" [Gilbert Crockatt and John Ushaw Monro]. 1692. *The Scotch Presbyterian Eloquence; Or, The Foolishness of their Teaching Discovered from their Books, Sermons, and Prayers*. London: Taylor.

Curtius, Ernst Robert. 1953. *European Literature and the Latin Middle Ages* (tr. W. Trask). London: Routledge & Kegan Paul.

Douglas, Gavin. 1957–64. *Virgil's Aeneid Translated into Scottish Verse* (ed. D.F.C. Coldwell) [Scottish Text Society 3rd series no. 25, 27–28, 30.]. 4 vols. Edinburgh: Blackwood.

Dove, Mary (ed. and trans). 2004. *The Glossa Ordinaria on The Song of Songs*. TEAMS Commentary Series. Kalamazoo: Medieval Institute, Western Michigan University.

Dunnigan, S.M. 2004. "Alexander Hume (c.1557–1609)" in the *Oxford Dictionary of National Biography*. Oxford: Oxford University Press. <http://www.oxforddnb.com/view/article/14133>. 11 June 2006.

Durkan, John. 1962. "The Cultural Background in Sixteenth Century Scotland" in Burns, J.H. (ed.) *Essays on the Scottish Reformation, 1513–1625*. Glasgow: Burns. 274–331.

Fleming, Morna R. "'Kin[g]es be the glas, the verie scoole, the booke, / Where priuate men do learne, and read, and looke' (Alexander Craig, 1604): The Translation of JVI to the Throne of England in 1603" in van Heijnsbergen, Theo and Nicola Royan (eds) *Literature, Letters and the Canonical in Early Modern Scotland*. East Linton: Tuckwell. 90–110.

Fradenburg, Louise Olga. 1991. *City, Marriage, Tournament: Arts of Rule in Late Medieval Scotland*. Madison: University of Wisconsin Press.

Gribben, Crawford. 2006. "The Literary Cultures of the Scottish Reformation" in *Review of English Studies* 57: 64–82.

Hazlitt, William. 1930–34. "On the Picturesque and Ideal" in Howe, P.P. (ed.) *Complete Works*. Vol. 8. London: Dent. 317–21.

Heller, Ben A. 1996. "Landscape, Femininity, and Caribbean Discourse" in *MLN* 111: 391–416.

Henryson, Robert. 1981. *Poems of Robert Henryson* (ed. D. Fox). Oxford: Clarendon Press.

The Holy Bible [King James]. 1612. London: Barker.

Hume, Alexander. 1902. *Poems of Alexander Hume* (ed. A. Lawson). Edinburgh: Blackwood.

Jack, R.D.S. (ed.) 1971. *Scottish Prose 1550–1700*. London: Calder and Boyars.

—. (ed.) 1988. *The History of Scottish Literature Volume I: Origins to 1660 (Mediaeval and Renaissance)*. Aberdeen: Aberdeen University Press.

—. 1997. "Critical Introduction: 'Where Stands Scottish Literature Now?'" in R.D.S. Jack and P.A.T. Rozendaal (eds) *The Mercat Anthology of Early Scottish Literature* 1375–1707. Edinburgh: Mercat Press. vii–xxxix.

James VI and I. 1994. *Political Writings* (ed. J.P. Sommerville). Cambridge: Cambridge University Press.

Jameson, Fredric. 1981. *The Political Unconscious: Narrative as a Socially Symbolic Act*. Ithaca, N.Y.: Cornell University Press.

Johnson, Samuel. 1905. *Lives of the English Poets*. (ed. G. Birkbeck Hill). 3 vols. Oxford: Clarendon.

Lacan, Jacques. 1977. *Ecrits: A Selection*. (tr. Alan Sheridan). New York: Norton.

Loar, Christopher F. 2004. "Nostalgic Correspondence and James Boswell's Scottish Malady" in *SEL: Studies in English Literature 1500–1900* 44: 595–615.

Lyall, Roderick J. 2001. "The Stylistic Relationship between Dunbar and Douglas" in Mapstone, Sally (ed.) *William Dunbar, "the nobill poyet": Essays in Honour of Priscilla Bawcutt*. East Linton: Tuckwell. 69–84.

—. 2005. "Henryson, the Hens, and the Pelagian Fox: A Poet and the Intellectual Currents of his Age" in Mapstone, Sally (ed.) *Older Scots Literature*. Edinburgh: Donald. 83–94.

Lynch, Michael. 1992. *Scotland: A New History*. London: Pimlico.

MacDonald, A.A. 1998. "Early Modern Scottish Literature and the Parameters of Culture" in Mapstone, Sally and Juliette Wood (eds) *The Rose and the Thistle: Essays on the Culture of Late Medieval and Renaissance Scotland*. East Linton: Tuckwell. 77–100.

—. 1991. "The Sense of Place in Early Scottish Verse: Rhetoric and Reality" in *English Studies* 72: 12–27.

Macfarlane, I.D. 1981. *Buchanan*. London: Cassell.

MacLaren, Ian ("John Watson"). 1894. *Beside the Bonnie Brier Bush*. Toronto: Revell.

MacQueen, James. 1988. "Scottish Latin Poetry" in Jack, R.D.S. (ed.) *The History of Scottish Literature Volume I: Origins to 1660 (Mediaeval and Renaissance)*. Aberdeen: Aberdeen University Press. 213–26.

Mapstone, Sally. 2005. "Invective as Poetic: The Cultural Contexts of Polwarth and Montgomerie's Flyting" in *Scottish Literary Journal* 26(2): 18–40.

—. "Older Scots and the Sixteenth and Seventeenth Centuries" in Mapstone, Sally (ed.) *Older Scots Literature*. Edinburgh: Donald. 413–23.

Melville, Elizabeth. "Ane Godlie Dreame" in *Poems of Alexander Hume*. 184–96.

Pearsall, Derek, and Elizabeth Salter. 1973. *Landscapes and Seasons of the Medieval World*. London: Elek.

Reid, David. 1989. "Prose after Knox" in Jack, R.D.S. (ed.) *The History of Scottish Literature Volume I: Origins to 1660 (Mediaeval and Renaissance)*. Aberdeen: Aberdeen University Press. 183–97.

—. "Rutherford as Enthusiast" in McClure, J. Derrick and Michael R. G. Spiller (eds) *Bryght Lanternis: Essays on the Language and Literature of Medieval and Renaissance Scotland*. Aberdeen: Aberdeen University Press. 337–51.

Reid Baxter, Jamie. 2000. "Politics, Passion and Poetry in the Circle of James VI: John Burel and his Surviving Works" in Houwen, L. et al. (eds) *A Palace in the Wild: Essays on Vernacular Culture and Humanism in Late-medieval and Renaissance Scotland*. Leuven: Peeters. 199–248.

Riddy, Felicity. 1989. "The Alliterative Revival" in Jack, R.D.S. (ed.) *The History of Scottish Literature Volume I: Origins to 1660 (Mediaeval and Renaissance)*. Aberdeen: Aberdeen University Press. 39–54.

Robertson, D.W., Jr. 1951. "The Doctrine of Charity in Mediaeval Literary Gardens: A Topical Approach through Symbolism and Allegory" in *Speculum* 26: 24–49.

Rutherford, Samuel. 1647. *Christ Dying and Drawing Sinners to Himself*. London: Crooke.

—. 1664. *Joshua Redivivus, or Mr. Rutherfoord's Letters Divided into Two Parts*. Rotterdam: s.n.

Sawday, Jonathan. 1995. *The Body Emblazoned : Dissection and the Human Body in Renaissance Culture*. London: Routledge.

Schama, Simon. 1995. *Landscape and Memory*. New York: Knopf.

Smith, G. Gregory. 1919. *Scottish Literature: Character and Influence*. London: Macmillan.

Spiller, Michael R.G. 1986. "The Donna Angelicata in The Kingis Quair" in Strauss, Dietrich and Horst W. Drescher (eds) *Scottish Language and Literature, Medieval and Renaissance* [Scottish Studies 4]. Frankfurt: Lang. 217–27.

Stock, B. 1995. "Reading, Writing, and the Self: Petrarch and his Forerunners" in *New Literary History* 26: 717–30.

Todd, Margo. 2002. *The Culture of Protestantism in Early Modern Scotland*. New Haven: Yale University Press.

Whyte, Alexander. 1894. *Samuel Rutherford and Some of his Correspondents*. Edinburgh: Oliphant, Anderson and Ferrier.

Robert Fergusson and the Romantic Ode[1]

Murray Pittock

Modern literary historiography of the Romantic period has neglected the four nations approach which has proved fruitful for understanding the cultural singularity and interrelatedness of Scottish literature in other periods. This essay takes issue with the prevailing Anglo-American critical trends and argues for the distinctiveness of Robert Fergusson's odes in relation to their Romantic successors. Detailed analysis of the differences and affinities which exist thematically and imaginatively between Fergusson's odes and those of English poets suggests the ways in which the form found distinctive Scottish Romantic expression.
Keywords: Akenside; Burns; Coleridge; criticism; Fergusson; genre; Gray; historiography; Keats; Macpherson; pastoral; Pindaric ode; Romantic ode; Romanticism.

The last thirty years have seen a substantial development in the study and understanding of a British history based across four nations. From J.G.A. Pocock's article "British History: A Plea for a New Subject" in the *Journal of Modern History* in 1975, to Norman Davies' *The Isles* a quarter of a century later, a strong trajectory has been established in historical study, which has led to the realisation of a complex and differentiated Britishness. Scottish history and Scottish literature have benefited from this development. These benefits have not been seen in Scotland alone, but wherever Scottish literature is studied: the *Edinburgh History of Scottish Literature* (2006) has almost half its essays contributed from outwith Scotland, while *Scottish Studies Review*, the premier journal in the area, also has a clear and increasing international profile of contributors, with, for example, articles from scholars in Egypt, Italy, Wyoming, Cambridge and the Sorbonne in its autumn 2001 issue. Substantial interventions in Scottish literature have been made by scholars such as Fiona Stafford at Oxford, Ian Duncan at Berkeley and Karen O'Brien at Warwick. Major scholarly editions of the Scottish Romantic writers, Scott and Hogg, have been extensively funded and appreciatively reviewed across the range of Anglo-American weeklies and scholarly journals. Oxford University

[1] This article first appeared substantially in this form in *The British Journal for Eighteenth-Century Studies* 28(1) (2005), and is used by permission of the editor.

Press has recently commissioned its own history of Scottish literature; while *Studies in Romanticism* ran a special Scottish issue in 2001.

And yet in some ways it is as if this change had never taken place: and this is most particularly true of the Romantic period, where the influence of Scottish writing, and its shaping role, was accepted well into the twentieth century, but is now generally in deep decline. As late as 1935–40, the number of articles published on Burns set him at the heart of the major Romantics in terms of scholarly interest: now he trails them badly (Pittock 2003: 191–211). A sea-change began to occur in the 1930s, one in significant measure linked to the rising profile of Coleridge and an emphasis on the inward rather than the social qualities of the imagination: Dennis Brown's 2003 article in *English* is symptomatic of this post-war consensus, with its identification of Coleridge as a "seminal 'Romantic'" in being linked to "contrastive psychological scenarios"; this also extends yet further the dimensions of the Coleridgean case by arguing that the poet's "*paysage intérieur*" separates him even from those "forerunners" with whom he seems to share an intertextual relationship (Brown 2003: 203). As so often since 1945, albeit in a different language, the invocation of the Romantic Imagination serves to annihilate continuity in literary history, as if Burns' "Despondency" had nothing to do with Coleridge's "Dejection" or the fascination of the Romantics with Burns (and Fergusson in "Resolution and Independence", as Robert Crawford suggests) had never occurred (Crawford 2003: 15). We have travelled a long way from W.J. Courthope's or J.W. Mackail's identification of Allan Ramsay as the founding father of Romanticism (Courthope 1895–1910; Mackail 1924).

The trend of viewing Romanticism as mainly subsisting in "a dim awakening of a forgotten or hidden truth of […] inner nature" (Dennis 2003: 205) has been challenged, by Marilyn Butler among others (Butler 1981), but it has not been substantially reversed, as Sharon Ruston's 2005 survey for the Higher Education Academy confirmed: despite lip-service to a diversity of Romanticisms, the textbooks, gatekeepers to the academy, routinely endorse the well-worn anaphora of interiority and imagination. A glance at publications which provide a guide to eighteenth-century and Romantic literary history reveals a complete, or almost complete, absence of Scottish material, even though increasingly tender attention is being paid to male figures who are marginal in the canon of literature in English, such as Stephen Duck (Curran 1993; O'Neill 1998; Womersley 2000). The leading review in the *Times Literary Supplement* on 15 September 2000 could even spend its time arguing whether Cowper or Smart was the best poet between Pope and Wordsworth, oblivious to either the claims or the influence of Burns, whose Kilmarnock Preface of 1786 provided, as Kenneth Johnston (1998) and others have noticed, a model for the *Lyrical Ballads* prefaces which followed. For Hazlitt, the Romantic age was one where "what that is Scotch is not approved ?" (Hazlitt 1904: XII: 230). In modern Anglo-American Romantic criticism, what that is "Scotch" is by contrast all but forgotten.

The omission is all the more strange because, although we now inhabit a critical world where diversity is prized and old boundaries neglected, the paradoxical fact remains that the observations made above are not a new case of special pleading, but very much a critical orthodoxy which was clearly recognised in the age of a far more narrow, chauvinist and centralist criticism. Courthope's *History of English Poetry* (1895–1910) devoted a quarter of its volume on Romanticism to a distinctively Scottish dimension, giving significant space to the subject of this essay, Robert Fergusson (1750–74), and in an earlier age, to Allan Ramsay (1684–1758). Courthope gives almost twenty pages to a discussion of Burns and Blake alone (1895–1910: IV: 52ff; V: 364–7, 410–11; VI, *passim*). Before the Second World War these writers were often discussed together: after 1945, Blake was adopted into Romanticism while Burns was increasingly ignored. Alternatively, Burns has been read as a "peasant poet" alongside figures such as William Barnes, in an identification which prevents understanding both of Burns' designing literary hybridity and of the long and complex defence of literary Scots as an authentic linguistic option, albeit one that might mark author or subject matter as "antiquarian" in a paradigm which bound the "vernacular revival" to Primitivism. Nonetheless within these limits Scots had a role largely accepted and even adopted by English writers: nineteenth-century novelists use quotations in it freely. Burns' presence, and the presence of Scottish Romanticism, in the critical reception of early periods is very different from that it has failed to enjoy since 1945. The issue which this essay in part addresses is therefore not one which consists of any plea for a compensatory expansion of the canon, but rather one which notes that Romantic literary history remains out of step with four nations historiography not only in the present, but in the past of its own critical practice. The issues drawn attention to by Raymond Bentman in his important article on "Robert Burns's Declining Fame" remain pertinent throughout the whole field of Scottish Romanticism (Bentman 1972: 206–24).

The present essay deals, however, not with Burns, but with his "elder brother in the Muse", Robert Fergusson, and specifically with Fergusson as a writer of odes. The thesis will be that Fergusson's "Ode to the Bee" and "Ode to the Gowdspink", written in the 1770s, are much closer in their themes to the established topoi of the Romantic Ode than to the odes of mid-century Anglophone poetry, and that Fergusson's wider achievement, well-recognised to a degree in Scottish literary studies, is a dimension now missing from our understanding of the poetry of the period as a whole. Susan Manning, in her recent essay on "Robert Fergusson and Eighteenth-Century Poetry" in Robert Crawford's 2003 collection, provides a valuable rectification of this: but whereas she places Fergusson's use of the ode with his eighteenth-century English predecessors and thinks it impersonal (though admitting Warton, Gray and Collins' interest in the "private [...] and existential") this essay takes a different approach, which examines what is distinctive about at least some of Fergusson's Scots odes in relation to their Romantic successors (Manning 2003: 105, 108).

In a wider British context, Ralph Cohen, in his essay "The Return to the Ode", notes that the odes of Thomas Warton, William Collins and Mark Akenside represented a definitive turn to the form in the 1740s in "British poetry", and without mentioning the term "pre-Romanticism" (apparently first used in the 1920s by Louis Cazamian), suggests a link between the lyricism of these poets and that of the Romantics (Cohen 2001: 203–24). Cohen does, however, make clear that he subscribes to the standard modern argument of a differentiated Romanticism, first made implicitly in Wordsworth's critique of Gray in the 1802 Preface to *Lyrical Ballads*:

If one compares Collins's "Ode Occasioned by the Death of Mr Thomson" (1748) with Wordsworth's early poem "Remembrance of Collins Composed upon the Thames near Richmond", written in 1789 and published in 1798, a shift becomes apparent from pastoral imagery to actual observation, from learned to ordinary language, from mythic imagination to private prayer (Cohen 2001: 219–20).

This case is fundamentally the same as that most fully stated by C.V. Deane in *Aspects of Eighteenth-Century Nature Poetry* (1967): that eighteenth-century poetry before the Romantics "was devoid of fresh nature-imagery", and that a heavy reliance on personification and abstraction gave "a chill effect of generalisation and conventional rhetoric" to poetry, while periphrasis also helped to lend a sense of distance, only relieved by ventures into the Claudian or Salvatorian picturesque, themselves hindered by a reliance on stock adjectives, such as those used in James Thomson's (1700–48) renderings of Salvator Rosa (Deane 1967: 1, 7, 9, 11–13, 64, 72).

The ode certainly did undergo the kind of revival that Cohen suggests, but he is also expressing the traditional view which separates the abstract or historic ode (Cowper's "Ode to Peace" or "Boadicea, An Ode", for example, or Thomson's "Liberty") from its Romantic successor (Cowper 1980: 406, 431). To some extent this separation is justified. Edward Young's account of the ode as a genre, for example, abstracts the ode into the realm of the "uncommon, sublime and moral": yet even in this context its "spirituous" remoteness from prose can equally be seen as foreshadowing inwardness or recommending abstraction. The eighteenth-century revival of the ode sought the balance ("peculiar, but not strained; moral but not flat: natural, but not obvious") evinced by Young and others but in the end became something else (Young 1852: II: 147–49, 152), the Romantic Ode: "a poem written on the occasion of a vocational or existential crisis in order to reassert the power and range of the poet's voice" (Preminger and Brogan et al. 1993: 855–57).

The power and range of that voice was to some extent conditioned by the conventions of the genre itself, particularly in its Pindaric rather than Anacreontic or Horatian modes. The odes of the 1740s and 1750s saw a return to a more formal understanding of the big bow-wow of the Pindaric Ode, which had been used irregularly by Abraham Cowley in his *Pindarique Odes* of 1656, but which now (following the more regular form successfully defended by William Congreve in his *Pindarique Ode to the Queen* (1706)) manifested itself once again in its more original form of strophe, antistrophe and epode, where "the metre and stanzaic form of the strophe was duplicated precisely in the antistrophe, while in the epode the poet created another, contrasting, stanzaic form" (Lonsdale ed. 1969: 158–59; Whitely 1993: 180; McDermott 1993: 191–92). Gray, in particular, utilised the Pindaric tradition (Terry 1993: 94; Fairer 1993: 158; Whiteley 1993: 182) and it has been argued that "Ode on a Distant Prospect of Eton College" (the same could perhaps be said of the "Elegy") foreshadows the Romantic lyric in its preoccupations (Newey 1993: 25; Manning 2003: 105). Yet at the same time the grandeur of the Pindaric Ode arguably somewhat compromised its claims to subjectivity (McDermott 1993: 195), while of course Gray was as much given to abstract personifications as any of his contemporaries. As a result, despite such claims, the close identification of the Romantic Ode with (in M.H. Abrams' words) a poem of "description and passionate meditation, which is stimulated by (and sometimes at its close reverts to) an aspect of the outer scene and turns on the attempt to solve a personal emotion or a general human one" remains dominant, and is predominantly applied only to the Lake Poets and their successors (Abrams 1957: 137).

Certain themes and images dominate the core Romantic odes, such as Coleridge's "Dejection", Keats' "Nightingale" and Shelley's "West Wind". Wind itself, particularly the collocation of wind and the Aeolian harp image, is one of them. Another is that of weather or the season as a representation of mood in the terms of the pathetic fallacy: another is identification with Nature. It is likely that the connection between wind, the Aeolian harp and mood, discussed in M.H. Abrams' powerful essay "The Correspondent Breeze" (1984), derives from Macpherson's Ossian poetry and not from the English sources Abrams cites (the original source is possibly religious, deriving from the association of wind with the Spirit of God, as Abrams suggests). Macpherson's art demonstrates the conjunction where the "music [...] evoked not by art, human or divine, but by a force of nature", is one chiefly of sentiment or mood, which in its intensity endows the whole Celtic world with the appearance of being the pathetic fallacy's holocaust, but in reality the property of being an avatar of "the persistent Romantic analogue of the poetic mind, the figurative mediator between outer motion and inner emotion" (Abrams 1984: 27, 38). Abrams' neglect of the power of Ossian as a Romantic avatar of harp and wind is of a piece with the separation to the point of dismissal of the Scottish contribution to Romanticism already noted, one which also highly complicated standard accounts of the "bard" in the period.

It was not only Gray and Macpherson (himself an author of Pindaric odes, such as "The Earl Marischal's Welcome to his Native Country" of 1760 (Simpson 1988: 47)), who foreshadowed some of the concerns of the Romantic Ode, but also Mark Akenside, who in *Odes on Several Subjects* (1745) produced work such as "To the Evening-Star" (Ode XV) which had a clear influence on Keats' "Ode to a Nightingale". Akenside also compared the poet's role to that of a bee, an image with its origins in Horace (*Odes* IV: ii), and Fergusson may have used this image of the poet-bee as "assuming to herself all the treasuries of Nature" in his "Ode to the Bee" (1773). Fergusson certainly also knew Horace's *Odes* and on occasion translated them. The likelihood that Fergusson had also read Akenside is increased by the similarity in language, form (to an extent) and subject matter of Akenside odes such as "To the Cuckoo" (III: "O rustic herald of the spring") to Fergusson's "To the Gowdspink", discussed below (Akenside 1996: 235, 292, 314).

There are nonetheless significant differences between Akenside and Fergusson. While (as I shall show below) the status of the bird in their odes is that of the "rustic herald" of a season, and comparisons are made between the bird and what it symbolises and a fairly conventional set of "nymphs and swains" (Akenside) or the more hybridised register of "herd lowns" (Fergusson) (Akenside 1996: 314; McDiarmid ed. [1954–56] 2005: II:178), the Scottish poet evinces both a greater personal interiority in keeping with the standard definition of the Romantic Ode, and also a greater sense of society, social responsibility and solidarity, which cuts across post-war understandings of Romanticism and thus potentially damages an attentive response to Fergusson's role and what he says in his poetry in these terms.

Robert Fergusson's poetic oeuvre was intensely varied for a man who died at only twenty-four, ranging from imitations of Shenstone, mock-heroics and Popean burlesque to the transformation of high cultural genres – elegy, eclogue, and Swift's octosyllabic couplets in "Auld Reikie". These achievements (and others, such as his revisitation of "graveyard" poetry in a political context in "The Ghaists") were in pursuit of a nativist agenda, begun by Allan Ramsay sixty years earlier (Daiches 1982: 39, 43–44, 46, 113; Freeman 1984: 151 ff; McDiarmid ed. [1954–56] 2005: II: 109, 141). Like Ramsay, Fergusson made strong claims for the importance of vernacular Scots by linking it to elevated subjects and high cultural forms: in this, Ramsay, Fergusson and Burns were far closer in outlook to Johann Herder than they were to Joseph Priestley. For Herder, a nation "could not exist without a distinct language and tradition of poetry", and this was exactly what Ramsay had set out to secure in the decades after the Union. For Priestley, "centralisation of language is a historical trend" in imperial states, and the pressure placed on Scots in the eighteenth century (from which it was in part rescued by Scottish Romanticism) bore witness to this. Yet even for Priestley, Scots was a "sister-language" rather than mere dialect, and by the end of the long eighteenth century its writers had helped to make it "distinctive enough to offer a powerful alternative tradition" (Baron 1995: 14–16, 23, 25). In this, Fergusson played a full part.

Fergusson canonised Edinburgh as a rival to London, creating for it simultaneous Latin and Scots personae, "Edina" and "Auld Reekie", and in so doing stating the capital's claim to native authenticity and universal significance: Fergusson's exaltation of the national against the international, the native against the European, the locality against the Grand Tour, has been ably demonstrated by Matthew Simpson in a recent article in *Eighteenth-Century Life* (2003). This exaltation of Edinburgh as an alternative metropolis was of a piece with other aspects of Scottish life and writing, from the conception of the New Town itself as giving Scotland a northern metropolis to rival that on the Thames, to the place for their city in a wider British life sought by *Blackwood's* and *The Edinburgh Review* half a century after Fergusson's death.

Fergusson's "Elegy, on the Death of Scots Music", with its masterly deployment of high cultural form to celebrate the codification of a native music, itself superior even to the idealised pastoral it evokes, shows how sophisticated Scottish manipulation of genre could be in the pursuit of a national literature. In similar complex vein, "Leith Races" adopts the mediaeval dream-vision and the encounter with the feminised nation typical of the *aisling* and other Jacobite poetry in pursuit of a world where both to "loup like Hebe" and to be among "scaw'd and bare-ars'd lowns" are typical of an experience which inflects the connotations of genre towards the lived life of local eyes. As Matthew McDiarmid pointed out long ago, "in his *Leith Races* Fergusson significantly personified his Comic Muse as a country girl with a healthy appetite for the simple festivities of her class" (McDiarmid ed. [1954–56] 2005: I: 132, II: 37, 160). Likewise, Ian Duncan has noted that the sequence of publication of Fergusson's Edinburgh poems ("Daft Days", "King's Birthday", "Leith Races", "Hallow Fair") in *The Weekly Magazine*, creates a "calendrical order, binding specificity of place to an immemorial, seasonal temporality", which in its turn designates the sequence of Edinburgh celebrations as "carnivalesque" cultural productions (Duncan 2003: 70). Fergusson's poetry thus habitually evoked the social world of locality: but it could also contain an interiority of spirit in its evocation of what it is that is valuable in Scottish life, and, by extension, his own. "Ode to the Gowdspink", first published in 1773, anticipates themes such as the application of the seasons to personal mood and political change (Shelley's "West Wind"), and the importance of the natural world and the use of seasons or animals (Keats's "Autumn", "Nightingale") as points both of departure and reflection for the poet's meditation.

Fergusson was thus doing more than imitating "Collins, Gray, and Shenstone" in his Odes (Courthope 1895–1910: IV: 52): and he was doing more than his contemporaries also. In Cowper's later "On a Goldfinch Starved to Death in his Cage" (1780; published 1782), the familiar themes of sentiment and sympathy are present, without the mock-heroic distancing of Gray's earlier "Ode to a Favourite Cat", present also in the uneasy tone of Anna Barbauld's "The Mouse's Petition" (1772) (cf. Bellanca 2003: 47–68). The sympathy of true feeling in Barbauld is, while similar to some aspects of Burns' "To a

Mouse", remote from Fergusson's use of the Gowdspink as an intensi-
fier of mood, experience and belief in the main subject of the poem,
the poet himself and the human condition (ll.49–58, 61–62):

Ah Liberty! thou bonny dame,
How wildly wanton is thy stream,
Round whilk the birdies a' rejoice,
An' hail you wi a grateful' voice.
The Gowdspink chatters joyous here,
And courts wi' gleesome sangs his peer:
The MAVIS frae the new-bloom'd thorn
Begins his *lauds* at ear'est morn;
And herd lowns louping o'er the grass,
Needs far less fleetching til his lass […]
But, reft of thee, fient flee we care
For a' that life ahint can spare. (McDiarmid ed. [1954–56] 2005: 178)

The Gowdspink free implies human closeness to Nature, the true
source of life and freedom, one which seeks change and experience:
the Gowdspink imprisoned implies the corruption of human experience by the desire to possess, the wish to crystallise the "gowden
glister" of a natural life into ownership, an ambition which tends to
disappointment. The irony is that the beauty of Nature is in its nature,
which the attempt to own destroys (ll.21–28):

'Mang man, wae's-heart! we aften find
The brawest drest want peace of mind,
While he that gangs wi' ragged coat
Is weil contentit wi' his lot.
When WAND wi' glewy birdlime's set,
To steal far aff your dautit mate,
Blyth wad ye change your cleething gay
In lieu of lav'rock's sober grey.

On a deeper level, the poem, with its fears of "winter's dreary
dreepin snaws" and the captivity which attends them, may reflect
Fergusson's own fears of the captivity and death of himself and his
genius, for it was published only a year before he died in the
Edinburgh Bedlam on 17 October 1774, and only a month or two
before his behaviour became unbalanced, and the gowdspink of his
gifts became imprisoned in his mind for ever. Fergusson is his own

protagonist in this ode: another indication of his relationship to the poetic practices we normally associate with the Romantic period.

The Ode begins with a celebration of the confluence of Nature's perpetual renewal in "caller verdure", with the Gowdspink's song "saneing" (blessing) the green of summer. The Gowdspink is a "ferlie", the "sey-piece" of Nature's skill, whose beauty and talent exceeds the contemplation of the beautiful or picturesque, ("seek the ROSE to bless our sight" or "yonder RUIN's lofty snout") and also perhaps the world of classical allusion, for the bird's "shining garments far outstrip / The cherries upo' HEBE's lip". Hebe is eternal, daughter of Zeus and Hera. She is probably used here by Fergusson because she occurs in Milton's *L'Allegro*, popular in poetic references at the time, and especially dear to Fergusson, who borrows the figure of "Mirth", a major substrate of his poetry, from this poem (Harvey 1946: 195; Harvey 1980; McGuirk 2003: 153n). Yet the eternity of Nature is nonetheless greater than Hebe, as it is not in Milton. The only other classical reference in the Ode, to Tantalus, is used to describe the Gowdspink's imprisonment by "Th' envious treachery of man" (l.30), who mistakes its "gowden glister" for the inanimate gold he treasures. Natural man is "weil contentit" (l.24), but those who seek to own and confine Nature by means of art ("birdlime", "traps", "cage": ll.25, 33, 38) lack "peace of mind" (l.22). The "lauds" of the mavis are a song of liberty almost like that of Shelley's skylark, though arising from an older tradition (l.57): "lauds" is also of course (in the context of Fergusson's Episcopalian and Jacobite politics) a deliberately un-Presbyterian reference. The "houff" and "bield" of the Gowdspink (l.36) are locations of explicitly Scots domesticity whence it is wrenched to the "fettering cage" (l.38), almost a paradigm for Fergusson's own impending position. The "dark chamber's dowy nook" (l.66) was soon to become every bit as real for the poet as for the bird, alike robbed of "fair freedom" (l.77) into the captivity of the cage of the madhouse. "Ode to the Gowdspink" moves us from the world of tradition, abstraction, and elevated, elaborate and public lyric poetry typical of the ode, to that of personal hope, doubt and fulfilment: a life attuned to Nature, and fearing the unnaturalness of society, a solitary poet's encounter with the solitary bird which reflects his own mind, the "feelingful meditation" characterised by

Abrams as that of the Romantic writer (Abrams 1993: 128). In this
sense the Gowdspink can even serve as an avatar of Baudelaire's poet
as albatross, "vaste oiseau de mer", helpless in the hands of society
when no longer free in flight, itself an image descended from the bird-
poet of Horace (*Odes* II: XX).

Apart from one mention each of "Liberty" and "Fortune" (ll.49,
73), there is no personification, and the retreat from classical allusion
is marked. Observation is direct and exact. The apparently simple
octosyllabic couplets and irregular length of the verse paragraphs
arguably conceal a Pindaric mode, with some evidence of a strophe/
antistrophe/epode development in the sequence nature/man/liberty.
Fergusson used Pindaric structure explicitly in his "Ode to Horror", so
it was quite within his capabilities and interests (McDiarmid ed.
[1954–56] 2005: II: 226).

Fergusson's "Gowdspink" was a seasonal poem, published on 12
August 1773. This was the case to with his "Ode to the Bee"
(McDiarmid ed. [1954–56] 2005: II:134), published on 29 April that
year, as the first bees made their return to the emerging flowers of
spring: both were written three days before their appearance in print.
In "Ode to the Bee", couplets are again almost bereft of personification ("Muse" and "Nature" only appearing in ll.59 and 62), abstraction
and classical allusion. The pastoral address to the "Herds" to
"blythsome tune your casnty reeds (l.1)" seems conventional enough
in its allusion to the tradition of Ramsay's Doric pastoral (Congleton
1952: 87, 113–14), but what succeeds it is a close series of natural
observations, probably based on James Hay's North Belton estate near
Dunbar (also near Broomhouse, where the poem was written).
Fergusson was a frequent visitor to North Belton, staying there, for
example, for the whole of August 1773, when "The Gowdspink" was
written and published. Both these odes are thus linked to a particular
landscape, and Fergusson's meditations on it in the context of his own
mind and art. The Bee, like the Gowdspink, is in a right relation with
nature, unlike that perpetually dissatisfied "feckless creature, man"
(l.23):

Whan fields ha'e got their dewy gift,
And dawnin breaks upo' the lift,
Then gang ye're wa's thro' *hight* and *how*,

Seek caller *haugh* or sunny *know*,
Or ivy'd *craig*, or *burnbank brae*,
Whare industry shall bid ye gae,
For hiney or for waxen store,
To ding sad poortith frae your door. (ll.15–22)

The Scottish landscape is evoked. The right use of it brings pleasure, and a living, though not wealth: the Bee's travel in the search for the honey Nature provides leads the reader's eyes across the countryside. If, following Horace and Akenside, the bee is the poet, then the intensity of the Ode's appreciation of its industry and status as an avatar of Spring gains a different and more personal dimension, highlighted by the simile comparing Bee and Muse in the last six lines:

Like thee, by fancy wing'd, the Muse
Scuds ear' and heartsome o'er the dews,
Fu' vogie, and fu' blyth to crap
The winsome flow'rs frae Nature's lap,
Twining her living garlands there,
That lyart time can ne'er impair. (ll.59–64)

Fergusson ponders on the state of man in comparison with the Bee, among reflections on age dwelling on an internalised misery and depression, quite possibly his own: "Yet thir, alas! are antrin fock / That lade their scape wi' winter stock [...] Wha hope for nae comforting, save / That dowie dismal house, the grave" (ll.27–28, 31–32). The poet then turns his eyes outward again, to landscape, nature and the bee's activity as cures for the darkness of the human heart:

Then, feeble man, be wise, take tent,
How industry can fetch content:
Behad the bees whare'er they wing,
Or thro' the bonny bow'rs of spring,
Whare vi'lets or whare roses blaw,
And siller dew-draps nightly fa',
Or whan on open bent they're seen,
On *heather-bell* or *thristle* green:
The hiney's still as sweet that flows
Frae thistle cald or kendling rose. (ll.33–42)

The address appears impersonal, but is in reality not so. The appearance of the bee as early as April (remembering the proverbial "a swarm of bees in May / Is worth a load of hay"), is a promise of great fertility in poetic "hiney-suckles" (1.48) as well as literal ones, and the last simile of the poem introduces the hope that Fergusson's Muse too will escape "lyart time" (1.64) and be, like the Bee, "Fu' vogie, and fu' blyth to crap / The winsome flow'rs frae Nature's lap" (ll.61–62). The eternity of Nature's round and its "living garlands" (1.63) provides (as does Keats in "Ode to a Nightingale") a contrast with the poet's state, but also promises a deliverance from that state into the perpetually recurring bounty of that Nature, symbolised in the early Bee. Fergusson calls for the "Instructive bee" to "attend me still, / O'er a' my labours sey your skill" (ll.47–48), and while on one level conventional enough, the hope is not for the material fortune of the Bee, but that "by fancy wing'd", the poet's Muse will be free and eternal in a perpetual spring, "To live, and work, and sing" (1.58).

Fergusson is not unique among Scottish writers in providing an early hint of the modes of poetic treatment which were to become inextricably associated with the passionate meditations of the Romantic subject: Beattie's *The Minstrel* is another such example, as Louis Cazamian and Ken Simpson have pointed out (Cazamian [1926–27] 1948: 984–85; Simpson 1988: 250), while the use of the bard and Aeolian harp images in Scottish writing sets up a largely overlooked complex relational dialogue with other British Romanticisms. But what is clear in these Odes is a relationship with Nature lighter in its use of personification than Keats, and like the English poet contrasting the "happy lot" of free Gowdspink or Bee with the "fever, and the fret" of human society. The "viewless wings of Poesy" championed by Keats are not so different from Fergusson's winged fancy which flies after the Bee "ear' and heartsome o'err the dews, / Fu' vogie, and fu'blyth". Fergusson's April and August, Keats' May, are alike specific seasonal aids to the two poets' reflection on the eternity of Nature and their own place as one of the envious productions of "lyart time". Fergusson's intense realisation of self in his half-created, half-perceived natural world does not need to be read forward into Romanticism to demonstrably relate to it: a mighty poet, in his misery, both mad and dead, and as such read by Wordsworth in 1802.

Bibliography

Abrams, M.H. 1984. *The Correspondent Breeze*. London and New York.
—. 1993. *A Glossary of Literary Terms*. Sixth edition. Fort Worth, Texas.
Baird, John D. and Charles Ryskamp (eds). 1980. *The Poems of William Cowper Volume I: 1748–1782*. Oxford: Oxford University Press.
Baron, Michael. 1995. *Language and Relationship in Wordsworth's Writing*. London and New York: Longman.
Bellanca, Mary Ellen. 2003. "Science, Animal Sympathy, and Anna Barbauld's 'The Mouse's Petition'" in *Eighteenth-Century Studies* 37(1): 47–68.
Bentman, Raymond. 1972. "Robert Burns's Declining Fame" in *Studies in Romanticism* 11: 206–24.
Brown, Dennis. 2003. "Coleridge's 'Romanticism' and Psychotherapy: Primal Science, Crime and Reputation" in *English* 52: 203–19.
Butler, Marilyn. 1981. *Romantics, Rebels and Reactionaries*. Oxford: Oxford University Press.
Cazamian, Louis. [1926–27] 1948. "The Pre-Romantic Period" in Cazamian, Louis and Emile Legouis (eds) *A History of English Literature: The Middle Ages and the Renascence: Modern Times* (tr. Helen Douglas Irvine, W.D. MacInnes and Louis Cazamian) London: Dent.
Cohen, Ralph. 2001. "The Return to the Ode" in John Sitter (ed.) *The Cambridge Companion to Eighteenth-Century Poetry*. Cambridge: Cambridge University Press. 203–24.
Congleton, J.E. 1952. *Theories of Pastoral Poetry in England 1684–1798*. Gainesville, Florida: Florida University Press.
Courthope, W.J. 1895–1910. *A History of English Poetry*. 6 vols. London.
Crawford, Robert (ed.) 2003. *Heaven-Taught Fergusson*. East Linton: Tuckwell Press.
Curran, Stuart (ed.) 1993. *The Cambridge Companion to British Romanticism*. Cambridge: Cambridge University Press.
Daiches, David. 1982. *Robert Fergusson*. Edinburgh: Scottish Academic Press.
Deane, C.V. 1967. *Aspects of Eighteenth-Century Nature Poetry*. London: Cass.
Dix, Robin (ed.) 1996. *The Poetical Works of Mark Akenside*. Madison/Teaneck: Fairleigh Dickinson University Press.
Duncan, Ian. 2003. "Auld Breeks and Daft Days" in Crawford, Robert (ed.) *Heaven-Taught Fergusson*. East Linton: Tuckwell Press. 65–83.
Fairer, David. 1993. "Thomas Warton, Thomas Gray, and the Recovery of the Past" in Hutchings, W.B. and William Ruddick (eds) *Thomas Gray: Contemporary Essays*. Liverpool: Liverpool University Press. 146–70.
Freeman, F.W. 1984. *Robert Fergusson and the Scots Humanist Compromise*. Edinburgh: Edinburgh University Press.
Harvey, A.D. 1980. *English Poetry in a Changing Society 1780–1825*. London: Allison & Busby.
Harvey, Sir Paul (ed.)1946. *The Oxford Companion to Classical Literature*. Oxford: Oxford University Press.

Hazlitt, William. 1904. *The Collected Works of William Hazlitt* (ed. A.R. Waller and Arnold Glover). 12 vols. London: n.p.

Hutchings, W.B. and William Ruddick (eds). 1993. *Thomas Gray: Contemporary Essays*. Liverpool: Liverpool University Press.

Johnston, Kenneth.1998. *The Hidden Wordsworth*. London and New York: Norton.

Lonsdale, Roger (ed.) 1969. *The Poems of Gray, Collins and Goldsmith*. London: Longman.

McDermott, Anne.1993. "The Wonderful World of Wonders: Gray's Odea and Johnson's Criticism" in Hutchings, W.B. and William Ruddick (eds) *Thomas Gray: Contemporary Essays*. Liverpool: Liverpool University Press. 188–204.

McGuirk, Carol. 2003. "The 'Rhyming Trade': Fergusson, Burns, and the Marketplace" in Crawford (ed.) 2003. *Heaven-Taught Fergusson*. East Linton: Tuckwell Press.135–59.

Mackail, J.W. 1924. "Allan Ramsay and the Romantic Revival" in *Essays and Studies by Members of the English Association*. Vol. 9. Oxford: Clarendon Press.

Manning, Susan. 2003. "Robert Fergusson and Eighteenth-Century Poetry", in Crawford (ed.). *Heaven-Taught Fergusson*. East Linton: Tuckwell Press. 87–111.

McDiarmid, Matthew P. (ed.) [1954–56] 2005. *The Poems of Robert Fergusson*. Edinburgh: Scottish Text Society.

Newey, Vincent. 1993. "The Solving of Thomas Gray" in Hutchings, W.B. and William Ruddick (eds.). *Thomas Gray: Contemporary Essays*. Liverpool: Liverpool University Press. 13–38.

O'Neill, Michael, (ed.) 1998. *Literature of the Romantic Period: A Bibliographical Guide*. Oxford: Oxford University Press.

Pittock, Murray. 2003. "Robert Burns and British Poetry" in *Proceedings of the British Academy* 121: 191–211.

Preminger, Alex and T.V.F Brogan et al. 1993. *The Princeton Encyclopedia of Poetry and Poetics*. Princeton, New Jersey: Princeton University Press.

Simpson, K.G. 1988. *The Protean Scot*. Aberdeen: Aberdeen University Press.

Simpson, Matthew. 2003. "'Hame Content': Globalisation and a Scottish Poet of the Eighteenth Century" in *Eighteenth-Century Life* 27(1): 207–29.

Terry, Richard. 1993. "Gray and Poetic Diction" in Hutchings, W.B. and William Ruddick (eds) *Thomas Gray: Contemporary Essays*. Liverpool: Liverpool University Press. 73–110.

Whiteley, Paul. 1993. "Gray, Akenside and the Ode" in Hutchings, W.B. and William Ruddick (eds) *Thomas Gray: Contemporary Essays*. Liverpool: Liverpool University Press. 171–87.

Womersley, David (ed.) 2000. *The Blackwell Companion to Literature from Milton to Blake*. Oxford: Blackwell.

Young, Edward. 1852. *The Poetical Works of Edward Young* [Aldine edition of the British Poets.]. London: William Pickering.

Burns and Barrie: "Deceptive Artists"

Kenneth Simpson

The critical writings of R.D.S. Jack have not only prompted renewed serious consideration of Scottish writers whose rhetorical artistry has been undervalued, but has
enabled recognition of parallels between two apparently dissimilar writers, Burns and
Barrie. Barrie's *Farewell Miss Julie Logan* offers a particularly powerful example of
the author's craftsmanship.
Keywords: James Barrie; Robert Burns; craftsmanship; Kailyard; persona; rhetoric;
Scottish literature.

Although at first glance there seems little reason to pair Burns and
Barrie, closer examination reveals points of comparison between the
poet from Ayrshire and the Kirriemuir playwright and novelist. Most
obvious are the similarities in origins and circumstances: each of
humble stock, with family roots in the north-east; each a "lad o'
pairts" with an insatiable desire for knowledge and formidable powers of recall; each indebted to a Masson for a schooling in rhetoric;
and Burns ending his days in Dumfries where Barrie would write
Peter Pan over a century later.

There are common interests in subject-matter: the relationship of
individual to community; the relationships between parish and world;
the fascination with the humanising of the abstract and the supernatural. For both writers evil has a human face and responses to it are
complex. Burns's attitude to the Devil fluctuates between jovial
familiarity ("Auld Hangie", "Auld Nickie-Ben" to whom he recommends reform) and admiration for "that great Personage, [Milton's]
Satan", characterised by "dauntless magnanimity, intrepid unyielding
independance, desperate daring, and noble defiance of hardship"
(Roy 1985: 1: 123). Burns wrote that his "favorite feature in Milton's
Satan [was] his manly fortitude in supporting what cannot be
remedied – in short, the wild broken fragments of a noble, exalted
mind in ruins" (Roy 1985: 1: 198); and of his own life he commented,
"The resemblance that hits my fancy best is, that poor, blackguard
Miscreant, Satan, who, as Holy Writ tells us, roams about like a
roaring lion, seeking, *searching*, whom he may devour" (Roy 1985:

2: 44). Surely he is kin to Barrie's Captain Hook ("not his true name"), a man "profoundly dejected [...] because he was so terribly alone" (Barrie [1911] 1995: 141). When Hook finds Peter alone and defenceless the narrator comments:

> The man was not wholly evil; he loved flowers (I have been told) and sweet music (he was himself no mean performer on the harpsichord); and, let it be frankly admitted, the idyllic nature of the scene stirred him profoundly. Mastered by his better self he would have returned reluctantly up the tree, but for one thing [...] – Peter's impertinent appearance as he slept. (Barrie [1911] 1995: 133)

It is tempting to compare Satan's view of the defenceless Eve in *Paradise Lost*:

> Such pleasure took the Serpent to behold
> This flow'ry plat, the sweet recess of Eve [...]
> Her graceful innocence, her every air
> Of gesture or least action overawed
> His malice, and with rapine sweet bereaved
> His fierceness of the fierce intent it brought.
> That space the Evil One abstracted stood
> From his own evil, and for the time remained
> Stupidly good, of enmity disarmed. (*Paradise Lost* 9: 455–65)

However, it is not only qualities such as these that particularly justify the linking of Burns and Barrie, but the extent to which the subtleties of their artistry have been illuminated by the scholarship of Ronnie Jack, often in ways that vigorously challenge popular interpretation. These issues form the focus of the first section of this paper. The second section aims to explore further in the work of James Barrie some of the insights offered by Professor Jack's critical perspective.

Despite the fact that Burns addresses us in the person of Mailie, a dying ewe, Holy Willie, Caesar and Luath, and the two bridges of Ayr, naively literalist reading of his work remains surprisingly prevalent: if the ploughman was taught by heaven he must always be speaking truth. So a multi-voiced poet is reduced to a spokesperson for the peasantry or – worse still – an icon representing what are, allegedly, Scottish qualities. In the words of Professor Jack, Burns "contains multitudes" (Jack 1997: 112). "That poor man's principles were abundantly motley", noted Ramsay of Ochtertyre (cited in

Kinsley 1974: 60: 136). The price paid for his rich range of voices and universality of appeal is that, while everyone can relate to something in Burns, the danger is that they will then insist, "My Burns is *the* Burns". So the egalitarian Burns recruits well; likewise the nationalist; possibly also the sentimental Jacobite. Fewer will relate to the Burns who, as Sylvander, assures Clarinda that their communion of sensibilities affords their entry to an elite, that of "people of nice sensibility and generous minds" as distinct from those possessed of "coarse minds" (Roy 1985: 1: 197). For the social realist approach or – even more so – that driven by a political agenda there are also voices in Burns that prove problematic.

I love to see a man who has a mind superior to the world & the world's men – a man who, conscious of his own integrity, & at peace with himself, despises the censures & opinions of the unthinking rabble of mankind. (Roy 1985: 1: 15)

– Burns, aged 23, to his former school-mate, Thomas Orr.

However respectable, Individuals in all ages have been, I have ever looked on Mankind in the lump to be nothing better than a foolish, headstrong, credulous, unthinking Mob; and their universal belief has ever had extremely little weight with me (Roy 1985: 1: 349);

– Burns, aged 29, to Mrs. Dunlop; and to William Dunbar he wrote, "We are not shapen out of the common, heavy, methodical Clod, the elemental Stuff of the plodding, selfish Race, the sons of Arithmetick and Prudence" (Roy 1985: 2: 3–4). This Burns is seldom cited.

Barrie has been equally misrepresented. The rich range of his writing is either dismissed as Kailyard parochialism or forced into the straitjacket of psychosexual interpretation. "The darkest interpretations of his nature gained enough credence to make the man more interesting than his work" (Jack 1991: 8): Professor Jack's comment on Barrie equally applies to Burns. Likewise, this assessment of Barrie might stand as a judgment on the literary critical fate of both writers: "A further tragedy is that those who wished to probe did so as biographers, psychologists, sociologists, and nationalists rather than literary critics" (Jack 1991: 24).

In contrast to such approaches, Ronnie Jack characteristically focuses on technique, but it is not technique in isolation. Central to his criticism is the awareness that what is said largely depends on how it is said; so meaning is apprehended by exploration of the expressive means. Allegory, narrative technique, irony in its various forms, rhetorical, linguistic and formal hierarchies: these are his recurrent concerns. So in his work on Burns, Jack insists that Burns be seen as artist, and his is the art that conceals its artifice; *ars est celare artem* recurs in his critical writing. "Burns", he writes, "possesses the *art* of conveying and recreating simplicity to the highest *poetic* degree" [my emphases] (Jack 1997: 111). "He is a dramatic poet, not a consistent logician nor a single-viewed politician" (Jack 1997: 112); and perhaps most important of all for Burns criticism, Burns is "an unrepentant rhetorician" (Jack 1994: 158). As he has shown, in "I never drank the Muses' stank / Castalia's burn an a' that", Burns uses the modesty topos, learned from Murdoch, whereby he disclaims the very complexity he is practising (Jack 1994: 156). Further substantiation can be found in items as diverse as "The Twa Dogs" and the Sylvander letters.

The same shrewd sensitivity to rhetoric is apparent in Jack's evaluation of Barrie. In his emphasis on technique and, in particular, rhetoric, he is reacting against what he rightly regards as the preoccupation of much Scottish literary criticism with evaluation of content. So, for Jack:

> The tendency to judge Barrie on what he says rather than how he says it is yet another evasion of detailed literary consideration of the texts. It is particularly marked among those approaching him within the context of Scottish literature. (Jack 1991: 18)

George Blake's *Barrie and the Kailyard School* is the worst offender: "instead of looking rationally at how Barrie writes, [...] [Blake] mocks what is being said" (Jack 1991: 20). Blake judges Barrie from the inappropriate standpoint of industrial realism, while for Jack, "variety and artifice characterise Barrie's non-dramatic works, so it is hardly enlightening to treat them all as failed attempts at anticipating

The Shipbuilders" (Jack 1991: 21). Once again, what emerges is just how constraining the social realist approach can be.

In his most recent work on Barrie, "James Barrie as Academic: 'Tom Nash' and 'The Rector of Diss'", Professor Jack shows the influence of Barrie's Edinburgh University education on his dramatic and narrative techniques. Of the M.A. degree of the University of Edinburgh and its Professor of Rhetoric and Belles Lettres at the time, David Masson, he writes:

Both fostered an inclusive, differentiated mode of argument modelled on the classical topos, *varius sis sed tamen idem*. A poet may, therefore, be at once fanciful *and* naturalistic, sentimental *and* cerebral, comic *and* serious, depending on the defined terms of reference. (Jack 2003: 12).

Masson's course "was taught from within the Philosophy department, where [Professor Campbell] Fraser's recent anthology of Berkeley was the major set text"; and "both [Masson and Fraser] believed, with Berkeley, that external reality and objective concepts did not exist except as perceptions in the minds of individuals" (Jack 2003: 13). How influential this would be can be seen not just from Barrie's plays but from his use of a sequence of increasingly subjective perspectives in his fiction. Jack refers to "the most basic understanding of Fraser's psychology course where 'memory' and 'phantasy' are held to overlap" (Jack 2003: 17). Thus for Barrie, vision is not static or consistent. In *The Road to the Never Land* Jack cites this key passage in *Sentimental Tommy*: "'It's easy to you that has just one mind', he retorted with spirit, 'but if you had as many minds as I have!'" (Jack 1991: 96). This is apparent, too, in the affinity in Barrie's theory and narrative practice with the perspectivism of Nietzsche in *The Will to Power*, section 520: "Continual transitions forbid us to speak of an 'individual' etc; the 'number' of beings is itself in flux".

If for Barrie identity is fissile, elusive even, then it is understandable that the writer should, like Burns, have recourse to personae. Jack notes, "From the very beginning [Barrie] invented different personae to sign the different voices and senses in his work" (Jack 2003: 15) In his essay "The Sentimentalist" Barrie gives a telling description of the chameleon, self-dramatising nature of the artist: "attacking a person or a custom at eight o'clock in one company, and becoming defendant at nine o'clock in another" (Barrie 1900: 4: 6–7). These words might have been written with Burns's whimsical, Shandean voice in mind. By heeding them, those who seek a single, consistent persona in either Burns or Barrie would be saved from a fool's errand.

In their propensity to role-playing and projection of self-images Burns and Barrie are kindred spirits. Burns directed his dramatic potential into the personae of his poems, letters and – one is tempted to add – his life. In the self-description prefacing his first Commonplace Book he writes that "his performances must be strongly tinctured with his unpolished, rustic way of life" (Burns 1965: 1); and to Lady Henrietta Don he writes, "I have sent you a parcel of my epistolary performances" (Roy 1985: 1: 103). This facility in the projection of self-images, wedded to the mastery of rhetoric, make Burns as much a "deceptive artist" as the Barrie so designated by Professor Jack (Jack 1991: 12). Burns's is an art of multiple levels. For some readers "To a Louse" merely re-enacts an episode in church; for others it is a benign satire on the vanity of aspirations as exemplified in Jenny, Lunardi, and the narrator. At first glance "The Death and Dying Words of Poor Mailie" is a record of a farmyard incident; closer examination identifies a subtle representation of the general human tendency to contradict theory in practice.

In Professor Jack's pioneering work on Barrie we find further common ground between the two writers. In *Sentimental Tommy* he identifies "a curiously complex view of art [...] which suggested that the artist was a purveyor of deceit, both in the sense of deceiving himself and his audience" (Jack 1991: 7). How apt this is in relation to Burns, especially the Burns of the later letters which depict the man as, psychologically, the victim of the facility of the writer. Burns exclaims, "God have mercy on me! a poor damned, incautious, duped, unfortunate fool! The sport, the miserable victim, of rebellious pride; hypochondriac imagination, agonising sensibility, and bedlam passions!" (Roy 1985: 1: 216). More poignantly:

My worst enemy is *Moimeme.* I lie so miserably open to the inroads and incursions of a mischievous, light-armed, well-mounted banditti, under the banners of imagination, whim, caprice, and passion, and the heavy-armed veteran regulars of wisdom, prudence, and forethought, move so very, very slow, that I am almost in a state of perpetual warfare, and alas! frequent defeat. (Roy 1985: 1:185)

Craftiness is inseparable from the writer's craft; and, in the case of Burns, it rebounds to the detriment of the man.

Jack's own critical preoccupations and penetrating literary sensitivities have prompted identification of shared characteristics in two apparently very diverse writers. They share a subtle sense of rhetorical nuance and play, a facility with voice and persona, a philosophical commitment to the multi-faceted and multi-perspective view. Critically both have suffered from critics who simplify them, fail to perceive their complexity, or apply inappropriately constricting criteria of judgment. Both are artists who are at times painfully aware of their own conflicts and complexities, and are able to manage deceit, both of themselves and of their audiences.

As the discussion so far has shown, through his scholarly career Professor Jack has offered a salutary re-focusing of critical perspective on rhetoric and craftsmanship. So to the text which, for me, represents the zenith of Barrie's achievements as craftsman. *Farewell Miss Julie Logan*, written in 1931, purports to be the diary of a minister in a tiny parish in a remote highland glen, a diary of events in the eighteen-sixties. The minister's name, Adam Yestreen, bespeaks retrospective vision; there is evidence of couthy Scots humour; and details from Barrie's earlier work reappear (the hens frozen to their perch at the start of chapter 4 evoke the bantam-cock similarly immobilised 43 years earlier on the first page of *Auld Licht Idylls*). Such details may prompt social realists and anti-Kailyarders to start sharpening their knives. But this novella serves a cathartic function for the author: it deliberately employs features of the earlier fiction for the purpose of depicting repression both personal and national, that of Yestreen, Scotland, and (one would venture to suggest) Barrie too. No Kailyard fiction offers this degree of revelation of the individual psyche. While in some of its details it may seem to replicate *Auld Licht Idylls*, its real affinities in Scottish literature are with James Hogg's *Memoirs and Confessions of a Justified Sinner* and Robert Louis Stevenson's *The Strange Case of Dr Jekyll and Mr Hyde*.

Barrie introduces Kailyard-like specificity for authenticity (the minister knows his parish) but also for humorous effect, using it to establish one part of a patterned thematic structure. Yestreen comically tugs the Doctor's beard to keep him awake while he tells the bizarre tale of "The Stranger". Gregory Smith's *Scottish Literature: Character and Influence* (1919) is lurking here with his theory of the interaction between the prose of experience and that of extravagance. A fuller example of this principle reveals its influence on the sequence and structuring of the material of the narrative and the ironic effects thereby achieved. So "Superstition and its Antidote" (Chapter 6) follows the account of "The Stranger" (Chapter 5) and precedes "Miss Julie Logan" (Chapter 7), drawing the two outer chapters into ironic juxtaposition with it. Likewise Chapter 8, "Christily goes Queer", undermines the reliability of the clergyman-narrator by demonstrating that it is his viewpoint that is distorted. Yet our view of his serious mental disturbance is complicated by the interposition of a humorous detail: Posty's wife has taken to bed, ill, on discovering that she is four years older than she thought she was . The use of such Kailyard-like details has the effect of grounding bizarre events in a specific locality. The effect is comparable to that achieved by Emily Brontë in *Wuthering Heights*: David Daiches in his introduction to the Penguin edition notes that "the domiciling of the monstrous in the ordinary rhythms of life and work [makes them] less monstrous and more disturbing" (Brontë [1847] 1965: 29). The same holds true for Barrie's novella.

Further heightening the disturbance level is the fact that it is from the minister himself, all unwitting, that we learn of the extent of his sexual repression. The text is a masterpiece of ironic self-revelation, in the tradition of Burns's "Holy Willie's Prayer" and John Galt's *Annals of the Parish*: the narrator says more about himself than he intends or realises. Yestreen uses the word "prudent" in his first sentence, only to claim, "I believe I could rope the winds of the manse to my bidding to-night, and by running from door to door, opening and shutting, become the conductor of a gey sinister orchestra" (Barrie [1931] 1989: 7). There is an ironic discrepancy between the claims that he makes for himself and the behaviour and personality that he presents. At the outset he dismisses "superstitious havers" (8). He assures his reader, "of course the old reprehensible songs that kow-tow to the Stewarts find no asylum with me" (9) – this from the man who is to associate Julie Logan with the Jacobite cause (an interesting point of contact with *Sentimental*

Tommy where Tommy fantasises by reconstructing the 1745 rebellion with himself in a central role).

Irony increasingly informs Yestreen's unwitting revelation of his psychological state. This is his description of his maid: "Christily is a most faithful young woman with a face as red and lush as a rasp, who knows her carritches both ways, and has such a reverence for ministers that she looks upon me more as an edifice than a mortal" (21): each of these clauses, words even, repays scrutiny in its revelation of unacknowledged feeling. Yestreen affirms: "'Wayward' […] what was wrong with it, for I like the word" (29) – this from the man acutely aware of his role as minister. "I do not believe in Spectrums" (31), he writes, while all the evidence contradicts this. He attempts via "more reasonable fancies" (36) to explain the fact that he sleeps with his fiddle, unknowingly reducing to the absurd the Scottish Enlightenment doctrine of sympathy: "it might be hard on a fiddle never to be let do the one thing it can do" (36). John Purser's reminder that in the Scottish cultural tradition "'fiddling' has always been a double entendre" is particularly apposite (Purser 1992: 202–3). Revealingly, Yestreen later says of Julie Logan, "My mind goes back in search of every crumb of her, and I am thinking I could pick her up better on my fiddle than in written words" (53); yet he then acknowledges, "ministers must be done quickly with the clutches of youth" (53).

Through his innocent narrator, Barrie offers acute insight into the psychological tensions arising from the frustration of the young man's sexual needs and the constraints of his vocation. He describes Julie Logan as "a long stalk of loveliness" (53), notes the "beloved huskiness in her voice", and reports that "she glides up a manse stair with what I take to be the lithe-someness of a panther" (54). Then, ironically, after an interlude in which he attempts to explain humour to her (a task for which his manifest deficiencies in humour render him singularly ill-qualified), he visualises her as his wife in church: "She is a tall lady, and I wondered whether the seat was too low for her; and such is my condition that, if I had brought nails and a hammer with me, I would have raised it there and then" (58). Such is his repression that he can replace reality with self-created fantasy. Male sexual tensions were similarly prominent in *Tommy and Grisel*, as

Andrew Nash has noted (Barrie 2000: x). In *Farewell Miss Julie Logan*, as in *The Little White Bird*, the narrator has constructed his ideal woman. Commentators have pointed out that Babbie in *The Little Minister* is an early version of the *femme fatale*, but Jack notes that "what remain for Babbie dark possibilities are fully realised in *Farewell Miss Julie Logan*". (Jack 1991: 59).

Landscape and locality are used by Barrie not only to authenticate experiences but also to represent them symbolically. This becomes evident in Chapter 4, "The Locking of the Glen": "The glen road, on which our intercourse with ourselves as well as with the world so largely depends, was among the first to disappear under the blankets [of snow]" (33). The effect of the blizzard is to transform familiar reality. Adam's choice of words is especially revealing: denied "intercourse" with "the world", he turns inward, and introversion fuels further his propensity to fantasy. "I am practically cut off from my kind", he writes, unaware of the resonances of his comment. He preaches to his tiny congregation from opposite sides of the burn, the physical isolation mirroring the mental. It is then that he hears the fiddle.

Beyond this powerfully nuanced management of local detail, by means of a range of references Barrie evokes a broader landscape – that of the Scottish nation, its history, and its culture. "The End of a Song" (Chapter 9) recalls the words of Lord Seafield, prompted by the last session of the Scottish Parliament as it voted to abolish itself in the union with England: "an end to an auld sang". Adam is "but half a Highlander" (9); Dr. John sees the 'Forty-Five as "the origin of all the clavers and clecking of nowadays" (24); the glen folk "liked best to be of no party unless they were of both" (25); the Stranger "is believed by the simple to have been the Chevalier himself" (25). In his alternation between attempted rational understanding and superstitious fancy Adam enacts within himself, in cultural and political terms, the tension between the old Scotland and the new.

At the climax of the Chapter 9, from outside the house of Mistress Lindinnock, the local laird, Adam sees reflected in the loch from the lighted windows a gathering of people "in the Highland dress of lang syne" (71). The mysterious group, dancing and conversing, are of uncertain reality: "near all colour had been washed out of them, as if they had been long among the caves and the eagles" (71). Viewing the group in the Great House awaiting an arrival, Adam expects "he who was fed from the eagle's nest" (73), the Chevalier himself. In fact it is Julie Logan, whom he has previously compared with Mary Stewart, who enters, "her garments ... in tatters" though "she was the one presence in the hall to them", and dominates the dance and the gathering (73).

Here we find the culmination of a recurring theme in Barrie, a derivative of his enduring interest in perspective – the situation and role of the spectator. In *Peter Pan* the narrator reminds the reader, "That is all we are, lookers-on" (Barrie [1911] 1995: 164); and when the Darling children are safe home, Peter "was looking through the window at the one joy from which he must be for ever barred" (171). But in *Farewell Miss Julie Logan* it is the most famous voyeur in Scottish literature that is evoked by Adam's night watch – Tam o' Shanter. "Heroic Tam", Burns's entranced spectator of the witches' dance, is safe until his life is threatened by the triumph of instinct over reason: with his roared approval of the dance's leader, "Weel done, Cutty-Sark!", he betrays his presence, thereby redirecting the young witch's energies from seductive dance to potentially fatal pursuit. Of Burns's poem Thomas Crawford has written:

In "Tam o' Shanter" realism, fantasy, humour and symbolism are skilfully inter-mingled in a work that is typical not only of Burns, but of the Scottish mind; for it is – next to "The Vision" – the most genuinely national of all his poems. (Crawford 1965: 222)

These terms might equally be applied to *Farewell Miss Julie Logan*, the most national of Barrie's works, particularly in respect of its engagement with the contesting claims of instinct and reason.

Adam explains the gathering – all part of his fantasy – as "the last sough of a song" (75). There is an ironic appropriateness in the use of the material of the native Scottish cultural tradition to make this point. The earlier Scotland, personified in Julie Logan through the comparison with Mary Stewart, is the seductress. As the last chapter, "A Quarter of a Century", makes plain, there is no escaping her clutches. Now allegedly "secure and serene" (87) and settled in his new parish in the industrial lowlands, where they even have a machine to disperse the snow, Adam anticipates that "time will no doubt efface every memory of Miss Julie of the Logan; and of mornings I may be waking up without the thought that I have dropped her in the burn" (88). Yet his testimony after an interval of twenty-five years indicates otherwise, as do the words with which his account ends:

Of course it is harder on young Adam. I have a greater drawing to the foolish youth that once I was than I have pretended. When I am gone it may be that he will away back to that glen. (88)

The irony of the novella's title is thereby confirmed: there is no farewell to Miss Julie Logan.

Farewell Miss Julie Logan exemplifies the deceptive artistry identified by Professor Jack. Of all Barrie's texts it particularly substantiates his claim that:

study of Barrie's methods suggests that Scottish Literature should cease condemning him within a static paradigm but alter the paradigm to welcome him and meet its own altering situation (Jack 1991: 246).

The term "quiddity" is one which recurs in the work of R.D.S. Jack and it is a concept to which he is particularly responsive. He is alert to the singularity and specificity of each work he explores, and has the subtlety of wit to engage with the nuances he identifies. In his scholarship we have proof aplenty that a mind may fill with knowledge but yet remain open.

Bibliography

Barrie, J.M. 1900. "The Sentimentalist" in *The Young Man* 4.

—. [1931] 1989. *Farewell Miss Julie Logan*. Edinburgh: Scottish Academic Press.

—. [1911] 1995. *Peter Pan*. London: Penguin.

—. [1931] 2000. *Farewell Miss Julie Logan: A Barrie Omnibus*. Edinburgh: Canongate Classics.

Brontë, Emily. [1847] 1965. *Wuthering Heights* (ed. David Daiches). Harmondsworth: Penguin.

Burns, Robert. 1965. *Commonplace Book 1783–1785*. London: Centaur Press.

Crawford, Thomas. 1965. *Burns: A Study of the Poems and Songs*. Edinburgh: Mercat Press.

Jack, R.D.S. 1991. *The Road To The Never Land: A Reassessment of J.M. Barrie's Dramatic Art*. Aberdeen: Aberdeen University Press.

—. 1994. "Burns as Sassenach Poet" in Simpson. Kenneth (ed.) *Burns Now*. Edinburgh: Canongate. 150–66.

—. 1997. "Castalia's Stank": Burns and Rhetoric" in Simpson, Kenneth (ed.) *Love and Liberty. Robert Burns: A Bicentenary Celebration*. East Linton: Tuckwell Press. 111–18.

—. 2003. "James Barrie as Academic: 'Tom Nash' and 'The Rector of Diss'" in *The Swansea Review* 22: 1–22.

Kinsley, James. 1974. "Burns and the Peasantry" in *Proceedings of the British Academy* 60: 135–53.

Purser, John. 1992. *Scotland's Music*. Edinburgh: Mainstream.

Roy, G. Ross (ed.) 1985. *The Letters of Robert Burns*. 2 vols. Oxford: Clarendon Press.

Smith, G. Gregory. 1919. *Scottish Literature: Character and Influence*. London: Macmillan.

J.M. Barrie and the Third Sex

Andrew Nash

This chapter explores the journalistic writing of J.M. Barrie, a relatively neglected aspect of his work, from the perspective of its preoccupation with gendered and sexual identities. It reveals Barrie's cultural, aesthetic, and psychological interests in the relationship between sexual and social constructions of identity; ideas of theatricality and gender; and in contemporary areas of cultural and political debate such as marriage, the New Woman, and the boundaries between homosocial and homosexual desires. In so doing, it helps to provide a new context for the interrelated questions of performance, emotion, and gender which inform his better-known dramatic and fictional work.
Keywords: R.L. Stevenson; journalism; sexology; sexual identity; social history; performance; Oscar Wilde.

Writing to Henry James in December 1892, Robert Louis Stevenson gave his estimate of the work of J.M. Barrie:

> But Barrie is a beauty, *The Little Minister* and the *Window in Thrums*, eh? Stuff in that young man: but he must see and not be too funny. Genius in him, but there's a journalist at his elbow – there's the risk. (Stevenson 1995: 451)

Critics have been only too eager to ignore the positive aspect of Stevenson's comment – to see it, in fact, as evidence of his own critical failings – and to seize on the negative remark; at least Stevenson was "aware of Barrie's faults" (Lindsay 1992: 352). Barrie's training as a journalist has often been viewed as a fault, and as having a deleterious effect on his writing; as one critic has stated, his "shortcomings" are "directly traceable to his journalistic concessions to the tastes of the reading public" (Geduld 1971: 15). But Barrie's journalism contains a wealth of neglected material, and now that he is no longer the *bête noire* of Scottish literature, it is possible to turn to it in search, not of faults, but of pointers to how one might approach and understand important aspects of his art.

It is well known that Barrie's early works of fiction, *Auld Licht Idylls* (1888) and *A Window in Thrums* (1889), set in his home-town of Kirriemuir, grew out of articles which he had previously published in various London newspapers and periodicals (Nash 1998). It was with these works that Barrie would first taste fame and they have since come to form the basis of much of the discussion of his work within the context of Scottish literature. But Thrums and regional Scottish life formed only a small part of Barrie's enormous output of journal and newspaper articles. In fact, the two most recurring subjects in his work on the press in the mid and late 1880s are authorship and the literary marketplace, and bachelorhood and gender relations. Isla Jack has opened up discussion of the first of these (Jack 1999) and I want to begin this essay by considering the second, taking as my focus the title of a series of articles that Barrie wrote first for the *Nottingham Journal* and then for the *Edinburgh Evening Dispatch*: "The Third Sex".

Barrie joined the staff of the *Nottingham Journal* in January 1883 and worked on the paper for almost two years. Gender issues were among the many subjects to which he turned his hand. R.D.S. Jack has drawn attention to his support for the women's rights movement (Jack 1995: 137–38) and other articles, on such topics as "Male Nursery Maids" (28 March 1883) and "Pretty Boys" (28 January 1884), reflect his interest in challenging – if mainly humorously – the social roles and identities of men and women. The article on "The Third Sex" (3 September 1883), however, is more striking because it engages with the terminology of Victorian sexology. The phrase "third sex" had long been used as a term to describe eunuchs or hermaphrodites but in the nineteenth century it came increasingly to be associated with gender inversion at the level of psychology and identity. The sexologist Karl Heinrich Ulrichs explicitly used the term in relation to same-sex desire (Hekma 1994), but it was also used more generally to refer to men and women who believed themselves to have a male identity in a female body or vice versa. As such, the term can be seen in the context of the new taxonomy of sexualities that grew up at the end of the nineteenth century. It forms part of what Michel Foucault has identified as the new "specification of individuals" (Foucault 1981: 47) that helped to establish the modern understanding of sexuality in terms not of sexual *acts* but of sexual *identities*. Barrie's use of the phrase thus suggests an awareness of contemporary debates on sexuality and an engagement with the modern conception of sexual identities as social constructions. Although his early articles do not develop this engagement fully, they are worth consideration because they can help us to understand Barrie's treatment of gender in his fiction and plays.

In the *Nottingham Journal* article, the "third sex" are "youthful clergyman" whom one might see playing lawn tennis or at garden parties. They are "passionately addicted to the wearing of flowers" and prove irresistibly charming to "giggling girls" who crowd round them and "provide them with slippers of the most beautiful pattern". They are the "third sex" because, in spite of their attractiveness to women, they are seemingly sexless and therefore, in society's eyes, useless. The article is essentially a debate on determinism – another topic that preoccupied the young Barrie in his journalism. (Jack 1989: 262) – and through the guise of his fictional author, "Hippomenes", Barrie proceeds to defend the usefulness of the "third sex". He proposes that

the happiest woman in the world would be the one who could hang a couple of them in her ears and wear them as rings of jet; and when one comes to think of it, this may have been the very purpose for which they were created. [...] The earring notion is probably new, but many attempts have already been made to account for the dandiacal body; we frequently pass notice-boards intimating that rubbish must not be shot in that vicinity and there is no reason why the third sex may not have been called into being for a somewhat similar purpose. A negative use is not necessarily small, and if it could be clearly proved that the third sex were created as a warning to the other two, their sphere would immediately become sharply-defined and honourable.

Some three years later Barrie used the same title for a series of six articles in the *Edinburgh Evening Dispatch*. Barrie was a freelance contributor to the *Dispatch* from 1886 to 1890, sending in unsigned articles as regularly as once a week. The articles on "The Third Sex" were published between 26 March 1887 and 4 June 1887. By this time the "third sex" had changed their identity from youthful clergyman to actors and actresses. Posing as the paper's "London Dramatic Critic", Barrie begins the first article by lamenting that "no novelists have yet managed to draw a player". Noting the failed attempts of Thackeray, Dickens, Charles Reade and the "lady novelists", he concludes:

If an English writer ever does succeed in drawing real actors, he will start with the assumption that they constitute a sex by themselves, not two sexes, for the men and women of the stage are very much alike.

The article goes on to describe a troupe of touring players whose various activities are related in the succeeding five articles. Running throughout these pieces – though never actually made the central focus – is the idea that men and women of the stage belong to a common gender because their identities exist in playing roles. Barrie's own experience of acting may have helped to develop this idea in his mind. In a speech given when he was awarded the freedom of Dumfries, he recorded that in his time with the Dramatic society of the Dumfries Academy he invariably played female parts and that at one performance "a male member of the audience asked for an introduction" (Barrie 1938: 84–85).

Barrie was clearly interested in the constructed nature of gender. In a much later article for the *Dispatch*, entitled "Men and Women" (18 June 1890), he wrote: "it is strange that such a difference should exist in the characteristics of two of the same species as there is between men and women". The subject that really floods his early journalism, however, is bachelorhood. The bachelor was a prominent figure in the literature and culture of the *fin de siècle* (Showalter 1990: 24–26), and the existence of numerous male-only clubs meant that even if men were not bachelors they could still spend a large part of their lives in a male-only social environment. Barrie wrote an article on "London Clubs" for the *Dispatch* (19 March 1887), and in *The Little White Bird* (1902) he placed a bachelor clubman at the centre of the story that was to witness the birth of Peter Pan. The social historian Peter Gay has argued that the fears of the men who sought refuge in male-only clubs were "fears not of being castrated but of being compelled to grow up, of having to abandon persistent adolescent ties with their distinctly, though largely unconscious, homoerotic pleasures" (Gay 1984: 288). Consideration of Barrie's journalism allows us to conclude – if it still needs concluding – that Barrie was far from being blissfully ignorant of the social and sexual implications of writing a story about a boy who would not grow up.

Marriage and bachelorhood are treated in a characteristically ironic and humorous way in Barrie's articles for the *Dispatch*. In "Is

Marriage a Failure. From the bachelor's point of view" (18 August 1888), a cynical bachelor judges the success of his friends' marriages on what he himself gains from the arrangements; from "this high point of view" he concludes that marriage must indeed be a failure. The article is almost certainly a response to the debate that was initiated by Mona Caird's article "Marriage" published in the *Westminster Review* for August 1888. Caird's article explored the historical development of the institution of marriage and challenged the assumption that women had no acceptable social alternative other than to marry. It provoked considerable debate. *The Daily Telegraph* opened a correspondence column entitled "Is Marriage a Failure" and received 27,000 letters in two months. The title of Barrie's article can hardly be coincidental, and it shows how much he was in touch with debates surrounding such topics as the New Woman.

In "Married and Done For. Poor George's Last Days. By a Confirmed Bachelor" (11 June 1887), marriage is presented as signifying death:

George, poor fellow! got engaged a few weeks ago, and already he is lost to his friends. The thing leaked out gradually but we had all too much good feeling to talk about it in his presence ... It was very sudden. He had been in his usual state of health on the previous day and had spoken brightly of his prospects as if he viewed the future without misgivings. When I left him in the afternoon it never struck me that anything was wrong ... I shuddered to think that it might have been myself ... a text came into my mind. It was "In the midst of life we are in death".

In "My Ghastly Dream: A Distressing Story" (21 September 1887), a bachelor has a recurrent nightmare: "Always I see myself being married, and then I wake up with the scream of a lost soul, clammy and shivering". This is a nightmare that afflicts the hero of *Tommy and Grisel* as well (Barrie 1900: 35). In several articles Barrie presents the bachelor as faced with a social compulsion to reject male-only society and pursue marriage as an inevitable destiny. In "My Ghastly Dream" the bachelor proposes to a girl the moment he learns that he has a rival for her affections. In "Popping the Question" (14 May 1887), a man desperate to get married writes to "lady writers of fiction" to find out how to propose; in "Why Ladies Don't Like Me: the Reflections of a Prig" (19 May 1888), a man tries, unsuccessfully, to convince himself that he doesn't care about the lack of female attention; and in "A Ladies Man; or the Pursuit of sentiment" (17 September 1887), a bachelor talks to a young lady "whilst looking longingly at a man and sighing".

The transition from homosocial bonding to the heterosocial bond of marriage is central to *My Lady Nicotine* (1890), a collection of sketches (most of which had appeared before as articles) centring upon an all-male smoking fraternity and telling the adventures of a man's final days as a smoking bachelor. There is a long-standing cultural association between smoking and sensuality (Klein 1993), and it is obvious from the title of Barrie's book that we are meant to view smoking as a substitute for sexual desire and the company of women. Marriage is seen as an infringement on the pleasures of male bonding. The men who smoke the Arcadia mixture with the narrator – some of them loosely based on Barrie's real friends – occupy the same lodgings as each other and holiday together on a houseboat. Smoking emerges as both a substitute and a remedy for sexual desire. The narrator declares: "after I smoked the Arcadia, the desire to pay ladies compliments went from me" (Barrie 1890: 30), and when Gilray, one of the members of the group, is rejected in a proposal of marriage, the men rally round and nurse him back to happiness with the Arcadia Mixture. In another story, Gilray purchases a rose for a woman he admires but shies away from approaching her and uses it as a pipe-cleaner instead.

However much the men try and avoid the complications of sexuality, a continual, and sometimes ambiguous, engagement with desire for women runs throughout *My Lady Nicotine*. As so often in Barrie's work, the ironic tone of the prose encourages us to see through the narrator's confidence in the superior claims of smoking: "On my life, love for a pipe is very like love for a woman, though they say it is not so acute" (Barrie 1890: 38). In the first chapter the narrator explains that he has given up his pipe following his marriage and has now come "to look upon smoking with my wife's eyes" (Barrie 1890: 4). Nevertheless, at the end of the book we see the narrator in his married state but still clinging to the homosocial routines of a male fraternity. Listening to the sound of his neighbour tapping his pipe through the wall, he simulates smoking by chewing on a briar; only after his neighbour has said good night with the final tap of his pipe does he "smile sadly" and join his wife in bed. (Barrie 1890: 276).

Whilst Barrie may have considered it as a largely ephemeral piece of juvenilia, *My Lady Nicotine* can now be seen as a text that engages – humorously – with important cultural concerns of its time, and in one chapter the text even dramatises the vexed issue of the boundaries between homosocial and homosexual desire. Marriot, the "sentimental member" of the group, has a habit of forcing the reluctant narrator to listen to his tales of failed romances. In "The Face that Haunted Marriott", the narrator has rushed to his bedroom to try and escape yet another tale about women and sex, but in this instance Marriot is at pains to point out that his story is not "a love affair – at least not exactly" (Barrie 1890: 209). His story is, however, very much about desire. Having being shown an old school photograph, Marriot is aroused by the face of a beautiful girl whose identity he cannot recall. On re-telling this story he is at pains to point out that he did not fall in love with the face: "it was not, I think, that kind of attraction" (Barrie 1890: 210). The reason becomes clear when it emerges at the end of the story that the beautiful young girl whom he thought he recognised in the photo has recently been presented to him as she now is – "a very short, very fat, smooth-faced man" (Barrie 1890: 215). The fear of the ambiguity of male sexual desire is illustrated here not just in the figure of Marriot, at pains to understand his "attraction", but also in the narrator himself, lying in his bed trying to avoid listening whilst Marriot flicks cigarette-ash on his pillow.

This story was first published in the *St James's Gazette* on 21 November 1888, under the title "A Face That Haunted Me" where it is the narrator who is haunted. The conclusion to this version has an edge to it that is not present in the humorous mode of *My Lady Nicotine*:

By-and-by, no doubt, I shall be able to dismiss this very odd affair with a smile. The mystery, however, occupied my mind for so long, and to-night's solution has so shaken me, that I confess I don't feel like laughing.

Ideas about marriage and male sexual and emotional desire naturally found their way into the novel Barrie was writing around the same period as *My Lady Nicotine* and the later *Dispatch* articles. As I have stated, the other major topic that recurs in Barrie's early journalism is authorship and creativity, and several of the articles on bachelors combine these two main themes. The "author" of "A Literary Revelation" (30 May 1888) is a novelist whose work has a controlling influence on his life. One of the effects is that

after devoting a whole chapter to a passionate love scene, I have said things to my wife for which a man deserves imprisonment ... The more I dwell on paper on the happiness of the married life the more eager am I to scowl at it as it is known to me in the concrete, and when I come to my senses my wife assures me that I spoke of our marriage as having ruined my life.

This inverse relationship between art and life is central to *The Little Minister* (1891), which in its narrative technique sets artistic creativity against sexual potency, and in its story stages a battle between the sexes. The apparent sexlessness of the minister, Gavin, is gradually broken down by the bewitching powers of the aristocratic lady, Babbie, who is able to conquer him through playing out the part of a gypsy girl. A study of his working notebooks reveals that it was the issue of power in male/female relationships with which Barrie struggled in his composition of this novel (Nash 1999b: 85–7). His presentation of Babbie as having a superior mind to Gavin is consistent with his many stage representations of the battle between the sexes which, as R.D.S. Jack has noted, present woman as having "*naturally* a complex mind which she uses to manipulate the simple male" (Jack 1995: 140). Once again this idea can be traced to an article in the *Dispatch*. In "The Stupid Sex" (23 July 1887), Barrie adopts the persona of a woman and puts a view of men that anticipates the idea behind the later play *What Every Woman Knows* (performed 1908). The fictional authoress of "The Stupid Sex" is in no doubt that "Women are far braver than men. They are also much cleverer; but as everybody of any sense admits that, I need say no more about it". The authoress explains that women flatter men into thinking that they have no courage: "It is so easy to get round them that we can't help doing it".

 The relationship between art and sexuality is taken further in *Tommy and Grisel* (1900), Barrie's most important full-length novel. Eve Kosofsky Sedgwick has identified this book as ground-breaking in its representation of the sexual warfare *within* a man (Kosofsky Sedgwick 1991: 198–99) and I have argued elsewhere that this sexual warfare is presented within the context of sentimentality and artistic creativity (Nash 1999a). In real life Tommy appears indifferent to female society, but in art he is able to write about women's desires with such insight that his book, *Letters to a Young Man about to be Married*, proves to be an outrageous best-seller, becoming known simply as "'Sandys on Women'" (Barrie 1900: 29). Everyone assumes that because of his book Tommy must have had extensive experience with women, but the only women with whom Tommy can fall in love are those of his own imagination:

While he sat there with eyes riveted he had her to dinner at a restaurant, and took her up the river, and called her "little woman," and when she held up her mouth he said, tantalisingly, that she must wait until he had finished his cigar. This queer delight enjoyed, back he popped her into the story (Barrie 1900: 16–17).

(One should again note the smoking reference). As R.D.S. Jack has commented, Tommy is "unable to sustain mature emotions because he is soon tempted by another sentimental part". Because he responds to life simply as raw material for art, he lacks spontaneity, and "if analysis stands in the way of spontaneity, role-playing prevents depth" (Jack 1995: 143).

Role-playing leads us inevitably to Barrie's drama and also back to the "third sex", for the stage became the perfect place for Barrie to develop his interest in the idea of gender and sexuality as perform-ance. Given the subject-matter of his journalism, it is no surprise that his early plays are obsessed by the issues of marriage and male desire. In *The Professor's Love Story* (performed 1893), a professor of science in his forties has, unbeknownst to himself, fallen in love with his secretary. That a man should fail to recognise his own amorous desires may seem far-fetched but it is not if one keeps in mind Barrie's contemporary and cognate work in the fields of journalism and the short story and sketch. *Walker, London* (performed 1892) is primarily a farce but it dramatises the plight of the bachelor who wants to escape the constraints of marriage and also explores the complications that arise from the taking upon of disguises and roles. A London barber decides to leave his fiancé temporarily on the eve of his marriage. His pre-nuptial honeymoon consists of pretending to be a famous African explorer and, in the process, making several proposals of marriage to women he naively assumes will not accept him. It is only when he *is* accepted that he realises the drawbacks of his game and happily departs with his fiancée, who has come to hunt him down.

For some of Barrie's stage characters, acting – embodying the "third sex" – becomes an escape out of the complications of sexuality. Jasper in *Walker, London* wants the women to whom he proposes to think of themselves as his sister. For other characters, however, the "third sex" is a tragic consequence of the way role-playing comes to constitute identity. Leonee Ormond has alerted us to a lost short story written around 1916 "about an actress whose stage self tries to take her over" (Ormond 1987: 40), and I want to conclude this essay by looking briefly at one of Barrie's more neglected plays, the one-act piece *Rosalind* (performed 1912), which deals explicitly with the figure of the actress and which points back to the discussion of the "third sex" in the *Edinburgh Evening Dispatch*.

Barrie had an extensive interest in Shakespeare, and it is no surprise that the plays that directly inspired two of his own pieces were among Shakespeare's most metatheatrical. *The Ladies' Shakespeare* (performed 1914) is a feminist re-working of *The Taming of the Shrew* (Jack 1995: 146–50); *Rosalind* features a middle-aged actress who is famed for her portrayal of Shakespeare's heroine in *As You Like It*. Beatrice has managed to maintain her stage career by carefully engineering the outward appearance of a youthful twenty-something – there being no parts in plays for "middle-aged ladies" (Barrie 1914: 125). Dissatisfied at never being able to be her "real self" (Barrie 1914: 124), she escapes from the limelight to a country cottage where she poses as her own mother, Mrs Page. Her refuge is interrupted, however, by a chance visit from Charles, a young Oxford man who, it emerges, has been courting Beatrice in her guise as a youthful actress, having fallen in love with her after seeing her act the role of Rosalind.

The theme is reminiscent of Wilde's *The Picture of Dorian Gray* (1891), where Dorian falls in love with the actress Sybil Vane only to discover that he is really in love with the roles she portrays. Contemporary reviewers noted a more explicit source, however, in Charles

Reade's *Nance Oldfield* (1883). In Reade's play a young man is sent to London by his father to prepare for the bar but quickly falls in love with a beautiful actress and neglects his study, devoting his entire world to the illusions of the theatre. His father persuades the actress to cure his son of his stage-struck adoration by presenting herself to him in the disguise of a plainly-dressed, dishevelled, middle-aged woman. Barrie's originality as a dramatist has been well noted, but that originality often took the form of an original inflection of existing themes. The contrast with *Nance Oldfield* is that in *Rosalind* it is Beatrice who takes centre stage. Barrie's play is far more subtle and interesting than Reade's because it focuses on the plight of the actress not the love-struck young man and so allows for a sophisticated presentation of the nature of illusion and identity. As in Reade's play, a young man is the victim of an illusion but to Charles – was Barrie's choice of name coincidental? – the middle-aged woman is a disguise when it is in fact the reality. At first Charles is unable to see beneath the disguise but by the end of the play he has come to believe that it is real woman, not the painted actress, that he loves. Beatrice, however, remains less confident that there is such a thing as the "real" woman:

CHARLES: Beatrice, until now I hadn't really known you at all. The girl I was so fond of, there wasn't any such girl.
MRS PAGE: Oh yes, indeed there was. (Barrie 1914: 142)

It is here that Barrie's transformation of Reade's theme becomes most interesting, for the course of the play suggests that for Beatrice the acted role of the young actress is as real as the "real" role of the middle-aged woman – or, alternatively, the "real" role of the middle-aged woman is as artificial as the acted role of the actress. A telegram recalls her to London to play Rosalind again and she retreats to her bedroom (off-stage) to dress. The above exchange takes place when only Charles is onstage. He proposes in a roundabout way to be her "Orlando to the end" and to accompany her "into the delicious twilight of middle-age", but when Beatrice comes back upon the stage, now dressed as the youthful and dazzling actress, her first words are defiant: "You naughty, Charles, I heard you proposing to Mamma". Amazed at the transformation Charles is led to exclaim:

"Good God! Is there nothing real in life?" (Barrie 1914: 142–46). The play leads us to conclude just that.

Barrie's actors and actresses cannot escape the artificiality of reality. Beatrice is in exactly the same predicament as Sentimental Tommy. As she tells Charles, the capacity for role-playing and the putting on and off of different emotions that comes with being an actress is what has prevented her from becoming a wife. Charles attempts to convince her that the middle-aged woman which he sees before him is her "real self" but it is not that simple:

MRS PAGE: (*warily*). Is it? I wonder.
CHARLES: I never knew any one who had deeper feelings.
MRS PAGE: Oh, I am always ready with whatever feeling is called for. I have a wardrobe of them, Charles. Don't blame me, blame the public of whom you are one; the pitiless public that has made me what I am. ... I would have been a darling of a wife – don't you think so, Charles? – but they wouldn't let me. I am only a bundle of emotions; I have two characters for each day of the week. Home became less a thing to me than a new part. Charles, if only I could have been a nobody. (Barrie 1914: 132–33)

The performance of emotion is linked here to the performance of gender, and I hope to have shown that the intersecting issues of performance, emotion, and gender, which lie at the heart of Barrie's work, can be traced to issues that he was exploring in his journalism. They can also be seen as evidence of his engagement with important contemporary cultural concerns. Numerous other plays might be considered within the same contexts, including *Quality Street* and *The Truth about the Russian Dancers*, to name just two of the more obvious examples. Far from being an indication of what is wrong in his writing, Barrie's journalism and early sketches have much to tell us about what is distinctive, modern and original about his literary achievement.

Bibliography

Barrie, J.M. 1890. *My Lady Nicotine*. London: Hodder & Stoughton.

—. 1900. *Tommy and Grisel*. London: Cassell.

—. 1914. *Half Hours*. London and New York. Hodder & Stoughton.

—. 1938. *McConnachie and J.M.B.: Speeches by J.M. Barrie*. London: Peter Davies.

Booth, Bradford A. and Ernest Mehew (eds). 1995. *The Letters of Robert Louis Stevenson, Vol. VII*. New Haven and London: Yale University Press.

Foucault, Michel. [1976] 1981. *The History of Sexuality: An Introduction* (tr. Robert Hurley). Harmondsworth: Penguin.

Gay, Peter. 1984. *The Bourgeois Experience: Victoria to Freud: Volume 1, The Education of the Senses*. Oxford and New York: Oxford University Press.

Geduld, Harry. 1971. *Sir James Barrie*. New York: Twayne.

Hekma, Gert. 1994. "'A Female Soul in a Male Body': Sexual Inversion as Gender Inversion in Nineteenth-Century Sexology" in Herdt, Gilbert (ed.) *Third Sex, Third Gender: Beyond Sexual Dimorphism in Culture and History*. New York: Zone.

Jack, Isla. 1999. "J.M. Barrie, New Journalism and 'Ndintpile Pont'" in *Scottish Literary Journal* 26(1): 62–76.

Jack, R.D.S. 1989. *The Road to the Never Land: A Reassessment of J.M. Barrie's Dramatic Art*. Aberdeen: Aberdeen University Press.

—. 1995. "Barrie and the Extreme Heroine" in Whyte, Christopher (ed.) *Gendering the Nation: Studies in Modern Scottish Literature*. Edinburgh: Edinburgh University Press. 137–67.

Klein, Richard. 1993. *Cigarettes are Sublime*. Durham: Duke University Press.

Lindsay, Maurice. [1977] 1992. *History of Scottish Literature*. London: Robert Hale.

Nash, Andrew. 1998. "The Compilation of J.M. Barrie's *Auld Licht Idylls*" in *The Bibliotheck* 23: 85–96.

—. 1999a. "From Realism to Romance: Gender and Narrative Technique in J.M. Barrie's *The Little Minister*" in *Scottish Literary Journal* 26(1): 77–92.

—. 1999b. "'Trying to be a Man': J.M. Barrie and Sentimental Masculinity" in *Forum for Modern Language Studies* 35(2): 113–25.

Ormond, Leonee. 1987. *J.M. Barrie*. Edinburgh: Scottish Academic Press.

Showalter, Elaine. 1990. *Sexual Anarchy: Gender and Culture at the fin de siècle*. London: Viking.

Stevenson, R.L. 1995. *The Letters of Robert Louis Stevenson* (ed. Bradford A. Booth and Ernest Mehew). Volume VII. New Haven and London: Yale University Press.

Professor R.D.S. Jack MA, PhD, DLitt, F.R.S.E., F.E.A.: Publications

"Scottish Sonneteer and Welsh Metaphysical" in *Studies in Scottish Literature* 3 (1966): 240–7.

"James VI and Renaissance Poetic Theory" in *English* 16 (1967): 208–11.

"Montgomerie and the Pirates" in *Studies in Scottish Literature* 5 (1967): 133–36.

"Drummond of Hawthornden: The Major Scottish Sources" in *Studies in Scottish Literature* 6 (1968): 36–46.

"Imitation in the Scottish Sonnet" in *Comparative Literature* 20 (1968): 313–28.

"The Lyrics of Alexander Montgomerie" in *Review of English Studies* 20 (1969): 168–81.

"The Poetry of Alexander Craig" in *Forum for Modern Language Studies* 5 (1969): 377–84.

With Ian Campbell (eds). *Jamie the Saxt: A Historical Comedy; by Robert McLellan.* London: Calder and Boyars, 1970.

"William Fowler and Italian Literature" in *Modern Language Review* 65 (1970): 481–92.

"Sir William Mure and the Covenant" in *Records of Scottish Church History Society* 17 (1970): 1–14.

"Dunbar and Lydgate" in *Studies in Scottish Literature* 8 (1971): 215–27.

The Italian Influence on Scottish Literature. Edinburgh: Edinburgh University Press, 1972.

Scottish Prose 1550–1700. London: Calder and Boyars, 1972.

"Scott and Italy" in Bell, Alan (ed.) *Scott, Bicentenary Essays.* Edinburgh: Scottish Academic Press, 1973. 283–99.

"The French Influence on Scottish Literature at the Court of King James VI" in *Scottish Studies* 2 (1974): 44–55.

"Arthur's Pilgrimage: A Study of *Golagros and Gawane*" in *Studies in Scottish Literature* 12 (1974): 1–20.

"*The Thre Prestis of Peblis* and the Growth of Humanism in Scotland" in *Review of English Studies* 26 (1975): 257–70.

"Petrarch in English and Scottish Renaissance Literature" in *Modern Language Review* 71 (1976): 801–11.

A Choice of Scottish Verse 1560–1660. London: Hodder and Stoughton, 1978.

"Henryson's 'Taill of the Cok and the Jasp' and Caxton's *Mirrour of the World*" in *Chaucer Review* 13 (1978): 157–65.

"Mary Queen of Scots – the Poetic Vision" in *Scotia* 3 (1979): 34–48.

"The Prose of John Knox: A Re-assessment" in *Prose Studies* 4 (1981): 239–51.

"Chaucer and *The Freiris of Berwick*" in *Studies in Scottish Literature* 17 (1981): 145–52.

With Andrew Noble (eds). *The Art of Robert Burns.* London: Vision Press, 1982.

"Burns and Bawdy" in Jack, R.D.S. and Andrew Noble (eds) *The Art of Robert Burns.* London: Vision Press, 1982. 98–126.

"James VI: Poet and Patron" in *Europaische Hofkultur im 16 und 17 Jahrhundert*. Hamburg: Hauswedell, 1982. 179–85.

"Robert Burns and the Idea of Freedom" in *Scotia* 6 (1982): 41–59.

Sir Thomas Urquhart: "The Jewel". Edinburgh: Scottish Academic Press, 1983.

"Appearance and Reality in *Humphry Clinker*" in Bold, Alan (ed.) *The Art of Tobias Smollett*. London: Vision Press, 1983. 209–27.

"William Drummond of Hawthornden" in *University of Edinburgh Journal* 31 (1983): 26–27.

"The Theme of Fortune in the Verse of Alexander Montgomerie" in *Scottish Literary Journal* 10:2 (1983): 25–44.

Alexander Montgomerie [Scottish Writers Series no. 7.]. Edinburgh: Scottish Academic Press, 1985.

"The Land of Myth and Faery: J.M. Barrie's dramatic version of *The Little Minister*" in *Scotia* 9 (1985): 1–16.

Scotland's Literary Debt to Italy. Edinburgh: Edinburgh University Press and Instituto Italiano di Cultura, 1986.

With M.L. McLaughlin, and C. Whyte (eds). *Leopardi: A Scottis Quair*. Edinburgh: Edinburgh University Press, 1987.

"Barrie as Journeyman Dramatist: A Study *of Walker London*" in *Studies in Scottish Literature* 22 (1987): 60–77.

"From Novel to Drama: J.M. Barrie's *Quality Street*" in *Scottish Literary Journal* 14:2 (1987): 48–61.

The History of Scottish Literature, Volume 1, Origins to 1660. Aberdeen: Aberdeen University Press, 1988.

"Pope's Mediaeval Heroine: *Eloisa to Abelard*" in Nicholson, Colin (ed.) *Alexander Pope*. Aberdeen University Press, 1988. 206–19.

Patterns of Divine Comedy: a study of Mediaeval English Drama. Cambridge: Boydell and Brewer, 1989.

"The Range of Robert Burns' Satires" in Peters, Ian and Thomas Stein (eds) *Scholastic Midwifery*. Tubingen: G. Narr, 1989. 256–69.

"The First MS of *Peter Pan*" in *Children's Literature* 18 (1990): 101–13.

The Road to the Never Land: A Re-assessment of J.M. Barrie's Dramatic Art. Aberdeen: Aberdeen University Press, 1991.

"Art, Nature and Thrums" in Schwend, Joachim (ed.) *Literatur im Kontext*. Frankfurt: P. Lang, 1992. 155–64.

"Lindsay's *Satyre* and Kemp's *Satire*" in *Chapman* 68 (1992): 81–86.

"The Hunt for Mrs Lapraik" in *Yale University Library Gazette* 67 (1992): 6–12.

"J.M. Barrie's *The House of Fear*" in *Studies in Scottish Literature* 27 (1992): 1–46.

With Kevin McGinley (eds). *Of Lion and Unicorn: Essays on Anglo-Scottish Literary Relations in Honour of Prof. John MacQueen*. Edinburgh: Quadriga, 1993.

"Of Lion and Unicorn: Literary Traditions at War" in Jack, R.D.S. and Kevin McGinley (eds) *Of Lion and Unicorn: Essays on Anglo-Scottish Literary Relations in Honour of Prof. John MacQueen*. Edinburgh: Quadriga, 1993. 67–99.

"Scottish Literature: The English and European Dimensions" in Brink, Jean R. and William Gantrup (eds) *Renaissance Culture in Context: Theory and Practice.* Aldershot: Scolar Press, 1993. 1–17.

"From Doon to Derwent: Burns and Wordsworth" in Macdonald, Murdo (ed.) *The Arts in Eighteenth Century Scotland: Essays in Honour of Basil Skinner.* Edinburgh: Quadriga, 1993. 69–84.

"James Barrie and the Napoleonic Heroine" in *Carlyle Annual* 13 (1993): 60–76.

"Burns as Sassenach Poet" in Simpson, Kenneth (ed.) *Burns Now.* Edinburgh: Canongate Academic, 1994. 150–66.

"Peter Pan as Darwinian Creation Myth" in *Literature and Theology* 8:2 (1994): 155–73.

"Barrie and the Extreme Heroine" in Christopher Whyte (ed.) *Gendering the Nation.* Edinburgh: Edinburgh University Press, 1995. 137–67.

The Poetry of William Dunbar [Scotnotes]. Glasgow: ASLS, 1996.

With P.A.T. Rozendaal (eds). *The Mercat Anthology of Early Scottish Literature: 1375–1707.* Edinburgh: Mercat, 1997.

"Castalia's Stank: Burns and Rhetoric" in Simpson, Kenneth (ed.) *Love and Liberty: Robert Burns – A Bicentenary Celebration.* Edinburgh: Tuckwell, 1997. 111–18.

"The Language of Literary Materials: Origins to 1700" in Jones, Charles (ed.) *The Edinburgh History of the Scots Language.* Edinburgh: Edinburgh University Press, 1997. 213–66.

"Translating the Lost Scottish Renaissance" in *Translation and Literature* 6:1 (1997): 66–80.

"Which Vernacular Renaissance? Burns and the Makars" in *Studies in Scottish Literature* 30 (1998): 9–17.

"'(A!), fredome is a noble thing!': Christian hermeneutics and Barbour's *Bruce*" in *Scottish Studies Review* 1 (2000): 26–38.

"Henryson and the Sense of an Ending" in Fleming, Morna (ed.) *The Cloak of Poetry.* Dunfermline: Robert Henryson Society, 2001. 61–84.

"Henryson and the art of precise allegorical argument" in Caie, Graham and Kenneth Simpson (eds) *The European Sun: proceedings of the seventh international conference on Medieval and Renaissance Scottish Language and Literature.* East Linton: Tuckwell Press, 2001. 1–18.

"*Versi Strani*: Early Scottish Translation" in Rose, Margaret and Emanuela Rossini (eds) *Italian Scottish Identities and Connections.* Edinburgh and Milan: Italian Cultural Institute, 2001. 111–20.

"Discoursing at Cross Purposes: *Braveheart* and Blind Hary's *Wallace*" in Goebel, Walter (ed.) *Renaissance Humanism – Modern Humanism(s).* Heidelberg: Winter, 2001. 41–54.

"Scottish Language and Literature, 1460–1640" in Lynch, Michael (ed.) *The Oxford Companion to Scottish History.* Oxford: Oxford University Press, 2001. 125–27.

"From Drama to Silent Film: The Case of Sir James Barrie" in *International Journal of Scottish Theatre* 2:2 (2002): 1–17.

"James Barrie as Academic: 'Tom Nash' and 'The Rector of Diss'" in *Swansea Review* 35 (2003): 1–22.

"Dunbar, William" in Matthew, H.G.C and Brian Harrison (eds) *Oxford Dictionary of National Biography*. 60 vols. Oxford: Oxford University Press, 2004.

"Montgomerie, Alexander" in Matthew, H.G.C and Brian Harrison (eds) *Oxford Dictionary of National Biography*. 60 vols. Oxford: Oxford University Press, 2004.

"Urquhart, Thomas" in Matthew, H.G.C and Brian Harrison (eds) *Oxford Dictionary of National Biography*. 60 vols. Oxford: Oxford University Press, 2004.

"The Castalians" in Matthew, H.G.C and Brian Harrison (eds) *Oxford Dictionary of National Biography*. 60 vols. Oxford: Oxford University Press, 2004.

"Barrie, James" in Matthew, H.G.C and Brian Harrison (eds) *Oxford Dictionary of National Biography*. 60 vols. Oxford: Oxford University Press, 2004.

"The Wallace" in Fazzini, Marco (ed.) *Alba Literaria: A History of Scottish Literature*. Maestre: Amos Edizioni, 2005. 19–31.

"Robert Henryson" in Fazzini, Marco (ed.) *Alba Literaria: A History of Scottish Literature*. Maestre: Amos Edizioni, 2005. 33–44.

With Tom Hubbard (eds). *Scotland in Europe* [Scottish Cultural Review of Language and Literature no.7.]. Rodopi: Amsterdam, 2006.

"Translation and Early Scottish Literature" in Hubbard, Tom and R.D.S. Jack (eds) *Scotland in Europe*. Rodopi: Amsterdam, 2006. 39–54.

"J.M. Barrie" in Brown, Ian and Susan Manning et al. (eds) *The Edinburgh History of Scottish Literature*. 3 vols. Edinburgh: Edinburgh University Press, 2006. II: 331–37.

"Music, Poetry and Performance at the Court of James VI" in *John Donne Journal* 25 (2006): 37–63.

"Petrarch and the Scottish Sonnet" in McLaughlin, Martin (ed.) *Petrarch in Britain: Interpreters, Imitators, and Translators over 700 Years* [Proceedings of the British Academy Vol. 146.]. Oxford: Oxford University Press, 2007. 259–73.

"Scottish Literature at the Crossroads: an Encouraging Voice" in Baker, William and Michael Lister (eds) *David Daiches: A Celebration of his Life and Work*. Brighton: Sussex Academic Press, 2007. 78–84.

"'In ane uther leid': Reviewing Scottish Literature's linguistic boundaries" in *Studies in Scottish Literature* 35–36 (2007): 164–83.

J.M.Barrie: Myths and the Mythmaker. Rodopi: Amsterdam (Forthcoming).

"The Case of Early Scottish Literature" in Vilhjálmsson, B et al. (eds) *Origins, Centres and Peripheries*. Norwich: Viking Press (Forthcoming).

"Translating Buchanan" in Greene, Roger (ed.) *Buchanan: Quincentenary Studies*. Glasgow (Forthcoming).

Index